The BIG Picture

2nd edition

Daniel Barber
Jake Hughes

With original material by Bess Bradfield and Carol Lethaby

Series editors:
Ben Goldstein and Ceri Jones

B1 PRE-INTERMEDIATE Student's Book   British English

Richmond
www.richmondelt.com/thebigpicture

CONTENTS UNITS 1–4

1 Communication

1.1 HOW DO YOU COMMUNICATE? p6
- G present simple and adverbs and expressions of frequency
- V communication collocations
- 66 third person -s

1.2 MAKING A GOOD IMPRESSION p8
- G present simple and present continuous
- V commonly confused verbs
- 66 -ing verb ending
- ✓ writing an email

1.3 SHOWING YOUR EMOTIONS p10
- V emotion adjectives
- ↗ approach a text
- ⇄ talk about specific information

1.4 WHAT DID YOU SAY? p12
- FL checking understanding
- 📹 Patrick speaks
- 66 sentence stress
- ✎ a personal profile

2 Back to nature

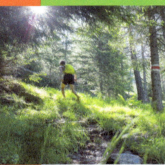

2.1 SURVIVAL p16
- G past simple
- V past time expressions
- 66 -ed endings

2.2 ANIMALS TO THE RESCUE p18
- G past continuous
- V animals
- 66 weak form of was/were
- ✓ completing a longer text

2.3 IMAGINED LANDSCAPES p20
- V geographical features
- ↗ identify key points
- ⇄ write about specific information

2.4 A GREAT STORY p22
- FL telling a story and reacting
- 📹 an unusual journey
- 66 showing interest
- ✎ an informal message

3 Icons

3.1 ICONIC PEOPLE p26
- G questions review
- V subjects and jobs
- 66 intonation in questions

3.2 ICONIC BUILDINGS p28
- G relative clauses
- V buildings and structures
- 66 relative pronoun stress
- ✓ understanding short texts

3.3 A HISTORY OF SYMBOLS p30
- G articles: a/an, the, no article
- ↗ pronoun referencing
- 66 /ðə/ and /ðiː/
- ⇄ talk about a text

3.4 THAT'S A GOOD POINT! p32
- FL agreeing and disagreeing
- 📹 the Moai heads
- 66 strong/weak expression
- ✎ a blog post

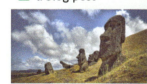

4 Learning by doing

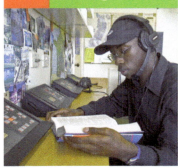

4.1 SKILLS OR QUALIFICATIONS? p36
- G going to and present continuous for plans and arrangements
- V education collocations
- 66 'gonna'

4.2 SCHOOL DAYS p38
- G must(n't) and (don't) have to
- V adjectives and dependent prepositions
- 66 have to/has to
- ✓ talking about yourself

4.3 LEARNING ABOUT CULTURES p40
- V -ed/-ing adjectives
- ↗ listen for specific information
- 66 word stress
- ⇄ simplify a text

4.4 WHAT ARE YOU DOING THIS WEEKEND? p42
- FL making arrangements
- 📹 Japanese high school life
- 66 expressing emotion
- ✎ a formal email

CONTENTS UNITS 5–8

5 Getting help

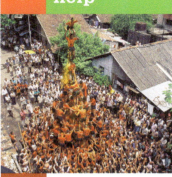

5.1 HELP! p46
- G *should* and *must* for advice
- V collocations with *have, take, do, make*
- P *shouldn't* and *mustn't*

5.2 ROBOT HELPERS p48
- G *will, may, might* for predictions
- V health problems
- P *'ll* contraction
- Listening for specific information

5.3 MAKING A DIFFERENCE p50
- V suffixes: *-ful* and *-less*
- Guess meaning from context
- Help a friend

5.4 A HELPING HAND p52
- FL asking for and giving advice
- Something for nothing
- P *do you* and *would you* in questions
- An opinion essay

6 Ages and changes

6.1 THE AGE OF RESPONSIBILITY p56
- G comparatives, superlatives, *as ... as*
- V personality adjectives
- P weak forms in comparatives

6.2 TRY SOMETHING NEW p58
- G present perfect with *ever* and *never*
- V phrasal verbs
- P irregular past participles
- Describing a photo

6.3 CELEBRATIONS p60
- V uses of *get*
- Listen for gist
- Discuss a story

6.4 THANKS FOR COMING! p62
- FL giving thanks
- Two very different brothers
- P sounding grateful
- A web forum comment

7 Homelife

7.1 HAVE YOU TIDIED UP YET? p66
- G present perfect with *just, already, yet*
- V housework collocations
- P sentence stress

7.2 A CITY FOR EVERYONE p68
- G present perfect with *for, since*
- V city features
- P contracted *have/has*
- Completing a factual text

7.3 A DIFFERENT KIND OF HOUSE p70
- G linkers
- Scan a text for specific information
- Work in a group

7.4 THANK YOU FOR CALLING p72
- FL telephone language
- Sharing your life with cats
- P sounding polite
- A promotional leaflet

8 Technology

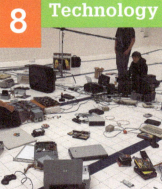

8.1 DIGITAL DETOX p76
- G *-ing* form and *to* + infinitive
- V free-time activities
- P weak form of *to*

8.2 GOOD TECH, BAD TECH p78
- G quantifiers
- V uncountable nouns
- P word stress
- Writing a narrative

8.3 GETTING AROUND p80
- V transport phrases
- Listen for numerical information
- Explain a diagram

8.4 WHAT DO YOU THINK? p82
- FL asking for and giving opinions
- A computer-made musical
- P weak form of *that*
- A for-and-against essay

3

CONTENTS UNITS 9–12

9 Healthy lifestyles

9.1 HAVE YOU EATEN ENOUGH? p86
- G too, too much/many, (not) enough
- V food
- /uː/, /ʌ/ and /ʊ/ sounds

9.2 WIN, LOSE OR DRAW p88
- G first conditional
- V sports
- intonation in clauses
- listening to a monologue

9.3 RELAX, BE HAPPY! p90
- G adverbs of manner
- find information in a text
- take notes

9.4 LOOK OUT! p92
- FL warnings and promises
- growing cities
- omission of /t/ sounds
- an invitation

©Brooklyn Grange Rooftop Farm.

10 Money and shopping

10.1 MONEY PROBLEMS p96
- G second conditional
- V money nouns
- would you

10.2 MAKING MONEY p98
- G so and such
- V money verbs
- emphasis with so and such
- writing an article

10.3 MONEY FOR NOTHING p100
- G indefinite pronouns
- identify reasons and results
- rewrite a text

10.4 WHAT A BARGAIN! p102
- FL shopping
- second-hand markets
- sounding sorry
- a complaint

11 A global market

11.1 ETHICAL FASHION p106
- G passives
- V describing clothes

11.2 A GLOBAL WORKFORCE p108
- G used to
- V verbs and dependent prepositions
- used to and use to
- listening to a radio interview

11.3 IMMIGRATION STORIES p110
- G past perfect
- identify a sequence of events
- summarize a text

11.4 OF COURSE YOU CAN! p112
- FL asking for and giving permission
- how to work and travel full time
- sounding polite
- a report

12 Entertain me!

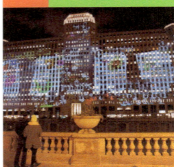

12.1 WHAT'S ON? p116
- G reported speech
- V entertainment
- weak form of that

12.2 STREET MUSIC p118
- G uses of the -ing form and infinitive
- V music
- understanding details in short texts

12.3 NEW WAYS TO HAVE FUN p120
- V gradable and extreme adjectives
- identify attitude and opinion
- emphasis of extreme adjectives
- work together

12.4 DON'T FORGET! p122
- FL giving instructions
- pottery challenge
- intonation in sequences
- a review

Communication

1

Grammar G
present simple and adverbs and expressions of frequency
present simple and present continuous

Vocabulary V
communication collocations
commonly confused verbs
emotion adjectives

Functional language FL
checking understanding

Skill
approach a text

Video
Patrick speaks

Writing
a personal profile

Exams
writing an email

The big picture: a special café

1 Look at the picture. In pairs, guess the answers to the questions.
   1 Where is the café?
   2 What is special about the café?
   3 What message are the people communicating in the picture?
   4 Are there other cafés like this in the world?

2 1.1 Listen and check your answers.

3 In pairs, discuss the questions.
   1 Would you like to visit a café like this? Why/Why not?
   2 Do you know any sign language? Would you like to learn?
   3 Where is your favourite café?
   4 What do you usually order there?

1.1 HOW DO YOU COMMUNICATE?

G present simple and adverbs and expressions of frequency
V communication collocations

Vocabulary

1 Match the expressions with the pictures.
1 ask for help ....
2 tell a story ....
3 send a message ....
4 make an announcement ....

2 Match the nouns in the box with the verbs to make more phrases.

V communication collocations

| advice | an appointment | a complaint | directions |
| an email | a joke | a letter | a lie | the truth |

Ask for	Send	Tell	Make
help	a message	a story	an announcement

🔊 1.2 Listen, check and repeat.

Reading

3 a Look at the pictures. In pairs, guess the answers to the questions.
1 What are the people's jobs? Where do they work?
2 What actions from the Vocabulary box do they do at work?

b Read the text and check.

A day in the life of ...
your questions answered

Each week, we send readers' questions to two people with interesting jobs. This week, a celebrity PA and a penguin researcher answer your questions about communication.

👤 Simon, personal assistant to a Hollywood actor

Does your job involve much communication? How many people do you speak to every day?
Well, I organize everything for my boss, so I speak to a lot of people. I make appointments for her meetings, her rehearsals, and I even organize her lunch dates with her friends and family!

What do you like about your job? What don't you like?
I really enjoy being busy. My boss can contact me at any time – she occasionally calls me in the middle of the night! I work hard and I hardly ever get a break, but I don't mind. It means I'm never bored! The worst thing about the job is saying no to people. Because I'm the PA to a famous actor, I get hundreds of calls from fans wanting to speak to her. Unfortunately, she doesn't want to speak to people, and I usually tell a lie and say she's busy. I don't really like lying.

👤 Sonia, a penguin researcher in Antarctica

How often do you speak to people face-to-face?
I hardly ever speak to people face-to-face, but I speak to penguins <u>every day</u> – does that count?

How do you communicate with people? Is there internet in Antarctica?
Yes, there is. I send an email to my boss <u>once or twice a day</u>. I almost always need to ask him for advice. I don't have any colleagues here in Antarctica! He usually replies after about ten minutes. I'd like to make video calls but the connection in Antarctica isn't fast enough. So <u>every day</u> I send an email to my family, too. My parents write back to me <u>every day</u>. My brother doesn't often reply, but I'm always happy when he does. He always tells me funny stories about life at home.

Are you happy or do you miss talking to people?
To tell the truth, I sometimes get a bit lonely, but I don't want to go home yet. It's so beautiful here ... and I don't want to leave the penguins!

4 Read the text again. Are the sentences true (T) or false (F)?
1 Simon only organizes work meetings for his boss. ....
2 Simon doesn't get much time to relax. ....
3 Simon's boss likes talking to people. ....
4 Sonia never communicates with people. ....
5 Sonia's brother hardly ever writes to her. ....
6 Sonia is always happy. ....

5 In pairs, discuss the questions.
1 Whose job is more interesting?
2 Would you like to do either of these jobs?
3 What questions would you like to ask Simon and Sonia?

Grammar

6 a Complete the sentences with the verbs in the box. Check your answers in the text.

| do | does | doesn't | don't | tell | tells |

1 .... your job involve much communication?
2 Unfortunately, she .... want to speak to people.
3 I usually .... a lie and say she's busy.
4 How often .... you speak to people face-to-face?
5 He always .... me funny stories.
6 I sometimes get a bit lonely, but I .... want to go home yet.

b Look at the sentences again and answer the questions.
1 Which letter is added to the verb in positive sentences when the subject is *he*, *she* or *it*? ....
2 What auxiliary verbs do we use in negative sentences? .... and ....
3 What auxiliary verbs do we use in questions? .... and ....

7 a Read the text and find the adverbs of frequency in the box. Choose the correct words to complete the rules.

| hardly ever | almost always | usually | often |
| always | occasionally | never | sometimes |

1 Adverbs of frequency go *before / after* the verb *be*.
2 Adverbs of frequency go *before / after* other verbs.

b Order the adverbs of frequency from 1–8.
1 .... 0%
2 ....
3 ....
4 ....
5 ....
6 ....
7 ....
8 .... 100%

8 Find the underlined expressions of frequency (*once a week*, *every day*, etc.) in the text. In which two places do they usually go in a sentence?

G present simple and adverbs and expressions of frequency

+ I'm **sometimes** late for appointments.
  She **hardly ever** answers her phone.
− We aren't good at talking **every day**.
  He doesn't **always** ask for help.
? Are you good at telling jokes?
  How often does she check her phone?

→ Grammar reference: page 132

9 a ◀)) 1.3 « third person -s » Listen and notice the three different sounds /s/, /z/ and /ɪz/ at the end of the verbs. Listen again and repeat.
1 she eat**s** 2 he spend**s** 3 she watch**es**

b ◀)) 1.4 Say the verbs in the box in the third person and put them in the correct columns. Listen, check and repeat.

| feel | go | like | practise | use | walk |

/s/	/z/	/ɪz/
eats	spends	watches

10 In pairs, use the phrases in the box to make sentences about people in your class. Remember to pronounce the third person -s correctly.

Marta eats in expensive restaurants.

eat in expensive restaurants
feel happy in the morning   go to bed late
spend a lot of time outside   like dancing
walk to class   watch a lot of sport
practise English outside class   use Twitter

Speaking

11 a In pairs, ask and answer *How often do you …?* with activities. Give reasons with your answers.
How often do you tell jokes?
I tell jokes every day.

make new friends	make promises
send text messages	tell jokes
tell lies	send emails
ask for help	ask for directions

b Swap partners. Ask and answer questions about your first partners.
How often does Carlos tell jokes?
Carlos always tells jokes. He's really funny!

1.2 MAKING A GOOD IMPRESSION

G present simple and present continuous
V commonly confused verbs

Vocabulary

1 Match pictures a–c with situations 1–3. In which situation is it most important to make a good impression? Why?

1 interviewing for a job
2 meeting someone at a party
3 meeting your partner's parents

2 a Choose the correct words to complete the sentences in the Vocabulary box.

b In pairs, say if you agree or disagree with the tips for making a good impression. Explain your answers.

V commonly confused verbs

1 When you meet someone for the first time, don't *discuss / argue* with them.
2 Don't *hope / expect* to become friends with someone immediately. It takes time!
3 Smile and be confident – don't *see / look at* the floor.
4 *Notice / Realize* how the other person speaks and try to copy his or her style.
5 Sometimes it's better not to *say / tell* people your opinion. Be prepared to lie a little bit!
6 When you don't *meet / know* a person well, find something you are both interested in.

🔊 1.5 Listen, check and repeat.

3 a Complete the sentences with the words you did not choose in the Vocabulary box.

1 I hardly ever _____ politics with new friends.
2 When I _____ someone new, I usually ask them about their family.
3 I often _____ people embrace when they meet each other, but I prefer to shake hands.
4 I always _____ 'nice to meet you' when I meet someone for the first time.
5 I _____ everyone likes me when they first meet me.
6 I try to be confident when I meet people, but they always _____ that I'm shy.

b Which sentences are true for you? Compare with a partner.

Listening

4 a 🔊 1.6 Listen to three conversations and match them with the situations in exercise 1.

b 🔊 1.6 Listen again and choose the correct words to complete the sentences. Which two meetings weren't successful? Why?

1 Yolanda prefers *sweet drinks / coffee*.
2 Maxi wants the job because it *pays well / has a big office*.
3 Sal and Marco are *brothers / friends*.
4 *Camille / Sal* is unhappy about the football match.

Grammar

5 a Choose the correct form of the verbs to complete the sentences from the conversations in exercise 4.
1 Why *do you want / are you wanting* the job, Maxi?
2 *I don't drink / I'm not drinking* anything with a lot of sugar in it.
3 *Do they play / Are they playing* right now?
4 *I really like / I'm really liking* this office.
5 France *already win / are already winning* 3–0!
6 Paul *talks / is talking* about you all the time!

b 🔊 1.7 Listen and check.

6 a Look at the sentences in exercise 5. Which verbs are present simple and which are present continuous?

b Complete the rules with present simple or present continuous.
1 We use the .... to talk about habits or something that is generally true.
2 We use the .... to talk about something that is temporary or happening now.
3 We use the .... for state verbs (e.g. *know*, *believe*, *want*).

G present simple and present continuous

Generally true or habits
I eat my lunch here every day.
Do young people often live with their parents?

Temporary or happening now
Why is nobody dancing?
We're not talking to each other at the moment.

State verbs
Do you want something to drink?
I don't believe you.

→ Grammar reference: page 132

🔍 notice

We sometimes use *always* with the present continuous to complain about someone's behaviour.
You're always telling me what to do!
Paul's always forgetting to wash my cup properly.

7 a 🔊 1.8 **-ing verb ending** Listen to the sentences. Notice the final /ɪŋ/ sound of the words in **bold**. Listen again and repeat.
1 Are you **listening**?
2 She isn't **eating** anything.
3 I'm **waiting** for someone.

b Say what five classmates are doing right now. Try to pronounce the /ɪŋ/ sound correctly.

8 🔊 1.9 Look at the picture. Do you think the two people are happy to see each other? Listen and check.

9 a 🔊 1.9 Complete the conversation with the present simple or continuous form of the verbs in brackets. Listen again and check.

D Elena? I (1) .... (not believe) it!
E Oh ... David. Hi.
D What (2) .... you .... (do) here? You (3) .... (not live) in **Santiago**.
E I (4) .... (visit) **my mother this week**. I (5) .... (meet) her for lunch now.
D Oh, how lovely. How is **your mother**? I (6) .... (remember) her so well.
E She's fine, thanks. I'm sorry, David, but I must go. I (7) .... (be) late.
D Oh. (8) .... you .... (want) to meet for **a coffee** tomorrow?
E Um ... I've got a **dentist appointment** tomorrow. I (9) .... (always go) when I'm back here.
D But what about **in the afternoon**? I (10) .... (not want) to miss you while you're here.
E Sorry, David, but I really have to go. **My mother** (11) .... (wait) for me. Why don't you call me?
D But I (12) .... (not have) your number. Elena! Elena! Oh ... she's gone.

b In pairs, act out the conversation, but replace the words in **bold** with your own ideas.

What are you doing here? You don't live in Buenos Aires.

Speaking

10 a In pairs, ask and answer present simple or present continuous questions.
1 what job / you / do / ?
2 why / you / learn English / ?
3 you / have any brothers or sisters / ?
4 you / watch a good TV series / at the moment / ?
5 what music / you / like / ?
6 your favourite sports team / play well / this season / ?
7 what / you / usually do / at the weekend / ?
8 what / your best friend / do / right now / ?

What job do you do?
I'm a chef.

b Swap partners. Talk about the similarities and differences between you and your first partner.

Maria is a chef, but I work as a teacher. We're both learning English because we want to work in a different country.

1.3 SHOWING YOUR EMOTIONS

🔤 emotion adjectives
🔧 approach a text

Reading

1 In pairs, look at the picture and answer the questions.
   1 How is the boy feeling? How do you know?
   2 How is the man feeling? How do you know?
   3 Which emotions are easy/difficult to see in a person's face and body?

🔧 approach a text

Before you read a text, try to become familiar with it.
- Look at pictures and read the title and headings. Predict the content of the text and each section.
- Read the first sentence of each paragraph. This sentence often gives you the main idea of the paragraph.

2 Read the Skill box. Then read the highlighted first sentence of each paragraph. Match the headings with paragraphs 1–4.
   a Improving relationships
   b Understanding other people
   c Always communicating
   d Understanding yourself

3 Choose the best summary for the text. Use the title and headings to help you. Read the text and check.
   a With the right body language, you can become successful in business.
   b Body language is important if you speak to people from different countries.
   c Body language is an important part of how we communicate and we can learn to control it.
   d Body language only tells other people how we feel.

4 Read the text again. Are the sentences true (T) or false (F)?
   1 Humans communicate more with their faces and bodies than with words.
   2 People in different countries make different expressions when they are happy or sad.
   3 There is more than one sign that someone is lying.
   4 Touching your neck is a sign of confidence.
   5 It's a good sign if two people are copying each other's body language.
   6 Looking at your phone makes you more attractive to other people.

5 In pairs, discuss the questions.
   1 How much of the information in the text did you already know?
   2 Which fact is the most surprising?
   3 Which fact is the most useful?

THE SECRETS OF BODY LANGUAGE
AND WHY YOU NEED TO KNOW THEM

1 As you read this article, your face and body are sending hundreds of messages to anyone watching. In fact, humans make and recognize about twenty-five thousand facial expressions every day! Compare this with how much we speak; the average person only says about fifteen thousand words a day. Clearly, we all need to know how body language works, because we are always 'speaking' with our gestures.

2 Body language is magical – learn it well and you can know what other people are thinking. Some emotions are quite easy to read. We all know what happens to our faces when we're **scared** by a horror movie, **annoyed** during an argument or **miserable** because we get some bad news. In the same way, everyone makes similar facial expressions when they're **cheerful** after hearing good news or **surprised** by a something they didn't expect. Those expressions are the same all over the world, but other body language is harder to understand. Imagine you are talking to a friend and you notice their feet are pointing away from you. Is that a good sign?

Vocabulary

6 Match the emotion adjectives in the box with the definitions.

> **V emotion adjectives**
>
> annoyed   calm   cheerful   confident
> embarrassed   miserable   nervous
> scared   stressed   surprised

1 .... relaxed, not feeling strong emotions
2 .... happy and feeling good
3 .... very sad
4 .... tired, worried and under pressure
5 .... when something unexpected happens
6 .... a little angry
7 .... feeling good about your abilities
8 .... feeling uncomfortable because you did something wrong
9 .... frightened
10 .... worried that something bad will happen

🔊 **1.10** Listen, check and repeat.

7 Which adjectives are positive and which are negative? In pairs, compare your answers.

Unfortunately not – your friend doesn't agree with you! Another useful thing to know is when someone tells a lie. Scratching your nose or looking away are signs that someone isn't telling the truth, and perhaps they're a little **embarrassed** about that.

3 ....
It's not just other people's signals you should look for, but also your own. For example, you may notice yourself touching your neck a lot or even pulling your shirt collar away from your neck. These are signs that you are **stressed**. Once you notice you are doing these things, it may be time to stop for a second, relax a bit and make yourself feel **calm**. In other words, by recognizing your own body language, you can change your behaviour for the better.

4 ....
Knowledge of body language can help us get on with other people better. When we are very comfortable with someone, we copy how he or she sits and moves. Research shows that we can even have more productive conversations if we do this consciously. And finally, looking up, not down, and opening our bodies instead of crossing our arms and legs and looking **nervous**, shows people we are **confident**. This helps to make us more attractive to other people. So, if you want people to like you, stop looking down at your phone, look up and smile!

---

8 In pairs, take turns to ask and answer the question *When do you feel …?* with the adjectives in the Vocabulary box.

When do you feel nervous?
I feel nervous just before I have an exam.

Writing

9 Read the blog about emotions and complete the sentences with the adjectives in exercise 6.

> Home   About   **Blog**   Archive   🔍
>
> Hi guys. I find it really useful to write about my feelings. So here is a list of some emotions that I often feel. I hope you enjoy reading about them. And please write your own list in the Comments box below. I'd love to hear from you!
>
> • I feel (1) .... when I'm waiting for a bus and someone pushes in front of me.
> • I feel (2) .... when I'm at work and my friends are all having fun.
> • I feel (3) .... when I know I can do something really well.
> • I feel (4) .... when I'm on a train and a stranger smiles and says hello.
> • I feel (5) .... when I'm waiting for the dentist and I hear the drill.
> • I feel (6) .... when the weather is warm and the sun is shining.
> • I feel (7) .... when I'm walking at night and I hear a strange noise.
> • I feel (8) .... when I'm late for an appointment and the traffic is moving slowly.
> • I feel (9) .... when my classmates are all answering questions and I don't understand.
> • I feel (10) .... when I'm lying on the beach and I can hear the sea.
>
> **Comments** ▼

10 a Write five sentences about your feelings. Use *I feel … when …*

b In pairs, compare your sentences. Say if you agree or disagree with your partner's sentences.

I feel embarrassed when I make a mistake in English.
Me too!

c Write a comment replying to the blog post.

⇄ **Mediation task:** Student A page 125, Student B page 126

1.4 WHAT DID YOU SAY?

checking understanding
Patrick speaks

The big picture: Patrick speaks

1. **1.1** Look at the picture of Patrick in class. Guess the answers to the questions. Watch the video and check.
   1. How old is Patrick?
   2. Where is he from?
   3. What is he learning to do?

2. In pairs, answer the questions with the adjectives in the box. Explain your answers.

annoyed	cheerful	confident	embarrassed
miserable	nervous	scared	stressed

   How does Patrick feel …
   1. at the start of the video?
   2. when he first goes to class?
   3. at the end of the video?

3. **1.1** Watch the video again and answer the questions.
   1. How does Patrick's father communicate with Patrick?
   2. Why is the presenter worried before the class?
   3. Which words does Raymond teach the class?
   4. What is Patrick's sign name?
   5. What does Patrick want to do in the future?

4. In pairs, discuss the questions.
   1. Why was the video almost silent?
   2. What was Patrick's life like before he learned sign language?
   3. How did you feel when you saw Patrick in the class?
   4. How do you think his father feels about the classes?
   5. Would you like to learn sign language? Why/Why not?

5. **1.2** Watch Rob and Lou talking about the video. Which topics from exercise 4 do they discuss?

6. **1.2** In pairs, order the sentences from the conversation. Watch the video again and check.
   a. ☐ Well, the video was almost silent.
   b. ☐ It was so nice to see Patrick smile. That was my favourite bit.
   c. ☐ It was clever the way they did it.
   d. ☐ **What do you mean?**
   e. ☐ **Do you mean** when he was in the sign language class?
   f. ☐ **Oh, I see.** Yes, it made you really think about what it's like to be deaf.
   g. ☐ **Yes, exactly.** I felt so happy for him.

7. Match the phrases in **bold** with the uses.
   1. to check information ....
   2. to confirm someone understands ....
   3. to say you don't understand ....
   4. to show you understand ....

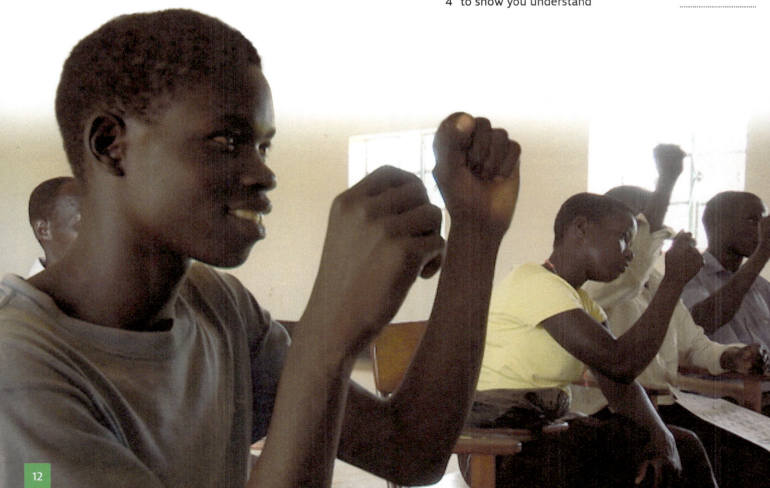

Functional language

8 🔊 1.11 Look at the pictures. What are the people doing? Listen to the conversations and check.

9 🔊 1.11 Complete the sentences with the words in the box. Listen again and check.

again	did	exactly	got	mean
right	see	understand		

1. Sorry, could you say that ...., please?
2. And .... you say 'after' the traffic lights?
3. I've .... it.
4. Do you .... I have to wait two weeks to see a doctor?
5. Oh, I .... what you mean.
6. I'm sorry, but I don't ....
7. Is that ....?
8. ....! So, which stamp would you like?

FL checking understanding

Check information
Is that right?
Do you mean ...?
Did you say ...?

Confirm someone understands
That's right.
You've got it.
Exactly!

Say you don't understand
Could you say that again, please?
What do you mean?
I'm sorry, but I don't understand.

Show you understand
(Now) I understand.
(I've) got it.
I see (what you mean).

10 🔊 1.12 ❝ sentence stress ❞ Listen to phrases from the Functional language box. Underline the stressed words. Listen again, check and repeat.

1. Could you say that again, please?
2. Is that right?
3. Now I understand.
4. You've got it.

11 a In pairs, match sentences 1–5 with replies a–e. Where do you think the conversations happen?

1. Could you say that again, please? ....
2. You mean there are two different stations? ....
3. Sorry, what do you mean? ....
4. But the museum is closed today. ....
5. So, I have to call the hospital. Is that right? ....

a. You've got it. Which one do you need?
b. I said, I'm going to the shops. Do you want anything?
c. That's right. Do you have the number?
d. I mean it's cold in here. Could you close the window?
e. Oh, now I understand. We'll come back tomorrow.

b In pairs, say the sentences and replies. Remember to use the correct sentence stress.

Speaking

12 a Choose an information card. Read the information to your partner. He/She must write down all the information correctly without looking at the card. Use the Functional language box to check understanding.

b Swap roles and repeat the task with the other information card.

Name:	Crazy Cars
Tel:	0808 157 08080
Email:	info@crazycars.com
Pick-up:	Monday–Sunday 08.00–19.00 (you can return cars 24 hours a day)
Prices:	£40–£75 per day
Fuel:	Car must be full of fuel when you return it.
Documents:	Passport <u>and</u> driver's license

Name:	The Happy Hotel
Tel:	313 555 8543
Office hours:	08.30–18.30
Email:	enquiries@happyhotel.com
Address:	14 Lakeshore Drive, Michigan, 48084
Prices:	from £70–£150 per night. (£50 deposit when you book)
Documents:	Passport <u>or</u> driver's license

📝 Writing bank: page 144

REVIEW UNIT 1

Vocabulary
Communication collocations

1 a Cross out the nouns that don't go with the verbs.

1 **ask for:**	help	directions	the truth
2 **send:**	a lie	a letter	an email
3 **tell:**	a story	a joke	a message
4 **make:**	advice	a complaint	an appointment

b Look at the correct collocations again. In pairs, say when and where you do them.

I ask for help in English class when I don't understand something.

Commonly confused verbs

2 a Choose the correct verb to complete the sentences.
1. Can you *say / tell* me what you're thinking?
2. Hi, Jin. It's really nice to *know / meet* you!
3. We don't have to decide now. Let's *argue / discuss* things first.
4. It's a difficult exam, so don't *expect / hope* to answer all the questions.
5. Did you *notice / realize* how tired he looks?

b Complete the sentences with verbs that you <u>didn't</u> use in exercise 2a. Which sentences are true for you?
1. I never .... with my parents. We get on well.
2. I .... that I become famous one day.
3. I don't .... many people in my English class.
4. I always .... 'thank you' to shop assistants.
5. I'm often late because I don't .... what time it is.

Emotion adjectives

3 🔊 **1.13** Listen to the speakers. Tick (✓) how they feel.

	a		b		c	
1	confident	☐	calm	☐	surprised	☐
2	cheerful	☐	confident	☐	stressed	☐
3	calm	☐	nervous	☐	annoyed	☐
4	miserable	☐	annoyed	☐	scared	☐
5	confident	☐	surprised	☐	cheerful	☐

Grammar
Present simple and adverbs of frequency

4 Complete the sentences with the verbs in the box in the present simple and the adverbs or expressions of frequency in the correct positions.

ask / never	be / almost always	call / once a week
~~send / hardly ever~~	tell / always	

1. Tricia *hardly ever sends* text messages. She prefers to talk to people.
2. I .... my mum .... It's good to keep in touch.
3. Jack is very honest. He .... the truth.
4. They find Maths difficult, but they .... for help.
5. The bus is really slow so I .... late for work.

5 In pairs, ask and answer the question *How often do you ...?* with the activities in the box.

speak English	write letters	have meetings
tell funny stories	make video calls	

How often do you have meetings?
We usually have meetings once a week.

Present simple and present continuous

6 Read the questions and tick (✓) the correct answer.
1. Is Poppy at the gym?
   a No, she's having lunch with a friend. ☐
   b No, she has lunch with a friend. ☐
2. How often do you go swimming?
   a I usually go every morning. ☐
   b I'm usually going every morning. ☐
3. Is Javier telling the truth?
   a No, I'm not believing him. ☐
   b No, I don't believe him. ☐

7 a Complete the sentences with the correct form of the verbs in brackets.
1. At the moment, I .... French. (learn)
2. I .... to have a long holiday this year. (want)
3. I .... to class every day. (walk)
4. I .... a book at the moment. (not read)

b Are the sentences true for you? In pairs, compare your answers.

Functional language
Checking understanding

8 a Complete the sentences with the words in the box.

got	mean	right	say

a Yes, that's ....
b Could you .... that again, please?
c I've .... it.
d Do you .... the post office?

b 🔊 **1.14** Complete the conversation with phrases a–d. Listen and check.

A Excuse me, is the place for sending letters near here?
B (1) ....
A (2) ....
B OK, go down this road and take the second turning on the left.
A (3) ....
B Of course. You go down this road. Then you take the second road on the left.
A (4) .... Thank you very much.

⏱ Looking back

- What do you want to look at in this unit again?
- Write down three new things you can say about yourself.

Back to nature

2

Grammar G
past simple
past continuous

Vocabulary V
past time expressions
animals
geographical features

Functional language FL
telling a story and reacting

Skill
identify key points

Video
an unusual journey

Writing
an informal message

Exams
completing a longer text

The big picture: getting away from it all

1 Look at the picture. In pairs, discuss the questions.
  1 Where do you think this is? What can you see?
  2 What time of day is it? What time of year is it?
  3 What is the man doing? What other activities can you do in a place like this?

2 🔊 2.1 Listen and check your answers.

3 In pairs, discuss the questions.
  1 What is the countryside like in your country? Are there any places like this?
  2 Where do you go if you want to 'get away from it all'?
  3 How often do you go there?
  4 What activities do you do there?

I sometimes go camping in the mountains with my friends. It's a nice change from city life.

2.1 SURVIVAL

G past simple
V past time expressions

Reading

1 Look at the pictures and titles in the two articles. In pairs, guess what the articles are about.

2 Read the articles and check your answers.

3 In pairs, discuss the questions.
   1 What do the stories have in common?
   2 How did the people survive?
   3 Do you watch survival programmes on TV?
   4 Could you survive in similar situations?

RIVER RESCUE

A few years ago, Rory and Chiara Maddocks and Rachel Hodson lost their way in a rainforest in central Malaysia. The forest was beautiful, but they were scared because they thought there were wild animals there. They didn't have anything with them – no food, water or tools, so they needed to get out quickly. How did the three people survive? They remembered tips from a TV programme – Ray Mears's *Extreme Survival*. They followed a river until finally they reached the sea, where they could get help. They swam out into the sea and luckily, some boys on a boat stopped and rescued them. After two nights in the forest, they were safe. When he got home, Rory wanted to watch more *Extreme Survival*. 'You never know when you might need it!' he said.

A COLD WALK HOME

When Christopher Traverse's snowmobile broke in the middle of winter, the Canadian was nervous. He realized that he was lost and he didn't have a mobile phone with him. Luckily, he remembered a TV show called *Survivorman*. As part of the show, a man called Les Stroud stayed in many wild, dangerous places. Christopher decided to use Les's ideas. He tried to make shelters out of trees and he slept in them. For water, he drank snow. He started early every morning and he walked all day. On the fourth day, he found a road … and the way home.

Grammar

4 Find the past simple forms of the verbs in the texts. Which verbs are regular and which are irregular?
   1 be
   2 break
   3 can
   4 decide
   5 lose
   6 realize
   7 stay
   8 stop
   9 swim
   10 think
   11 walk
   12 want

5 Find a question and a negative sentence in the texts. Then choose the correct words to complete the rules.
   1 *Irregular / Regular* verbs end in *-ed*.
   2 We make negative sentences in the past with *didn't* + *infinitive / past form*.
   3 We make questions in the past with *did* + subject + *infinitive / past form*.

G past simple

+ They **walked** along a river.
  They **saw** the sea.

− He **didn't have** a mobile phone with him.
  They **didn't have** anything with them.

? **Did** they **have** any water to drink?
  How **did** the three people **survive**?

→ Grammar reference: page 133

6 🔊 2.2 **-ed endings** Listen to the sentences. Notice the pronunciation of the sounds in **bold**: /t/, /d/ and /ɪd/. Listen again and repeat.
   1 They reach**ed** the sea. /t/
   2 They remember**ed** tips from a TV programme. /d/
   3 Christopher decid**ed** to use Les's ideas. /ɪd/

16

7 2.3 Say the words in the box and put them in the correct columns. Listen, check and repeat.

finished	needed	realized	started	
stayed	stopped	tried	wanted	washed

/t/	/d/	/ɪd/

8 Read about Megan Hine. Complete the text with the past simple form of the verbs in the box.

catch	climb	decide	die	do	finish
get	not have	learn	live	try	wash

Who is she?
Megan Hine is a survival expert. She visits some of the wildest places on Earth for TV survival programmes. Her job? To find water, food and shelter, and to keep people alive!

How ⁽¹⁾............ Megan .... to survive in the wild?
She started very young. When she was only 6 years old, she ⁽²⁾............ the highest mountain in Wales. In 2006, she ⁽³⁾............ on her own in a forest for three months. She ⁽⁴⁾............ fish with her hands! She woke up at 5.00 a.m. each day and ⁽⁵⁾............ in a cold lake. She ⁽⁶⁾............ a shower at all in those three months!

Is her job dangerous?
Yes, it is. In December 2007, she ⁽⁷⁾............ very ill when an insect bit her. A few years ago, she almost ⁽⁸⁾............ when a family of lions ⁽⁹⁾............ to eat her in her tent in Namibia.

What ⁽¹⁰⁾............ she .... in 2016?
She did something completely different. She ⁽¹¹⁾............ to write a book: *Mind of a Survivor*. I ⁽¹²⁾............ it last night. It's amazing.

Vocabulary

9 Read the text in exercise 8 again. Match actions 1–6 with the time that they happened.

1 climbed a mountain in Wales   a at 5.00 a.m.
2 lived in a forest   b when she was six
3 woke up in the forest   c a few years ago
4 got ill   d in 2006
5 almost died   e last night
6 finished *Mind of a Survivor*   f in December

10 Complete the Vocabulary box with the time expressions from exercise 9.

> **V past time expressions**
>
> **In + season/month/year**   **Point in time + ago**
> - in the summer   - two days ago
> - ⁽¹⁾............   - ⁽⁴⁾............
> - ⁽²⁾............
>
> **On + day/date**   **When + past clause**
> - on Sunday   - when I was a child
> - on 3 April   - ⁽⁵⁾............
>
> **At + celebrations/   Last + night/week/month/
> time of day**   year**
> - at New Year   - last week
> - ⁽³⁾............   - ⁽⁶⁾............
>
> 2.4 Listen, check and repeat.

> **🔍 notice**
>
> When we don't want to say exactly when, we can add the word **about**:
>
> **about** six years ago   when I was **about** ten

11 Complete the questions with the past simple form of the verbs in brackets. Then, in pairs, ask and answer the questions. Ask follow-up questions.

When was the last time you …
1 .... outside? (eat)
2 .... a wild animal? (see)
3 .... dinner? (cook)
4 .... some new shoes? (buy)
5 .... someone a present? (give)
6 .... a funny video on social media? (share)

When was the last time you ate outside? Last year.
Did you have a barbecue? Yes, I did!

Speaking

12 Think of a time when you were in the countryside. In pairs, ask and answer questions.

1 where / go?   4 enjoy it?
2 when / go?   5 anything interesting happen?
3 what / do?   6 what / weather like?

Where did you go? I went to … . I had a great time!

2.2 ANIMALS TO THE RESCUE

G past continuous
V animals

Vocabulary

1 What animals can you see in the pictures 1–4? Use the words in the Vocabulary box to help you.

2 Put the animals in the box in the correct columns.

V animals

ant	bee	butterfly	camel	dolphin
gorilla	kitten	lamb	mosquito	puppy
seal	shark	spider	tiger	whale

Bugs	Young animals	Sea animals	Wild animals

🔊 2.5 Listen, check and repeat.

Listening

3 Look at the pictures a–c below. In pairs, answer the questions.
1 What animals can you see?
2 What are they doing?
3 What are the humans doing?
4 Which situation do you think is the most dangerous? Why?

4 🔊 2.6 Listen and match the story to one of the pictures a–c.

5 🔊 2.6 Are the sentences true (T) or false (F)? Listen again and check.
1 Nan Hauser was alone when she saw the whale.
2 The whale pushed her hard.
3 She was scared.
4 The whale saw the shark before Nan saw it.
5 There are many stories of whales protecting humans.

Grammar

6 a 🔊 2.7 Choose the correct form of the verbs to complete the sentences. Listen and check.

1. In October 2017, Nan Hauser *studied / was studying* whales near the Cook Islands.
2. She and a photographer *swam / were swimming* near their boat when she *saw / was seeing* a whale.
3. She *turned / was turning* around to look at the whale one more time while she *got / was getting* out of the water.

b Read the sentences again. Answer the questions.

1. Which verbs describe an action in progress at a time in the past? ...., ... and ....
2. Which verbs describe a completed action which happened at the time of another action in progress? .... and ....

> **G   past continuous and past simple**
>
> **Action in progress at a time in the past:**
> In 2015, I **was working** at the San Diego zoo.
>
> **Completed action at the time of another action in progress:**
> We **saw** a bear while we **were driving** to work.
> We **were driving** to work when we **saw** a bear.
>
> → Grammar reference: page 133

7 Choose the correct form of the verbs to complete the other stories about animals and humans.

Saved by the cat!

One night in 2010, the Lineham family in Birmingham in England ⁽¹⁾*slept / were sleeping* when Graham Lineham ⁽²⁾*heard / was hearing* something. Their cat Sooty ⁽³⁾*made / was making* a noise at the bedroom door. Graham ⁽⁴⁾*opened / was opening* the door and smelled smoke. He immediately ⁽⁵⁾*woke / was waking* his family and they all ⁽⁶⁾*escaped / were escaping* before it was too late.

Gorilla to the rescue

On 16 August 1996, Binti Jua, a female gorilla, ⁽⁷⁾*sat / was sitting* with her baby Koola at Brookfield Zoo near Chicago when one of the zoo's visitors, a three-year-old boy, ⁽⁸⁾*fell / was falling* into the cage. Binti ⁽⁹⁾*walked / was walking* over to him, ⁽¹⁰⁾*picked / was picking* him up and ⁽¹¹⁾*took / was taking* him to the door of her cage. The zoo staff ⁽¹²⁾*waited / were waiting* for him there.

8 🔊 2.8 ❝ **weak form of *was/were*** ❞ Listen to the sentences. Notice how *was* and *were* are pronounced. Listen again and repeat.

1. The family were sleeping.
2. The cat was making a noise.

9 In pairs, ask and answer the question *What were you doing …?* with the times in the box.

> an hour ago   at 6.00 this morning
> at 9.00 last night   this time last week
> on the first day of this month   in 2017
> at midnight last New Year's eve

What were you doing an hour ago?
I was walking to class.
What were you doing at 6.00 this morning?
I was sleeping, of course!

Speaking

10 a Look at the pictures. In pairs, make notes to describe the story of what happened. Use as many past continuous and past simple phrases as you can.

b Swap partners and tell your new partner your story. Are they similar?

This happened last summer when my family were camping in the mountains …

c 🔊 2.9 Listen and compare your stories with what happened.

2.3 IMAGINED LANDSCAPES

V geographical features
🔧 identify key points

Listening

1. Look at the pictures of film and TV series locations. In pairs, answer the questions.
   1. How would you describe them?
   2. Do you know which films and series used them?
   3. Which countries are they from?

2. 🔊 2.10 Listen to a radio programme and check. Match the place names 1–3 with the pictures a–c. Which would you like to visit most? Why?
   1. Gaztelugatxe ....
   2. Wadi Rum ....
   3. Koh Phi Phi Le ....

🔧 identify key points

When people speak, you can't always understand every word, but it's important to understand the main points.

- Listen for words that are repeated, or words with a similar meaning.
- Listen for emphasis on important words.
- Listen for stories, examples and explanations to emphasize key points.

3. 🔊 2.10 Read the Skill box. Listen again and choose the correct words to complete the sentences.
   1. They film in Gaztelugatxe in the *winter / summer / spring*.
   2. There isn't a *path / castle / church* on the island. It's computer generated.
   3. Wadi Rum is famous because it's the location of *one / two / a lot of* films.
   4. Tourists also come to see the *cave art / cliffs / camels*.
   5. Before they made *The Beach*, Koh Phi Phi Le had a *beautiful and natural / big and sandy / dirty and spoiled* beach.
   6. *Famous actors / Lots of tourists / The government* destroyed the beach on the island.

Vocabulary

4 Look at the pictures. Complete the descriptions with the words in the box.

geographical features

cave	cliffs	coast	jungle	ocean
path	rocks	sand	stream	valley
waves	waterfall			

a This beach is on the south (1)............. . It's famous for its tall (2)............. and beautiful yellow (3)............. . Not many people swim here because the (4)............. is often cold, but lots of surfers come here because of the big (5)............. .

b This is a tropical forest, or (6)............., in Brazil. There are tall hills covered in trees on both sides, but between them is a low (7)............. . In the middle, there is a long river which is full of (8)............. so it's dangerous for boats, but there's a small (9)............. next to the river where you can walk.

c I took this photo when I was standing in a (10)............. in Thailand. Outside, you can see an amazing (11)............. – it's very noisy. The water falls into a (1)............. and flows away.

🔊 **2.11** Listen, check and repeat.

5 In pairs, describe two regions in your country that are famous for their landscapes.

Niagara Falls is three different waterfalls in the United States and Canada. I think they're the most beautiful in the world!

Writing

6 Look at the picture and read about a trip. How many geographical features can you find in the text?

Last year, my friend Lupita and I (1)............. (go) on a trip to Chiapas in the south of Mexico. We travelled from Mexico City to Tuxtla Gutiérrez by bus. The journey took more than twelve hours, but while we (2)............. (travel), we saw lots of trees and (3)............. (hear) birds and monkeys.

We spent two days at the famous Mayan ruins. The landscape was amazing, with the temples hidden in the jungle. This was the best part of our trip.

On the last day, we (4)............. (decide) to go to Misol-Ha, a waterfall in the jungle. It was a beautiful morning and when we (5)............. (arrive), the sun (6)............. (shine) on the rocks and trees at the bottom of the waterfall. There was a cool stream so we swam in it before lunch. When we (7)............. (walk) back along a path, we (8)............. (see) a huge spider. Lupita screamed and I laughed!

7 Read the text again and complete it with the past simple or continuous form of the verbs in brackets.

🔍 notice

Travel is usually a verb: *We **travelled** from Mexico City to Tuxtla Gutiérrez by bus.*

A **journey** describes going from one place to another: *The **journey** took more than twelve hours!*

A **trip** is the whole time you were away: *This was the best part of our **trip**.*

8 a Write about a trip you enjoyed a lot. Include the following information.

1 Where did you go?
2 How did you get there?
3 Who did you go with?
4 What was the landscape like?
5 What was the best thing about the trip?

b In pairs, compare your texts. Which trip was more exciting?

⇆ Mediation task: All students, page 127

2.4 A GREAT STORY
telling a story and reacting
an unusual journey

The big picture: an unusual journey

1 **2.1** Look at the picture of an unusual journey. In pairs, guess the answers to the questions. Watch the video and check your answers.
   1. Which country is this?
   2. What is the landscape like?
   3. Which animals are travelling?
   4. Why are they making this journey?

2 **2.1** Are the sentences true (T) or false (F)? Watch again and check.
   1. Timothy Allen is a photographer. ....
   2. The journey takes twenty days. ....
   3. The Kazakhs have 1,000 animals. ....
   4. Everyone travels by camel. ....
   5. They sleep in hotels at night. ....
   6. The temperature is -40°C at night. ....

3 In pairs, discuss the questions.
   1. Do you remember any of Timothy's photos? Which ones?
   2. Why was it important for him to travel with the Kazakhs?
   3. What problems do you think he had?
   4. Would you like to go on a journey like this? Why/Why not?
   5. What's the most difficult journey you've ever had?

4 **2.2** Watch Lou and Rob talking about the journey. Choose the correct words to complete the sentences.
   1. Rob and Lou liked the picture of *the man on a horse / some cows*.
   2. They think Timothy communicated *in English / with a translator*.
   3. Rob *would / wouldn't* like to go on a similar journey.
   4. Lou tells a story about a problem with *her cat / her car*.
   5. She walked in the snow to *a village / her parents' home*.

5 **2.2** Was Rob interested in Lou's story? Watch the video again and match the expressions in the box with the sentences.

   | Go on. | No way! | Lucky you! | Oh no! |
   | Really? | That's awful! | | |

   1. It reminds me of a terrible journey I had. ....
   2. Suddenly, something ran into the road! ....
   3. When I got out of the car, there was nothing there! ....
   4. I got out again, and I could see that the car only had three tyres. ....
   5. There was snow up to my knees! ....
   6. They were really kind and helped us change the wheel. ....

Functional language

6 🔊 2.12 Look at the pictures about another story. In pairs, guess what happened. Listen and check.

7 🔊 2.12 In pairs, order the sentences. Listen again and check.
- a ☐ One day, we decided to go to Jenny's house.
- b ☐ Anyway, at lunchtime we decided to have a picnic.
- c ☐ Did I ever tell you about the wasps?
- d ☐ It happened last year when we were studying for our exams.
- e ☐ In the end, I had to go home on the metro with wet clothes!
- f ☐ We were just starting to eat when suddenly we saw lots of wasps.

FL telling a story and reacting

Telling a story	Reacting to a story
That reminds me of …	Surprise: *Really? / No way!*
Did I ever tell you about …?	Interest: *Go on. / Then what happened?*
It happened …	
One day, …	Bad news: *Oh no. / That's awful!*
Anyway, …	
I was … when suddenly …	Good news: *That's great. / Lucky you!*
In the end, …	

8 🔊 2.13 Look at the Functional language box. Complete the conversation with the correct words. Listen and check.

- **A** That (1) _____ me of something that happened to me.
- **B** What? Did you jump in a lake, too?
- **A** No! It (2) _____ when I was visiting my grandparents. We had a picnic, too.
- **B** (3) _____ on.
- **A** Well, we were sitting in a field when (4) _____ there were all these cows everywhere!
- **B** (5) _____?
- **A** Yeah, it was frightening!
- **B** Oh (6) _____!
- **A** I had to climb a tree. I was so scared.
- **B** (7) _____ way!
- **A** It's true! In the (8) _____, the cows walked away and I climbed down, but I didn't want my lunch after that!

9 a 🔊 2.14 **❝ showing interest ❞** Listen to the sentences and the responses. Tick (✓) the response which sounds more interested: A or B.

1. Last week, I passed my English exam. A ☐ B ☐
2. I missed the train and was late for the interview. A ☐ B ☐
3. They asked me if I wanted to be in the film! A ☐ B ☐
4. It happened when I was working in San Diego. A ☐ B ☐

b 🔊 2.15 Listen and repeat the interested responses.

Speaking

10 a Look at the topics and think of a story about something that happened to you or someone you know.

- a terrible journey
- an embarrassing situation
- an accident
- something you lost
- a funny situation in a shop or restaurant
- a surprise when you met someone

b Prepare to tell your story. Use the questions to help you.
- Where were you?
- What were you doing?
- What happened?
- What did you do?
- How did you feel?
- How did the story end?

c In pairs, tell your stories and react to your partner's story.

REVIEW UNIT 2

Vocabulary
Past time expressions

1 Look at the clock showing the date and time now. Complete the timeline with the past time expressions in the box.

on 1 June   last week   two hours ago
in January at 10.00   yesterday

↑ Now
1 ....
2 ....
3 ....
4 ....
5 ....
6 ....
One year ago

2 Write five sentences that are true for you using the past time expressions in the box. In pairs, compare your answers.

in the summer   an hour ago   when I was ten
at new year   last night

I worked in a café in the summer.

Animals

3 a Put the letters in the correct order to make animals.
1 NDPOILH ....   5 MAELC ....
2 OALILGR ....   6 HKASR ....
3 MLBA ....   7 UYTREBFLT ....
4 RGIET ....   8 PPYUP ....

b In pairs, say if the animals are: wild animals, sea animals, young animals or bugs.

Geographical features

4 Look at the picture and tick (✓) the geographical features you can see.
a valley ☐
b waterfall ☐
c rocks ☐
d trees ☐
e cliffs ☐
f waves ☐
g stream ☐
h sea ☐

5 Describe a landscape in your country to a partner. Why do you like it?

Grammar
Past simple

6 a Complete the sentences with the past simple form of the verbs in brackets.
1 I .... a nature programme on TV last night. (watch)
2 I .... interested in nature when I was young. (not be)
3 I .... the countryside last year. (not visit)
4 I .... a pet animal when I was a child. (have)
5 I .... anywhere this summer. (not travel)

b Make the sentences true for you. In pairs, compare your answers.

I didn't watch a nature programme on TV last night. I watched a football match.

Past continuous and past simple

7 In pairs, answer the question *What were you doing …?* with the past time expressions.
1 in the summer of 2020?
2 before the English class began?
3 at 3.00 p.m. yesterday?

I was living at home in the summer of 2020.

8 Complete the sentences with the correct form of the verbs in brackets.
1 He .... a crocodile while he .... (see / swim)
2 It .... in the forest when we .... (not rain / arrive)
3 I .... through the trees when I .... my phone. (walk / lose)

Functional language
Telling a story and reacting

9 🔊 2.16 Choose the correct words to complete the conversation about an accident. Listen and check.

A Did I ever ⁽¹⁾*tell / remind* you about the time I fell in a lake?
B ⁽²⁾*Really? / Go on.* When was that?
A I was fishing with my dad and I saw a fish jump. I was excited, so I stood up quickly and slipped.
B Oh ⁽³⁾*no / yes*. That's ⁽⁴⁾*awful / great*! Were you scared?
A Yes, the water was so cold and it was difficult to swim. ⁽⁵⁾*Anyway / One day*, everything was OK as there was a rowing boat nearby and I managed to climb inside.
B ⁽⁶⁾*Lucky / Happy* you!

10 Think of a time when you got lost. In pairs, tell your story and react to your partner's story.

🕐 Looking back

- How many irregular past verbs from this unit can you remember?
- Think of three interesting things that happened to you recently. Can you describe what happened?

Icons

3

Grammar G
questions review
relative clauses
articles: *a/an*, *the*, no article

Vocabulary V
subjects and jobs
buildings and structures

Functional language FL
agreeing and disagreeing

Skill
pronoun referencing

Video
the Moai heads

Writing
a blog post

Exams
understanding short texts

The big picture: lunch at the top of a skyscraper

1 Look at the pictures. In pairs, answer the questions.
  1 Do you recognize the photos?
  2 Where are the people?
  3 What are they doing?
  4 What are the differences between the pictures?

2 🔊 3.1 Listen and check your answers.

3 In pairs, discuss the questions.
  1 Would you have lunch at the top of a skyscraper?
  2 What is the most unusual place you've eaten lunch?
  3 Read the definition of *icon*. Can you think of another iconic photo? Describe it to your partner.

icon (noun) An *icon* can be an image, a person or a building that people recognize immediately. It usually represents something.

25

3.1 ICONIC PEOPLE

G questions review
V subjects and jobs

Vocabulary

1 Complete the jobs with the word endings.

V subjects and jobs

-ect	-er	-ete	-ian	-ist

Subject	Job
art	art.........
science	scient.........
athletics	athl.........
politics	politic.........
law	lawy.........
journalism	journal.........
architecture	archit.........
design	design.........
building	build.........
music	music.........
engineering	engine.........

🔊 3.2 Listen, check and repeat.

2 a 🔊 3.3 Look at the pictures and describe the people. Listen and check.

Serena Williams is an athlete from the USA.

Serena Williams

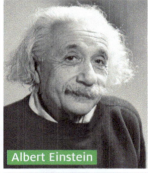
Albert Einstein

Bob Marley

Malala Yousafzai

b Do you think the people are icons? Why?

c In pairs, think of an iconic image, person or building for each of the subjects in exercise 1.

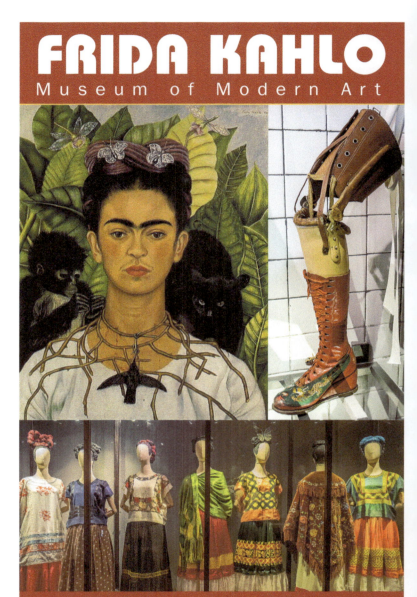

FRIDA KAHLO
Museum of Modern Art

4 MAY – 31 JULY

Listening

3 Look at the poster for an art exhibition. In pairs, answer the questions.
 1 What do you know about Frida Kahlo?
 2 How would you describe her paintings?
 3 Would you like to visit the exhibition? Why/Why not?

4 🔊 3.4 Listen to an interview about the exhibition. Why is Frida Kahlo an icon?

5 🔊 3.4 Listen again. Are the sentences true (T) or false (F)?
 1 It's easy to buy tickets for the exhibition today.
 2 There are lots of products with Frida Kahlo's image on.
 3 Frida Kahlo was a doctor before she was an artist.
 4 She started painting because she couldn't walk.
 5 A lot of her paintings are about her personal feelings.
 6 The exhibition doesn't have any of her paintings.

Grammar

6 a Complete the questions with the auxiliary verbs in the box. In pairs, answer the questions.

are	did	do	was	can

1 .... tickets for the exhibition selling well?
2 Why .... people love Frida so much?
3 What problems .... she have?
4 What .... she planning to study?
5 What .... you see in the exhibition?

b Which question has the answer *yes* or *no*? Look at the other questions again. Put the words in the box in the correct order.

auxiliary verb question word	main verb subject

1 .... 3 ....
2 .... 4 ....

7 a Choose the correct words to complete two more questions from the interview.

1 *Is / Does* she an icon?
2 How old *she was / was she*?

b Choose the correct words to complete the rules.

1 We *use / don't use* the auxiliary verb *do* with the verb *be* in questions.
2 The subject comes *before / after* the verb *be* in questions.

G questions review

Wh- questions
Where do your parents live?
When did she learn to sing?
Why was he playing the guitar?
What can you say in Spanish?

Yes/No questions
Do you know any famous people?
Are you listening to me?
Did she take a photo?
Is he an artist?

→ Grammar reference: page 134

🔍 notice

Prepositions usually go at the end of questions:
*What's the exhibition **about**?*
*What are you waiting **for**?*

8 🔊 3.5 **" intonation in questions "** Listen to a Yes/No question and a *Wh-* question. Does the intonation go up or down at the end? Listen again and repeat.

1 Are tickets for the exhibition selling well?
2 Why do people love Frida so much?

9 Look at the picture. Who is the mural of? Why is he an icon? Read the text and check.

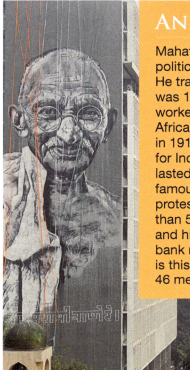

AN INDIAN ICON

Mahatma Gandhi was an Indian politician and civil rights leader. He travelled to London when he was 18 to study law and later worked as a lawyer in South Africa. When he returned to India in 1915, he began a campaign for Indian independence which lasted for over thirty years. He is famous for his idea of peaceful protest. In India, there are more than 50 streets named after him and his face is on stamps and bank notes. And of course, there is this mural of him which is 46 metres tall!

10 a Put the words in the correct order to make questions.

1 study / South Africa / he / law / did / in / ?
2 in / what / South Africa / he / doing / was / ?
3 campaign / last / did / how / the / for / long / ?
4 famous / is / for / what / he / ?
5 can / where / face / you / his / see / ?
6 mural / how / is / tall / the / ?

b In pairs, ask and answer the questions. Remember to use the correct intonation in the questions.

Speaking

11 a Think of a famous person, alive or dead, but don't say who it is.

b In pairs, ask and answer the questions. Try to guess your partner's famous person.

Is he/she alive or dead?
Is he/she a man or a woman?
What is/was his/her job?
What is/was he/she famous for?

3.2 ICONIC BUILDINGS

G relative clauses
V buildings and structures

Vocabulary

1 Look at the pictures. Match them with the words in the box. Do you recognize any of them?

V buildings and structures

bridge	castle	cathedral	mosque
palace	ruins	skyscraper	stadium
statue	tower		

1 .... 6 ....
2 .... 7 ....
3 .... 8 ....
4 .... 9 ....
5 .... 10 ....

🔊 **3.6** Listen, check and repeat.

2 Choose five buildings or structures from the Vocabulary box and think of an example of each in your country. In pairs, compare your answers.

Listening

3 a Look at the pictures. In pairs, answer the questions.
   1 What types of building are they?
   2 Which countries are they in?
   3 Why are they famous?

b 🔊 **3.7** Listen to a podcast and check. Which building do you think is the most interesting? Why?

Grammar

4 🔊 **3.8** Complete the sentences from the podcast with the numbers in the box. Listen and check.

| 200,000 | 20,000 | 1211 | 200 | 1831 | 1950 |

1 Brazil played Uruguay in the .... World Cup. This was at a time **when** everyone thought Brazil were the best team in the world.
2 Unfortunately for most of the .... people **that** were in the stadium, Uruguay won 2–1!
3 People became more interested in the cathedral in ...., the year **when** *The Hunchback of Notre Dame* was published.
4 You soon see why it gets its name – because of the .... blue tiles **which** cover the walls.
5 In 2001, it was declared safe for another .... years by the engineers **who** fixed it.
6 But what if I tell you that this castle, built in ...., is the place **where** Count Dracula lived?

5 Look at the words in **bold** in the sentences in exercise 4 again. Complete the rules with the words in the box.

| that | when | where | which | who |

1 Use .... or .... to talk about things.
2 Use .... or .... to talk about people.
3 Use .... to talk about places.
4 Use .... to talk about times.

G relative clauses

*This is the bridge **which/that** joins Denmark and Sweden.*
*This is the book **which/that** I bought from the shop at the castle.*
*She's the architect **who/that** designed the new skyscraper.*
*Is this the stadium **where** Arsenal won the FA cup?*
*Wednesday was the day **when** we went to the cathedral.*

→ Grammar reference: page 134

6 🔊 **3.9** 🗣 **relative pronoun stress** 🗣 Listen to the questions and sentences. When is the underlined word stressed? Listen again and repeat.
1 a <u>Who</u> do you live with?
  b This is the friend <u>who</u> I live with.
2 a <u>When</u> did you buy this?
  b I bought this <u>when</u> I started my new job.
3 a <u>Where</u> did you park the car?
  b It's on the street <u>where</u> Jon lives.
4 a <u>Which</u> hotel did you stay in?
  b That's the hotel <u>which</u> we stayed in.

7 a Look at the picture below of Bristol in the UK. What buildings can you see?

b Choose the correct words to complete the questions and answers. In pairs, practise asking and answering the questions with the correct stress.
1 Do you know a place *where / who* I can get a good view of the city?
  The place *where / when* you can see the whole of Bristol is the top of Cabot Tower.
2 Is there a cinema *who / which* shows foreign films?
  Yes, the place *that / when* shows the best variety of films is the Watershed.
3 Are there any special days *that / when* everyone gets together to celebrate something?
  Yes, the Harbour Festival is a time *when / which* the streets are full of people.
4 Are there any famous people *who / where* live here?
  Not many, but the one person *which / who* everyone wants to see is Banksy, the graffiti artist.
5 What is the one thing *that / who* every visitor must see?
  The one thing *who / that* most tourists love is walking across the famous Clifton Suspension Bridge.

c In pairs, take turns to ask the questions again. Give answers about where you live.

Speaking

8 a Complete the circles with examples which are important to you.

- a name
- a date
- a place
- an object
- an activity

b In pairs, take turns to guess why each word is important to your partner.

Is 9 February 2015 the day when you got married?
No, it isn't. It's the day my son was born.

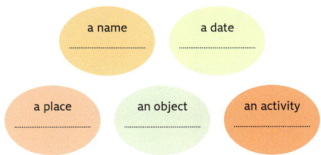

Exam practice: page 158

3.3 A HISTORY OF SYMBOLS

G articles: *a/an, the,* no article
🔧 pronoun referencing

Reading

1 Look at the pictures. In pairs, answer the questions.
   1 How many signs and symbols do you recognize?
   2 Where do you normally see them?
   3 What do they mean?

2 Read the text and match pictures a–f to the first five paragraphs.

3 Choose the best summary of the text.
   a Pictures are more useful than words.
   b Using symbols is part of human nature.
   c Most symbols are very old.

4 Read the Skill box. Then in pairs, find pronouns 1–8 in **bold** in the text. Underline what they refer to.

🔧 **pronoun referencing**

Writers often use pronouns to avoid repeating names, objects and ideas. It's important to understand what they refer to when you read.

- Personal pronouns: *The lawyer read **the contract** yesterday. **It** was thirty pages long.*
- Demonstrative pronouns: *The skyscraper is **500 m tall**. **This** is more than the Empire State building.*
- Possessive adjectives: *I like **the company**, but **their** prices are too expensive.*

5 Are the sentences true (T) or false (F)? Use your answers to exercise 4 to help you.
   1 Humans started using symbols a very long time ago.
   2 Scientists were looking for one of the most important historical sites in the world.
   3 The cave paintings of people and animals are examples of complex ideas.
   4 People in most countries understand the word 'OK'.
   5 Spoken words are not really symbols.
   6 Logos are symbols which represent businesses.
   7 Most people don't recognize the Nike logo.
   8 Humans need symbols in many different areas of our lives.

6 In pairs, think of other signs and symbols that you see every day.

Why humans need symbols

1 These days, symbols are everywhere, from the icons on our phones which we tap to open an app, to the road signs we see on our way to work. But using symbols is nothing new. In fact, ⁽¹⁾**it's** as old as human life itself.

2 In 1970, when a team of scientists discovered a natural cave in southern Italy, ⁽²⁾**they** didn't know they had found one of the most important historical sites in the world. Inside the cave, the walls were covered with drawings made over 5,000 years ago. Among the pictures of people and animals, there were also strange symbols – spiral shapes, for example, which scientists believe represent life. ⁽³⁾**This** showed that using symbols to represent complex ideas is natural to humans.

3 We use symbols a lot more than you may realize. Think about the words you're reading right now. Each word, and even the individual letters that we use to make the words, are symbols. Take just two letters, for example – OK. ⁽⁴⁾**These** are seen on buttons around the world and speakers of almost any language understand that they mean 'acceptable' or 'good'. Even the words we speak are a type of symbol because ⁽⁵⁾**they**'re noises which represent something else.

4 Words are not the only symbols that are used around the world. Imagine you're at an airport in a foreign country. You need the toilet, but where do you go? The airport will almost definitely have signs of a man and a woman standing together which you can follow.

5 Companies have realized how important symbols are, too. Almost every business has a picture (often called a logo) that represents ⁽⁶⁾**it**. Their aim is for people to see them and immediately think of the company. Once the connection between the logo and the company is clear, a company can even stop using their name and simply show the logo, such as the sports company Nike, which just uses ⁽⁷⁾**its** famous 'swoosh' logo on its products and adverts.

6 From prehistoric art to everyday language, from airport signs to company logos, symbols have many different functions. Humans have used them for a very, very long time. ⁽⁸⁾**They**'re not just useful, but they're actually necessary in almost every aspect of human life.

Grammar

7 a Choose the correct words to complete the sentences. Check your answers in the text.

1 Imagine you're at *a / an* airport in *a / an* foreign country. *An / The* airport will almost definitely have signs.
2 Think about *the words / words* you're reading right now.
3 *The words / Words* are not the only symbols that are used around *the world / world*.

b Look at the sentences again. Complete rules 1–5 with *the*, *a*, *an* or no article.

1 We use .... or .... to talk about a person or thing for the first time.
2 We use .... to talk about a person or thing we have already mentioned.
3 We use .... to talk about people and things in general.
4 We use .... to talk about specific people and things.
5 We use .... for things where only one exists or it's clear which one we mean.

> **G** articles: *a/an*, *the*, no article
>
> I have **a** new phone and I downloaded **an** app yesterday.
> **The** app helps me organize my time.
> I'm interested in cave paintings.
> **The** cave paintings in southern Italy are very important.
> I used **the** internet to find out about **the** company.
>
> → Grammar reference: page 134

8 Choose the correct options to complete the blog post. Do you agree with the writer?

There are lots of ⁽¹⁾*the / –* icons used in ⁽²⁾*the / –* technology that are clever and creative. I like ⁽³⁾*a / the* house icon on the internet that represents the homepage of ⁽⁴⁾*a / the* website. It looks just like a child's drawing of ⁽⁵⁾*a / –* house! I like ⁽⁶⁾*a / the* bin, too – that's ⁽⁷⁾*a / the* place where you put ⁽⁸⁾*a / –* things that you don't want. It's ⁽⁹⁾*a / the* very clear icon. ⁽¹⁰⁾*The / –* symbols that Facebook and Twitter use are also fine because they're attractive and everyone recognizes them. But there is one icon which just doesn't work these days: ⁽¹¹⁾*– / the* floppy disk icon for 'save' because ⁽¹²⁾*the / –* computers don't use ⁽¹³⁾*– / the* floppy disks any more. They stopped using them in 2002! Most ⁽¹⁴⁾*the / –* young people don't know what they are. I think someone should design ⁽¹⁵⁾*a / the* new icon. There must be ⁽¹⁶⁾*an / –* icon out there that's more modern. Here are some ideas I came up with. What do you think? Which do you like best? Or do you have ⁽¹⁷⁾*the / a* better idea?

9 3.10 /ðə/ and /ðiː/ Listen to the phrases. Notice how *the* is pronounced differently before vowel and consonant sounds. Listen again and repeat.

1 the icons /ðiː/
2 the words /ðə/
3 the airport /ðiː/
4 the logos /ðə/

Writing

10 a Complete the sentences with *a*, *an*, *the* or – (no article).

ICONIC LANDMARKS … AT THE WRONG TIME?

This is ⁽¹⁾............... picture of Piazza San Marco. It is ⁽²⁾............... popular place for ⁽³⁾............... tourists in Venice, Italy. There is ⁽⁴⁾............... man and ⁽⁵⁾............... woman in the picture and they are looking at ⁽⁶⁾............... beautiful building in ⁽⁷⁾............... piazza. I think they are ⁽⁸⁾............... tourists. ⁽⁹⁾............... funniest thing in ⁽¹⁰⁾............... picture is that ⁽¹¹⁾............... people are standing in water because, unfortunately, Venice often floods.

b In pairs, write a short description of the picture below.

Tower Bridge, London, UK

⇄ Mediation task: Student A page 125, Student B page 126

3.4 THAT'S A GOOD POINT!

agreeing and disagreeing
the Moai heads

The big picture: the Moai heads

1 Look at the picture of an iconic place. In pairs, think of three adjectives to describe the statues.

2 **3.1** In pairs, guess the answers to the questions. Watch the video and check.
1 What are the two names of the island?
2 Where is this island?
3 Why are the statues famous?
4 Why did people build them?

3 **3.1** Watch the video again and complete the sentences with the correct words.
1 The statues are .... of years old, and there are almost .... statues on the island.
2 The .... of the statue is buried seven to eight metres underground.
3 The film made on the island in the 1990s was called ....
4 The statue for the film is still underwater because it was .... and ....
5 The statues are iconic because they're one of the world's last great ....

4 In pairs, discuss the questions.
1 How do you think the people built the statues?
2 How would you describe the landscape on the island?
3 Would you like to visit the island? Why/Why not?
4 What other iconic statues do you know? Where are they? Which would you most like to visit?

5 **3.2** Watch Rob and Lou talking about the video. Who is more interested in the statues? Why?

6 **3.2** Watch the video again. Do Rob and Lou agree (A) or disagree (D) about the opinions? Do you remember any phrases they used to agree and disagree?
1 A trip to Rapa Nui is much better than looking at photos. ....
2 The statues are iconic because they are mysterious. ....
3 The statues were built to protect the people on the island. ....
4 Lou will need a lot of money to visit Rapa Nui. ....

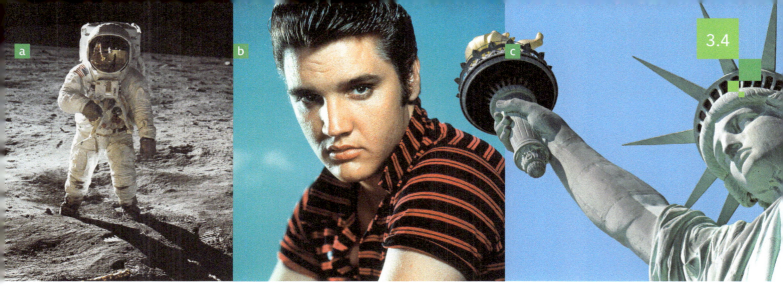

Functional language

7 🔊 **3.11** Look at the pictures. Match them with the questions. Listen and check.

1 What's the most famous photo in the world?
2 What's the most beautiful statue in the world?
3 Who's the most iconic musician of all time?

8 a 🔊 **3.11** In pairs, match the sentences with the responses. Listen again and check.

1 I think it has to be a photo of a famous person, like Kim Kardashian or Justin Bieber.
2 I think the Little Mermaid in Denmark is really beautiful.
3 Now this is an easy question to answer. It's Elvis Presley.
4 I think it's probably the first man on the moon.

a **True, but actually** it doesn't look that great when you see it in real life.
b **I'm not sure I agree with that**. It's a cool photo, but you can't see his face!
c **No way!** Those photos aren't iconic. They're just photos of celebrities!
d **I totally agree.** He really is an icon.

b Look at the phrases in **bold**. Which do we use to agree, disagree or partly agree?

FL agreeing and disagreeing

Agreeing	Disagreeing	Partly agreeing
That's a good point.	I'm not sure I agree with that.	I see your point, but …
I totally agree.	I'm afraid I disagree.	I know what you mean, but …
That's (so) true.	I don't think so.	True, but actually …
Absolutely!	I completely disagree.	
I suppose so.	No way!	

9 🔊 **3.12** 🎤 **strong/weak expression** 🎤 Listen to the statements. Do they express strong (S) or weak (W) agreement or disagreement? Listen again and repeat.

1 Absolutely! I totally agree.
2 I'm not sure I agree with that.
3 No way! I completely disagree.
4 I suppose so.

10 a Read the sentences. Do you agree strongly (AS), agree weakly (AW), disagree strongly (DS) or disagree weakly (DW)?

1 You must always tell the truth to your friends.
2 Learning English is a lot of fun!
3 Money is more important than love.
4 Music is better now than it was 30 years ago.
5 Breakfast is the most important meal of the day.
6 Watching football is boring.
7 Travelling alone is dangerous.
8 Dogs are better pets than cats.

b In pairs, read out the sentences and agree or disagree with them. Remember to express if it is strong or weak agreement or disagreement.

Speaking

11 In groups of three, discuss the topics. Give your opinion, then your classmates will agree or disagree and give their opinions. Continue the conversations for as long as possible.

- a good film
- a restaurant or café that you like
- an actor that you don't think is good
- a food that you really like
- a country that you want to visit
- a music group that you don't like

I think Black Panther is a great film.
I'm afraid I disagree. The story is really silly!
That's true, but the action is amazing! And the actors are brilliant.
No way! They're awful.

📝 Writing bank: page 146

REVIEW UNIT 3

Vocabulary
Subjects and jobs

1 **a** Look at the subjects and write the correct words for the jobs.

1 architecture .... 4 athletics ....
2 science .... 5 politics ....
3 design .... 6 music ....

b In pairs, think of people for the jobs. Write sentences to describe them.

Winston Churchill was a famous British politician.

Buildings and structures

2 Complete the sentences with the words in the box.

bridge   palace   ruins   skyscraper   statue

1 Every day in Sydney, thousands of cyclists use the .... to cross the harbour.
2 The Sphinx is a giant .... in Egypt with the body of a lion and the head of a person.
3 Buckingham .... is the home of the British Queen, but she doesn't live there all the time.
4 The Burj Khalifa in Dubai is over 800 metres high and the tallest .... in the world.
5 No one knows who built the ancient .... at Stonehenge, but they are thousands of years old.

3 In pairs, think of a famous building or structure in your country. Describe it to your partner.

Grammar
Questions review

4 **a** Put the words in the correct order to make questions.

1 do / do / you / what / weekend / the / at ?
....
2 live / you / parents / do / with / your ?
....
3 moment / what / you / studying / the / are / at ?
....
4 work / who / with / do / you ?
....

b In pairs, ask and answer the questions.

Relative clauses

5 Tick (✓) the sentences which are correct. Correct the incorrect relative pronouns in **bold**.

1 It's a famous painting **who** is in the Louvre in Paris. ☐
2 He's the architect **that** designed the new museum. ☐
3 Is this the cathedral **which** William and Kate got married? ☐
4 It was 1985 – the year **when** he wrote his first book. ☐
5 Was that the day **where** you moved house? ☐

6 Write four sentences describing famous people or places. In pairs, try to guess your partner's people or places.

It's the bridge that …
She's the athlete who …

Articles: *a/an, the,* no article

7 Choose the correct articles to complete the sentences: *a, an, the* or – (no article).

1 Sam Maxwell is *an / a* engineer. He's *the / a* person who designed this bridge.
2 Mum's at *the / –* restaurant I told you about. She's having *a / the* meal with *– / the* friends.
3 We're buying *a / the* new table and *– / the* chairs. *The / –* chairs are very comfortable.
4 **A** Where are *the / –* keys to *a / the* garage?
   B They're on *the / a* kitchen table.
5 Look at *the / –* moon. It's beautiful. I love *the / –* nights like this.

Functional language
Agreeing and disagreeing

8 🔊 3.13 Complete the conversation with the words in the box. Listen and check.

mean   point   suppose   sure   totally   true

A I don't think students should use mobile phones in class.
B I (1).................. agree. I think that they stop students from concentrating.
C I know what you (2).................., but actually, mobile phones can be quite useful.
B How?
C Well, there are some really good apps for learning languages, and you can find so much information on the Web.
A Yes, that's (3).................., like online dictionaries.
B I see your (4).................., but they can make students lazy. They look up words on their phones and don't try to learn vocabulary.
C I'm not (5).................. I agree with that. I learn lots of words by using the dictionary on my phone.
A I (6).................. so.

9 In pairs, read out the sentences and use expressions to agree or disagree. Try to explain why.

1 Students mustn't use their mobile phones in class.
2 Online dictionaries are better than printed dictionaries.
3 Learning Chinese is more useful than learning English.
4 Writing in English is more difficult than speaking.

Looking back

- Think of three things you learned in this unit.
- Is there anything you want to look at again?
- Tell a partner about your favourite famous person/place.

Learning by doing

4

Grammar G
going to and present continuous for plans and arrangements
must(n't) and *(don't) have to*

Vocabulary V
education collocations
adjectives and dependent prepositions
-ed/-ing adjectives

Functional language FL
making arrangements

Skill
listen for specific information

Video
Japanese high school life

Writing
a formal email

Exams
talking about yourself

The big picture: learning languages

1 Look at the picture. In pairs, guess the answers to the questions.
   1 Where is the person?
   2 Which language is he learning?
   3 Is it a good way to learn a language? Why/Why not?
   4 Why does he want to learn this language?

2 ◄)) 4.1 Listen and check your answers.

3 In pairs, discuss the questions.
   1 Do you ever have English classes like this?
   2 Is it important to have good pronunciation when you speak English?
   3 Who do you speak to in English?
   4 Why do you want to learn English?
   5 What motivates you to study English?

4.1 SKILLS OR QUALIFICATIONS?

G *going to* and present continuous for plans and arrangements
V education collocations

Vocabulary

1 🔊 **4.2** Look at the blog title and picture. In pairs, order the sentences. Listen and check.

University wasn't for me

HOME BLOG ABOUT

Posted by Ben Frankle 14 July

There are lots of ways to 'get an education'

a ◯ So I went to university to study languages, but I didn't get a degree.
b ◯ It's very practical, so I don't have to revise for exams or write essays.
c ◯ Unfortunately, I failed my German exams and I decided to leave.
d ◯ Now, I'm doing a part-time cooking course at college.
e ◯ I'm learning lots of new skills and I'm doing work experience in a hotel.
f ◯ At first, I thought I wanted a career in tourism.
g ◯ I passed my exams at secondary school and got good grades.
h ◯ When I get my qualification, I want to work as a chef.

2 Complete the phrases with the verbs in the box. Check your answers in the text.

V education collocations

| do (x2) | fail | get (x2) | go | learn |
| revise | study | pass | want | write |

1 .... a career in ...
2 .... / .... exams
3 .... good grades
4 .... a degree/qualifications
5 .... a course
6 .... skills
7 .... work experience
8 .... for exams
9 .... to university/college
10 .... essays
11 .... a subject

🔊 **4.3** Listen, check and repeat.

🔍 notice

Compulsory education includes **primary school** and **secondary school**.

After that, you can choose to go to **university** to do a degree, or go to **college** to do a more practical course.

3 Complete the sentences so they are true for you. In pairs, compare your answers.
1 I always wanted a career in ....
2 When I was at secondary school, I loved studying ....
3 The best place to revise for an exam is ....
4 When I failed my .... , I felt ....
5 The last essay I wrote was about ....
6 I'd like to do a part-time course in ....

Listening

4 a 🔊 **4.4** Look at the pictures. What sort of careers do Beth and Tom want? Listen and check.

b Who plans to get more work experience? Who plans to get more qualifications?

5 🔊 **4.4** Listen again and choose the correct options to complete the sentences.
1 Beth thinks it will be difficult to …
  a get a place at university.
  b get a job in computer animation.
2 Her plan is to work while she is at university because …
  a she wants work experience.
  b she needs money.
3 Tom already …
  a repairs phones as a hobby.
  b has a job when he finishes school.
4 Tom isn't doing a course at college because …
  a the industry changes very quickly.
  b he wants to make money quickly.

Grammar

6 a Whose plans are these: *Beth's* or *Tom's*?
1 **I'm going to design** my own website.
2 **I'm going to look for** a part-time job while I'm there.
3 **I'm not going to take it easy** this summer.
4 **I'm not going to stay there** for a long time.

b Look at the words in **bold**. What form of the verb comes after *be going to*?

7 a Read two more sentences. What tense are they in?
a I'm living with my parents at the moment.
b I'm doing an intensive Photoshop course in July.

b Answer the questions.
1 Which refers to an action happening now?
2 Which refers to an arrangement (with a fixed time and place) in the future?
3 Is it also correct to use *going to* + infinitive for an arrangement?

G *going to* and present continuous for plans and arrangements

Plans

+ I'm going to study Law at university.
− I'm not going to study Maths.
? Are you going to get a degree?
Y/N Yes, I am. / No, I'm not.

Arrangements

+ I'm meeting Juan tonight.
− We aren't going out tonight.
? Are you revising for the exam tonight?
Y/N Yes, we are. / No, we aren't.

→ Grammar reference: page 135

8 🔊 **4.5** 🗨 *'gonna'* 🗨 Listen to the sentences. Notice how *going to* is pronounced when before an infinitive. Listen and repeat.
1 I'm **going to** design my own website.
2 I'm **going to** Rochester Art School in September.

9 a Complete the conversations with the present continuous or *going to* forms of the verbs in brackets.
1 **A** Jo and I _____ (go) to a festival tomorrow. We have our tickets. Can you come?
   B Sorry, no, I can't. I _____ (play) football with my team tomorrow morning.
2 **A** What job _____ you _____ (do) when you finish your studies?
   B No idea! I _____ (give) myself some time to decide.
3 **A** Sally _____ (travel) to Malta in November for a two-week English course.
   B Great! Where _____ she _____ (stay)?
   A She _____ (live) with an Irish family.
4 **A** I _____ (not write) my History essay this evening. I _____ (go) to the cinema.
   B When _____ you _____ (do) the essay, then?
   A On Sunday … Oh no! I can't! My sister _____ (visit) me that day!
5 **A** I _____ (buy) some new shoes soon. My trainers are so old.
   B Great! _____ you _____ (try) the new shoe shop in the town centre?

b In pairs, practise the conversations. Try to pronounce *going to* as 'gonna' before an infinitive.

Speaking

10 In pairs, ask and answer the question *What are you doing …?* with the time expressions in the box.

next month   next week   next year
this evening   tomorrow

11 a Imagine that you want an interesting career. Plan your career path. Choose from the jobs in the box or think of your own idea.

actor   architect   astronaut
musician   nurse   scientist

Astronaut: 1 degree in Physics → 2 apply for a job at NASA → 3 learn Russian!

b In pairs, say your career plan, but don't say the job. Your partner will try to guess the job.

I'm starting a degree in Physics next month.
Are you going to be a scientist?
No. After university, I'm going to apply for a job at NASA.
Are you going to be an astronaut?
That's right!

4.2 SCHOOL DAYS

G must(n't) and (don't) have to
V adjectives and dependent prepositions

Vocabulary

1 In pairs, ask and answer the questions about your school days.
   1 Which subjects were you good at? Which were you bad at?
   2 Were you worried about exams?
   3 Were you ever disappointed with your exam grades?
   4 Were you ever surprised by your exam grades?
   5 Were you keen on sports?
   6 Were you interested in most things or were you bored with some subjects?

2 Look at the questions in exercise 1 again. Match the prepositions in the box with the adjectives.

   V adjectives and dependent prepositions

about	at	by	from	in
of	on	to	with	

   1 afraid ....   5 different ....   9 keen ....
   2 angry ....   6 disappointed .... 10 similar ....
   3 bad ....   7 good ....   11 surprised ....
   4 bored ....   8 interested ....   12 worried ....

   🔊 4.6 Listen, check and repeat.

Reading

3 a Look at the title and the picture. In pairs, discuss the questions.
   1 Where is the girl?
   2 What is she doing?

  b Read the text and check your answers.

4 Read the text again. Are the sentences true (T) or false (F)?
   1 At the Circus School, students don't have to study normal subjects. ....
   2 Students must get the highest grades when they study at the school. ....
   3 Students learn about life, and they work hard, but enjoy school. ....
   4 They don't pay any money to go to the school. ....
   5 Carla is from a poor family and sold things in the street. ....
   6 Carla wants to get a good job. ....

5 Would you like to go to Circus School? Why?
   I wouldn't like to go to Circus School. I'm not very athletic and I'm not good at dancing!

WHEN SCHOOL IS A CIRCUS

When you were at school, did you ride a bicycle in class? Did your teachers let you run and jump in the classroom? Of course not! But when Carla does these things, her teacher isn't angry with her. In fact, she's disappointed with her if she doesn't!

The school where Carla goes in Rio de Janeiro, Brazil, is very different from most schools. Students from the ages of 4 to 24 learn how to dance, sing and do acrobatics in a circus. That sounds exciting, but it isn't easy. 'Students have to work hard,' says Ester, one of the teachers at the school. 'Our students at Circus School have to go to normal classes too and study traditional subjects like languages and Maths as well – that's very important. They don't have to get the highest grades, but they do have to try their best. They mustn't be late for class, and they must always be polite.'

Ester thinks that Circus School teaches students many useful things. 'Students learn how to work with other people, and they learn about themselves, too. They see that some things in life can be difficult, but if you work hard, things can get better. Best of all, they learn that school – and life – can be exciting and enjoyable!'

Circus School is a charity. That means the school is free for these students. Most of them come from areas of the city where many children leave school without any qualifications. Carla lives in a tiny room with her mother and brothers. She left secondary school when she was ten and she sold drinks to drivers in the street. 'It was tiring working all day.' Now, thanks to the Circus School, she's hoping for a better future. 'I'm probably not going to be a circus star!' she smiles. 'But I want to get good grades and get a good job. I'm very happy I don't have to stand in the street all day any more!'

Grammar

6 a Find the sentences in the text and complete them.
1 Students at Circus School .... go to normal classes, too.
2 They .... get the highest grades.
3 They .... be late for class.
4 They .... always be polite.

b Look at the sentences again and answer the questions.
1 Which sentences are about students' obligations? .... and ....
2 Which sentence is something which isn't allowed? ....
3 Which sentence is about something which isn't necessary? ....

> **G** *must(n't)* and *(don't) have to*
>
> Students **have to** study English and Maths.
> They **don't have to** study Music.
> They **mustn't** eat or drink in class.
> They **must** ask to go to the toilet.
>
> → Grammar reference: page 135

7 Read about school rules around the world and choose the correct words to complete the sentences.

> 1 In some schools in the USA, students *must / don't have to* wear special indoor shoes in the school building. This helps keep the school clean.
> 2 Chinese students *mustn't / have to* sleep for 30 minutes in their classrooms after lunch. Short naps during the day are good for you, but these students *must / mustn't* sleep at their desks, and they're uncomfortable.
> 3 Some teachers in the UK *don't have to / mustn't* use a red pen to correct students' work because red makes students unhappy. They *have to / don't have to* use softer colours like purple or green.
> 4 Children in a primary school in Sydney, Australia *must / mustn't* stand on their hands in the playground because the school says it is dangerous.
> 5 Students in Japan *mustn't / don't have to* stay in every night, but if they want to go out, some students *don't have to / have to* ask their teacher – even at the weekend!
> 6 Students in France *mustn't / don't have to* have tomato ketchup on their food at lunchtime because it isn't healthy and it is 'too American'.

8 In pairs, discuss the questions.
1 Do you have any of the rules in exercise 7 in your country?
2 Which rules do you think are a good idea?
3 Which rules do you think are silly?

We have to wear slippers in school – we mustn't wear shoes inside. I think it's a good idea!

9 🔊 4.7 ❝ **have to/has to** ❞ Listen to the sentences. Notice how *have to* and *has to* are pronounced in the sentences. Listen again and repeat.
1 Students don't **have to** wear a uniform at my school.
2 My cousin **has to** wear a green jacket and tie.

10 a In pairs, add four more school rules that are common in your country.
1 Students have to …   3 They mustn't …
2 They must …   4 However, they don't have to …

b In groups of four, compare your answers. Are any rules the same?

Most students have to wear a uniform to school.

Speaking

11 In pairs, think of some rules for your classes to improve your English. Use the phrases below or your own ideas.

speak your own language	watch films in English
study at home	visit English-speaking countries
buy a good dictionary	aim for perfect pronunciation
read long novels in English	apply for official exams

OK, Rule 1: English learners mustn't speak their own language. They have to try to speak English.

✅ Exam practice: page 159

4.3 LEARNING ABOUT CULTURES

- V -ed/-ing adjectives
- listen for specific information

Listening

1. Look at the picture and read the information. In pairs, answer the questions.
   1. What can you see in the picture?
   2. Where is the museum?
   3. What can visitors learn about?
   4. Would you like to visit the museum? Why/Why not?

2. 🔊 4.9 Listen to the audio guide to the museum. Number the topics in the order you hear about them.
   - a ☐ Romani clothes
   - b ☐ Romani music
   - c ☐ Roma people around the world
   - d ☐ the Romani language

listen for specific information

We often have to listen for specific information and take notes.
- Before you listen, think about what type of information you need to listen for: is it a number, a person, a time, a place, etc.?
- Listen for 'clues'. For example, if the information is an age, you might hear *old* or *years*.
- When you hear the information, write it down, but keep on listening.

3. a Read the Skill box. Then look at the notes in exercise 3b. In pairs, decide what kind of information you need to complete them.

   b 🔊 4.9 Listen to the audio guide again and complete the notes.

   Exhibit A
   › The Roma people originally came from (1) ....
   › They moved to Europe (2) .... years ago.
   › Today, more than (3) .... live in the USA.

   Exhibit B
   › Roma people prefer small musical instruments, like the (4) ....
   › Their music inspired some famous musicians like Django Reinhardt.

   Exhibit C
   › Many Romani clothes are (5) .... because it's a lucky colour.
   › At the museum, children can learn traditional Romani skills.

   Exhibit D
   › Many Roma people don't (6) .... or (7) .... the language.
   › They enjoy telling (8) .... about their history and traditions.

Museum of Romani Culture

If you're visiting the Czech city of Brno, why not visit the Museum of Romani Culture? Here you can learn about the fascinating history of the Roma people in the Czech Republic and around the world. The museum is found in the city's Romani district. Audio guides are available.

4. In pairs, answer the questions.
   1. Did you know much about the Roma people and their culture?
   2. Which of the exhibits is the most interesting? Why?
   3. Are there any museums in your town? What can you learn about?

Vocabulary

5. Read the reviews of the Museum of Romani Culture. Complete the reviews with 1, 2, 3, 4 or 5 stars.

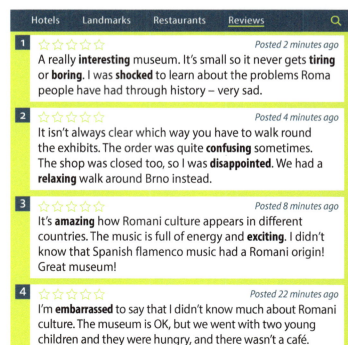

| Hotels | Landmarks | Restaurants | Reviews |

1 ☆☆☆☆☆ *Posted 2 minutes ago*
A really **interesting** museum. It's small so it never gets **tiring** or **boring**. I was **shocked** to learn about the problems Roma people have had through history – very sad.

2 ☆☆☆☆☆ *Posted 4 minutes ago*
It isn't always clear which way you have to walk round the exhibits. The order was quite **confusing** sometimes. The shop was closed too, so I was **disappointed**. We had a **relaxing** walk around Brno instead.

3 ☆☆☆☆☆ *Posted 8 minutes ago*
It's **amazing** how Romani culture appears in different countries. The music is full of energy and **exciting**. I didn't know that Spanish flamenco music had a Romani origin! Great museum!

4 ☆☆☆☆☆ *Posted 22 minutes ago*
I'm **embarrassed** to say that I didn't know much about Romani culture. The museum is OK, but we went with two young children and they were hungry, and there wasn't a café.

6 Look at the adjectives in **bold** in exercise 5 again and complete the rules with *-ed* or *-ing*.
1 We use the ending .... to describe how we feel.
2 We use the ending .... to describe things that make us feel a certain way.

7 Which adjectives are positive and which are negative? In pairs, compare your answers.

V *-ed/-ing* adjectives

1 amazing/amazed
2 boring/bored
3 confusing/confused
4 exciting/excited
5 relaxing/relaxed
6 disappointing/disappointed
7 embarrassing/embarrassed
8 interesting/interested
9 shocking/shocked
10 tiring/tired

🔊 4.10 Listen, check and repeat.

8 a 🔊 4.11 **word stress** Listen to the adjectives. Notice how the underlined syllables are stressed. Listen again and repeat.

1 <u>bor</u>ing (Oo)
2 an<u>noyed</u> (oO)
3 ex<u>cit</u>ed (oOo)
4 <u>in</u>terested (Ooo)

b 🔊 4.12 In pairs, say the adjectives in the box and put them in the correct columns. Listen, check and repeat.

amazed   confused   confusing   embarrassed
interesting   shocking   tiring

Oo	oO	oOo	Ooo
boring	annoyed	excited	interested

9 a Choose the correct words to complete the sentences.
1 I saw an exhibit at the History Museum about life during the war. It was very *shocked / shocking*.
2 My job is very *tired / tiring*. I work ten hours a day.
3 I love horror films. The special effects in some are really *amazed / amazing*!
4 The concert was *disappointed / disappointing*. The singer arrived an hour late!
5 I was *amazed / amazing* that lots of people liked *Avengers: Infinity War*. I didn't think it was very good.
6 I'm *bored / boring* when I visit art galleries for more than an hour!
7 It's *embarrassing / embarrassed* that some people know nothing about other cultures!
8 I don't understand a lot of modern art. I think it's very *confused / confusing*!
9 I love going to the beach. It's very *relaxed / relaxing*.
10 I'm very *interested / interesting* in history. I think I'll study it at university.

b Change the sentences in exercise 9a so they are true for you. Use *-ing/-ed* adjectives.

I saw an exhibit at the Science Museum about computer technology. It was very interesting!

Writing

10 a Read the review. Complete the first sentence with one of the items in the box.

book   film   museum   online course
school   TV programme

b How many words from the Vocabulary box can you find in the text?

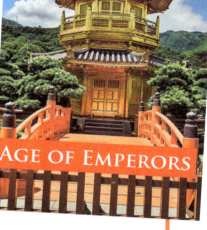

You'll like this 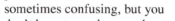 if you are interested in Chinese and south-east Asian history. There are ten chapters, and each chapter is about a different period in history. It starts three thousand years ago and ends almost in the present. The chapters are an amazing journey through time. The stories about the people (emperors, soldiers, etc.) are really interesting. The explanations of political events are sometimes confusing, but you don't have to read every chapter. You can jump to the parts that you're most interested in, and there's a test at the end of each chapter. It's useful to do the tests, but they are very easy, so I was sometimes bored by the questions.

11 a In pairs, write a similar review about one of the ideas in the box in exercise 10a. Try to use as many *-ed/-ing* adjectives as possible.

b Swap your review with another pair. Read each other's review and decide if it makes you want to find out more about the topic.

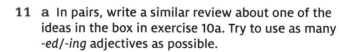

4.4 WHAT ARE YOU DOING THIS WEEKEND?

FL making arrangements
Japanese high school life

The big picture: Japanese high school life

1 Look at the picture. In pairs, answer the questions.
   1 Where do you think the girl is going?
   2 Do many people travel this way in your country?
   3 What is she wearing?
   4 What questions would you like to ask her?

2 **4.1** Watch the video and tick (✓) the topics Sophie talks about.
   1 her journey to school ☐
   2 school clothes ☐
   3 her favourite subjects ☐
   4 school food ☐
   5 her friends ☐
   6 problems she had ☐

3 In pairs, try to remember two things Sophie liked and two things she didn't like about the exchange.

4 **4.1** In pairs, choose the correct words to complete the sentences. Watch the video again and check.
   1 In Japan, when students arrive at school, they *must / mustn't / don't have to* take off their shoes.
   2 In the winter, students *must / mustn't / don't have to* wear a jacket over their uniforms.
   3 Students usually *bring lunch to school / go home for lunch / buy lunch at school*.
   4 At the end of each day, students have to *learn languages / clean the classroom / do homework*.

5 In pairs, discuss the questions.
   1 What are the similarities and differences between high school in Japan and in your country?
   2 Did anything about Sophie's school surprise you?
   3 Would you like to go on an exchange to another country? Why/Why not?
   4 What country would you like to study in? Why?

6 **4.2** Watch Lou and Rob talking about the video. Are the sentences true (T) or false (F)?
   1 Both Lou and Rob wore a school uniform. ....
   2 Rob was surprised that students clean their classrooms. ....
   3 They agree to meet with Chia on Friday evening. ....
   4 They decide to go to an art gallery and eat Japanese food. ....

7 **4.2** In pairs, order the sentences. Watch the video again and check.
   a ☐ That sounds great.
   b ☐ Wednesday's OK, but I'll have to ask Chia, of course.
   c ☐ There's a new exhibition at the art gallery I want to see.
   d ☐ I'm free on Wednesday. How about then?
   e ☐ If she can make it, what do you want to do?
   f ☐ What are you doing on Friday?
   g ☐ What about next week some time?
   h ☐ Sorry, I'm busy. I'm going to visit my grandparents for the weekend.

Functional language

8 🔊 **4.13** Listen to three conversations. Match them with the pictures.

1 .... 2 .... 3 ....

9 🔊 **4.13** In pairs, match the sentences with the responses. Listen again and check.

1 What are you up to this weekend? ....
2 How about next weekend? ....
3 Do you fancy going to the cinema? ....
4 When's good for you? ....
5 What are you doing on Monday? ....
6 What time suits you? ....

a I can do 1.30.
b I have to work that day.
c I'm free on Thursday evening.
d Sorry, I'm busy.
e Nothing special.
f That sounds great!

FL making arrangements

What are you doing / up to …?	Nothing special. / Not much.
	I'm … / I have …
Do you fancy / feel like …?	That sounds great! / I'd love to.
What / How about …?	I'm afraid I can't. / Sorry, I'm busy.
When's good for you?	I'm free … / I can do …
What time suits you?	… is tricky. / I can't make it …

🔍 notice

How / What about …? and *Do you feel like / fancy …?* are followed by the *-ing* form of the verb.

*How about **going** for a walk?*
*Do you feel like **having** pizza?*

10 🔊 **4.14** 🗣 **expressing emotion** 🗣 Listen and notice how the intonation changes in the underlined responses. Repeat the responses.

1 **A** Some friends and I are going camping in the mountains. Do you want to come?
  B Oh, <u>I'm afraid I can't</u>. I'm taking my brother to the airport on Sunday morning.
2 **A** How about next weekend?
  B <u>That sounds great</u>! Are you going again?

11 In pairs, make arrangements and excuses for the activities below. Remember to use the correct intonation.

Do you feel like going for a bike ride tomorrow?
I'm afraid I can't. I'm meeting some friends from university.

1 going for a bike ride tomorrow
2 playing tennis in the park this afternoon
3 going to a concert tonight
4 having a coffee tomorrow
5 watching a film later
6 going for a walk after class

Speaking

12 Complete your calendar with nine events. Use the suggestions in the box or your own ideas.

coffee with …	dentist	
decorate bedroom	dinner at …	
English class	haircut	party at …
picnic at …	play …	visit …

	Thursday	Friday	Saturday
9.00–12.00			
12.00–3.00			
3.00–6.00			
6.00–9.00			

13 In pairs, arrange to meet each other. Don't show your partner your calendar.

Do you fancy going for a coffee Thursday evening?
Thursday evening is tricky. I have my English class. What about Friday morning?

✏ Writing bank: page 147   43

REVIEW UNIT 4

Vocabulary
Education collocations

1 Complete the sentences with the verbs in the box.

| fail | go | revise | write |

1 Do you plan to .... to college, or find a job?
2 I usually .... for exams in the library. It's quiet and peaceful.
3 For homework, I'd like you to .... an essay about a famous artist.
4 Did she .... all her exams?

2 Complete the sentences so they are true for you. In pairs, compare your answers.
  1 Of all the subjects I studied at school, ... was my favourite.
  2 I always feel really .... when I pass an exam.
  3 When I get my qualifications, I want to ....
  4 A skill that I'd really like to learn is ....

Adjectives and dependent prepositions

3 Choose the correct prepositions to complete the sentences.
  1 Kurt is really good *with* / *at* / *to* speaking Spanish.
  2 Are you worried *about* / *with* / *on* your driving test?
  3 I'm so disappointed *at* / *with* / *of* your essay, Paula.
  4 Is this similar *with* / *to* / *of* your idea?
  5 Pip can't swim so she's afraid *at* / *by* / *of* water.

-ed/-ing adjectives

4 Choose the correct adjectives and complete the sentences with your own ideas.
  1 .... is a really *interested* / *interesting* subject.
  2 I felt *disappointed* / *disappointing* when ....
  3 One of the most *excited* / *exciting* things I've done is ....
  4 I usually feel *tired* / *tiring* when ....

Grammar
going to and present continuous for plans and arrangements

5 a Fill in the diary with your plans for next weekend.

	SATURDAY	SUNDAY
morning		
afternoon		
evening		

b In pairs, tell your partner about your plans. Use the present continuous or *going to* for each sentence.

must(n't) and *(don't) have to*

6 Choose the correct words to complete the sentences.
  1 You *mustn't* / *have to* eat chocolate, it's bad for you!
  2 My office is quite relaxed. You *mustn't* / *don't have to* wear a suit and tie, but you *mustn't* / *don't have to* wear jeans – they aren't allowed.
  3 He *doesn't have to* / *mustn't* be late for the interview. He really wants this job.
  4 Did you say 'thank you'? You *has* / *must* be polite.

7 Complete the sentences with *must*, *mustn't*, *have to* or *don't have to* so that they're true for your country.
  1 Children .... go to school.
  2 Students .... stay at school until they're 18.
  3 Primary school students .... study English.
  4 Secondary school students .... take exams.

Functional language
Making arrangements

8 🔊 4.15 Complete the conversation with the words in the box. Listen and check.

| doing | fancy | going | good |
| sounds | special | tricky | up |

A What are you (1) .... to this Saturday?
B Oh, nothing (2) .... I have to clean the flat and then I'm visiting my parents.
A What are you (3) .... in the evening?
B Nothing, why?
A Do you (4) .... trying that new Italian restaurant?
B Nice idea, but that's a bit (5) .... because I'm on a diet.
A OK, well how about (6) .... to the cinema, then?
B That (7) .... great. When's (8) .... for you?
A Shall we meet in town at 7.30? We can have a drink first.
B Perfect, see you then.

9 In pairs, make arrangements for the weekend.

🕐 Looking back

- What was your last English lesson like? What was the most interesting thing you learned?
- Do you have to go to school or work tomorrow? What are you going to do there?

Getting help 5

Grammar
should and must for advice
will, may, might for predictions

Vocabulary
collocations with have, take, do, make
health problems
suffixes: -ful and -less

Functional language
asking for and giving advice

Skill
guess meaning from context

Video
something for nothing

Writing
an opinion essay

Exams
listening for specific information

The big picture: human pyramids

1 Look at the picture. In pairs, guess the answers to the questions.
 1 Where are the people and what are they doing?
 2 How do they do it?
 3 How many people are there at the bottom of the pyramid?
 4 How high can people go?

2 🔊 5.1 Listen and check your answers.

3 In pairs, discuss the questions.
 1 Do you like being high up or do you find it scary?
 2 Would you like to be in a human pyramid?
 3 What festivals are there where you live? What happens in the festivals?
 4 Can you think of other activities in which everyone has to help each other?

I think human pyramids are really scary. I'm afraid of heights!

5.1 HELP!
G should and must for advice
V collocations with have, take, do, make

Vocabulary

1 Look at the people in the box. In pairs, say when you would ask the people for advice.

| family | friends | teacher | expert | stranger |

I always talk to my friends first when I need advice on schoolwork.

2 **a** Read the introduction to the 'Be Happy' podcast. Do you ever read or listen to things like this?

b Read the three emails to Marina. Do you know anyone with similar problems?

3 Complete the table with the words in the box. Check your answers in the text.

V collocations with *have, take, do, make*

advantage of	~~an argument~~	my/your best	a break
a chance	a class	a decision	an effort	an exam
an excuse	exercise	fun	a mistake	money
a nap	a problem	someone a favour
something wrong	my/your time

have	take	do	make
an argument			

🔊 5.2 Listen, check and repeat.

4 **a** Complete the sentences with the words in the box.

advantage	argument	break
chance	decision	excuse
exercise	favour	mistake
money	something	

1 Don't worry if you make a .... It's the best way to learn.
2 You can have a big .... with someone and still be good friends.
3 If you do someone a .... once, they try to take .... of you again and again.
4 A job isn't just about making .... You have to enjoy the work, too!
5 You'll always be healthy if you do .... for fifteen minutes every day.
6 If you do .... wrong, don't make an .... Just say you're sorry.
7 It's important to take a .... every couple of hours at work.
8 It's better to take a .... than not make a ....

b Do you agree with the sentences? In pairs, compare your answers.

I don't agree with number 5. It's also important to eat healthy food.

▶ BE HAPPY

Marina Gonzales talks about happiness and how to achieve it. Each week she responds to three emails from people who need help and advice on how to be happy. Let's look at this week's emails:

✉ Dear Marina,
I moved to another city last year to go to university, but I'm lonely and miserable. People say I should take my time and take advantage of all the university clubs and events, but it's hard! My flatmates don't talk to me. They're always out or in their bedroom having a nap. Maybe I'm doing something wrong. I have to take exams next month, but I just want to move back home and be with my old friends. I've really made an effort at university, but it's not working. Please help. I need to make a decision.
Harry, 19

✉ Dear Marina,
I changed jobs last year, but I think I made a mistake. The office is so busy and nobody ever takes a break. I always try to do my best, but I don't finish all my work and then I have to make excuses to my boss! I'm making more money in this job, but I have to work in the evening and at the weekend, so I hardly ever have fun outside of work. I'm not happy, but I don't know if I can find another job. Should I take a chance and quit?
Tanya, 24

✉ Hi Marina,
I have a problem. Everyone thinks I'm really lucky: I have a nice house, I'm in good health, I hardly ever have arguments with my boyfriend … but I feel that my life doesn't have much meaning. In my spare time, I take dance classes and I do exercise every morning. I still feel like something is missing from my life. Can you do me a favour and tell me what it is?
Esther, 22

Listening

5 Look at the pictures and answer the questions.
1 What activities are the people doing?
2 How often do you do these activities?
3 Do they make you happy?

6 a 5.3 Listen to Marina give advice. What advice does she give? Match pictures a–c with the people.
1 Tanya .... 2 Harry .... 3 Esther ....

b Do you think the advice is useful? Why?

7 5.3 Match the pieces of advice from the podcast with Tanya (T), Harry (H) or Esther (E). Listen again and check.
1 But please remember – you mustn't compare their lives to your own!
2 So, you should find out who needs help in your community.
3 I think you should join a club.
4 You must take breaks at work!
5 You shouldn't feel silly.
6 I don't think you should quit your job.

Grammar

8 Look at the sentences in exercise 7 again. Answer the questions.
1 Which sentences refer to a good idea? Which sentences refer to a bad idea?
2 Which two sentences are making strong suggestions?
3 Do the words *I (don't) think* make the suggestions in 3 and 6 more or less direct?

G should and must for advice

Strong advice
You **must** tell me what's wrong!
You **mustn't** tell anyone. It's a secret!

Direct advice
You **should** drink more water.
You **shouldn't** look at your phone in bed.

Indirect advice
I think you **should** apply for this job.
I don't think you **should** go out tonight.

→ Grammar reference: page 136

9 5.4 *shouldn't and mustn't* Listen to two pieces of advice. Notice how *shouldn't* and *mustn't* are pronounced. Listen again and repeat.
1 You shouldn't talk with your mouth full.
2 You mustn't blame yourself.

10 a Match problems a–e with advice 1–5.
a I have an exam tomorrow morning and I'm really nervous.
b I'm really tired. I went to bed at 4 a.m.!
c It was my mother's birthday yesterday and I forgot to call her.
d My brother is studying in a different city. He's lonely.
e I moved house last week and I hurt my arms lifting the boxes.

1 .... call one of his friends and have a chat. (indirect advice)
2 .... do something relaxing so you sleep well tonight. (direct advice)
3 .... lift anything heavy for the next week. (strong advice)
4 .... call her today and say sorry! (strong advice)
5 .... stay out so late. (indirect advice)

b Complete the advice with the instructions in brackets.

c In pairs, say the problems and give advice. Remember to pronounce *mustn't* and *shouldn't* correctly.

Speaking

11 a Read the situations. In pairs, make a list of possible problems.
1 I have a problem at work/college …
2 I have a problem with my boyfriend/girlfriend …
3 I have a problem with my flatmate …
4 I have a problem with my family …

b In groups, take turns to choose a problem from your list. Ask the group for advice. Give each other advice, using the prompts.

You should …   You must …   I think you should …
You shouldn't …   You mustn't …   I don't think you should …

I have a problem with my flatmate. He never does any housework!
I think you should make a list for each day of the week. And then share the housework with him.

47

5.2 ROBOT HELPERS

G *will*, *may*, *might* for predictions
V health problems

Vocabulary

1 In pairs, think of five ways to stay healthy.
You have to get enough sleep.

2 Match the sentences in the box with the pictures.

V health problems

1 I have a cold/the flu.
2 I have a temperature.
3 I have a headache.
4 I have stomach ache.
5 I have toothache.
6 I have a cough/a sore throat.
7 I have backache.
8 My ear hurts.
9 I burned my hand.
10 I broke my leg.
11 I cut my finger.
12 I have a pain in my knee.

🔊 5.5 Listen, check and repeat.

3 In pairs, take turns to say a health problem and give advice. Use the ideas in the box.

put it under cold water   not exercise
take medicine and stay warm   go to the dentist
lie down in a dark room   put a plaster on it
not move it   not play tennis
drink lots of water   go to hospital

I burned my finger.
You should put it under cold water.

Reading

4 Look at the pictures and read the first paragraph of the text. How do you think robots are helping with healthcare? Read the text and check.

THE ROBOT WILL SEE YOU NOW

The world's population is growing very fast. More babies are being born and people are living longer than before. Healthcare systems around the world have too much work and not enough staff. But will robots be the solution? We look at the different ways robots already help and how they might help in the future.

HELPING DOCTORS AND SURGEONS

Robots already do simple surgery because they can move more easily than human hands. As they improve, they will probably be used for more complicated surgery.

Experts believe that doctors might use 'robot pills' in the future. A patient will take one of these tiny pills, and the doctor will be able to see where exactly it goes in the body. The doctor will then be able to send medicine to the correct place.

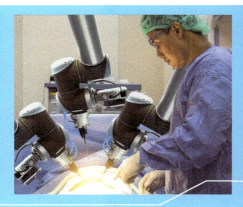

HELPING NURSES

Robots already help nurses with simple tasks. For example, they carry medicine from one part of the hospital to another. But this isn't all they can do. When you have an infection, a robot can find the best place on your body to take blood if necessary. When you break your leg and can't walk, a robot can lift you out of bed and carry you across the room. These 'robot assistants' will definitely get better but, because most patients prefer to speak to a human, robots won't replace nurses completely.

Grammar

5 a Match the halves to make sentences. Check your answers in the text.

1. Will robots be the ....
2. Doctors might use ....
3. Robots won't replace ....
4. Soon we may all have ....
5. Robots will read the ....

a robots in our home.
b 'robot pills' in the future.
c solution?
d information on our phones.
e nurses completely.

b Choose the correct words to complete the rules.

1. We use *may / might / will* to ask questions about predictions for the future.
2. We use *will* and *won't* for *possible / certain* predictions for the future.
3. We use *may (not)* and *might (not)* for *possible / certain* predictions for the future.

G will, may, might for predictions

Questions:	*Will* our team *win*?
Certain predictions:	She*'ll be* late. I'm sure! It *won't rain* tomorrow.
Possible predictions:	The traffic *may be* bad. The shops *might not open* at the weekend.

→ Grammar reference: page 136

notice

We use *definitely* and *probably* after *will* and before *won't*.
Robots and humans will **definitely / probably** work together.
Robots **definitely / probably** won't replace humans.

6 🔊 5.6 *'ll contraction* Listen to the pairs of sentences. Notice how *'ll* is pronounced. Listen again and repeat.

1. I see.   I'll see.
2. You go.   You'll go.
3. We want to. We'll want to.

7 a In pairs, match 1–8 with predictions a–h.

1. scientists   a be the most popular language
2. the government   b do tasks around the house
3. the world's population c build more homes in this city
4. phones   d only study courses online
5. English   e find a cure for cancer
6. most cars   f increase to more than 8 billion
7. summers   g drive themselves
8. students   h get hotter

b Take turns to ask and answer questions about what in exercise 7a will happen in the next ten years.

Will scientists find a cure for cancer?
They probably won't find a cure because there are a lot of different kinds of cancer.

HELPING AT HOME
Robots already do a number of jobs in the home, especially for elderly patients. They can talk to patients, remind them to take their medicine and even make a doctor's appointment for them. Soon we may all have robots in our home, and they will connect to our smartphones. Our phones can already collect basic information about our health, but in the future, there will be even more information on them. Robots will read the information on our phones and look for signs of illness. For example, your robot may notice that you've got a temperature and it will start asking questions. You will tell your robot what's wrong: 'I have a pain in my chest,' for example or 'My arm hurts.' The robot will then contact a human health professional with the information. Robots definitely won't solve all the problems our healthcare systems face, but they might solve some of them. They won't replace humans entirely, but people and robots will probably work together in hospitals and homes to give us all an improved health service.

Speaking

8 In groups, take turns to make predictions about you and your classmates.

| She will definitely ... | You may ... |
| He might not ... | She probably won't ... |

Ana will definitely find a job when we graduate.

5.3 MAKING A DIFFERENCE

V suffixes: -ful and -less
→ guess meaning from context

Vocabulary

1 Look at sentences A and B. Which do you agree with more?

> A Trying to solve the world's problems is **useless**. Nothing ever changes.
>
> B I am **hopeful** about the future of the world. We can all make a positive difference.

2 Look at the adjectives in bold. Complete the rules with -less or -ful suffixes.

1 .... means that there's a lot of the quality.
2 .... means that there's nothing of that quality.

3 Complete the table. Use a dictionary to help you.

V suffixes: -ful and -less

Root word	-ful	-less
1 care		careless
2 help	helpful	
3 end	–	endless
4 gratitude	grateful	–
5 home	–	
6 hope		hopeless
7 use	useful	
8 pain		painless
9 colour		colourless
10 forget		–
11 peace		–
12 thought	thoughtful	

🔊 5.9 Listen, check and repeat.

4 a Complete the sentences with words from the Vocabulary box.

1 I like wearing .... clothes because it's more interesting than wearing black all the time!
2 I can sometimes be very .... I'm always dropping or breaking things.
3 I sometimes like to just sit somewhere very quiet and think. I find it so ....
4 The list of things I have to do today is .... ! I don't think I have time to do them all!
5 I'm very .... to my parents and my family for everything that they've done for me.
6 I'm quite a .... person. I never remember people's names when I meet them for the first time.
7 I like it when people send me messages on my birthday. It's really .... of them.
8 I broke my arm when I was a child. It was so .... !

b Are any of the sentences true for you? In pairs, compare your answers.

Number 5 is true for me. My parents don't have a lot of money, but they're paying for me to go to university.

Reading

5 a Look at the pictures and read the title. What do you think the text is about?

a People playing football in a competition to make money to give to homeless people.
b Homeless people from all over the world watching a football tournament.
c Homeless people playing in a football tournament.

b Read the text and check your answer.

THE HOMELESS WORLD CUP

Around the world, ⁽¹⁾**roughly** 100 million people are homeless. Although most of us think that we should try to get these people off the streets and back into work, few people know how they can ⁽²⁾**meaningfully** help homeless people.

Mel Young from Scotland and Harald Schmied from Austria had a great idea. They are the founders of the Homeless World Cup (HWC). The HWC is an international football tournament for people who are homeless. The event began in 2003 in Austria and it is held every year. More than 500 players from over 50 countries around the world play against each other. Every player has experienced homelessness at some time. Thousands of people come to watch the matches, and millions more watch online.

The main purpose of the HWC is to ⁽³⁾**improve** the lives of the people involved. Homeless people often lose confidence and feel helpless. Young and Schmied saw football as a way to help people feel good about themselves and learn skills that are useful in a job. When people become involved in football, they start to form new relationships. They also have new responsibilities, such as supporting their ⁽⁴⁾**teammates** and attending matches and training sessions on time. Thirty-one of the original 141 players from the 2003 tournament had a job one year after the tournament. 83% of participants say the HWC has helped them improve relationships with their family and friends and 94% say the tournament had a positive impact on their lives. 71% of participants continue to play football and some have even become professional players or ⁽⁵⁾**coaches**.

5.3

6 Read the text again. Are the sentences true (T) or false (F)? Correct the false sentences.
1 Mel Young and Harald Schmied are from the same place.
2 The first HWC was in Austria.
3 The HWC helps players improve their lives.
4 There were fewer than 150 players in the first HWC.
5 Over 90% of the players in the HWC say it has helped them with their friends and family.
6 Everyone who watched the 2016 HWC felt more positive about homeless people afterwards.

guess meaning from context

Whatever your level, there will always be words you don't know the meaning of. It's not always efficient or possible to check in a dictionary. Asking yourself questions can help you to make an 'educated' guess.
- What class is the word (noun, verb, adjective, adverb)?
- Is it similar to another English word you know? Does it have a prefix or a suffix?
- Guess which word would make most sense in this context.

7 a Read the Skill box. Look at the words in **bold** in the text. Are they nouns, verbs, adjectives or adverbs?

b Look at the words in exercise 7a again, read the sentences carefully and guess the meaning of the words.

The HWC is not only about helping homeless people to improve their lives. It is also a **(6)powerful** method for changing the way others see homelessness. Many people think and say **(7)unkind** things about homeless people, but 83% of spectators at the 2016 tournament in Scotland said they now have a more positive attitude to homeless people. This is all as a result of going to the event and watching the games. When spectators hear about the difficult challenges that the participants have to **(8)overcome**, it helps to show the human side of homelessness.
The HWC is a perfect example of a simple idea that helps people to change their lives in a positive way.

8 Match the words in exercise 7 with the definitions. Which words were easiest to guess? Which tips did you find most useful?
a make something better than before
b people who help others to improve at a sport or a skill
c in a serious, important or worthwhile way
d not exactly
e deal successfully with something difficult
f strong
g people who play in the same team
h not nice (to other people)

The last tip was the most useful. I guessed 'overcome' because I knew the word 'challenges'.

Writing

9 a Complete the text with the words in the box.

peaceful   helpless   hopeful
unnecessary   hopeless

SMALL TAX, BIG DIFFERENCE

Millions of people in the world live in poverty. We all want to end poverty, but most of us feel (1)..................... What can we do? Philippe Douste-Blazy doesn't think it's a (2)..................... situation – he has an idea. He thinks there should be a very small extra tax on any items that are expensive and (3)...................... So, when we buy a £1,500 holiday, we pay an extra £1.50. We probably won't notice that we're paying a bit more, but when all the extra charges are put together, it will make billions of pounds! This money will then go to the poorest parts of the world to help end poverty. Less poverty will mean fewer wars, so the world will be more (4)..................... Ideas like this can make us feel (5)..................... about the future.

b In pairs, discuss whether this idea will 'make a difference'. Why/Why not?

Yes, I think it will make a difference because it's a very small tax on a lot of items.

10 a Look at some more ideas for helping other people. Which idea do you like best?
1 visit a lonely elderly person in your community and spend time with him or her
2 cook and serve hot food for homeless people in your city
3 help local children who can't read very well

I like number 3. I really want to help young people.

b Write a similar paragraph to the one in exercise 9a about your favourite idea.

Mediation task: All students, page 127   51

5.4 A HELPING HAND

FL asking for and giving advice
something for nothing

The big picture: something for nothing

1 Look at the picture. In pairs, guess the answers to the questions.
   1 Who are the two people?
   2 Why are they happy?
   3 Why are they in the street?

2 **5.1** Watch the video and check your answers to exercise 1.

3 **5.1** In pairs, answer the questions. Watch the video again and check.
   1 Why does Josh post pictures online?
   2 Do the haircuts change people's appearance a lot?
   3 How do the people feel after the haircut?
   4 What does Jade do to help the project?
   5 How does the project help Josh?

4 In pairs, discuss the questions.
   1 How can a haircut help a homeless person?
   2 Are there many homeless people in your city?
   3 What do people do when they see a homeless person?
   4 What does 'Help others, help yourself' mean? Do you agree?
   5 Would you like to volunteer in your community? Why/Why not?
   6 Do you have a skill that could help a group of people?

5 **5.2** Watch Rob and Lou talking about the video. Choose **two** correct options to make sentences about the conversation.
   1 Rob says a haircut helps homeless people because …
      a they feel good about themselves.
      b it helps them get a job.
      c they interact with other people.
   2 Lou says her volunteer work …
      a is in the library.
      b is only for old people.
      c makes her feel good.
   3 Rob decides …
      a he wants to help Lou teach computer skills.
      b he can offer music lessons.
      c he will volunteer at a children's club.

6 **5.2** Watch the video again. Tick (✓) the advice Lou gives Rob.
   1 He should think about what he's good at. ☐
   2 He should join a volunteer group. ☐
   3 He should offer expensive music lessons. ☐
   4 He should call the children's club now. ☐

Functional language

7 🔊 **5.10** Look at the pictures of people asking for advice. In pairs, guess what the problems are. Listen and check.

8 a 🔊 **5.10** Choose the correct words to complete the sentences from the conversations. Listen again and check.

Conversation A
1 What do you *advice / suggest*?
2 If I *am / were* you, I would use this lamb here.
3 Then why *do / don't* you use this beef?

Conversation B
4 It's a good *idea / advice* to tell her it's going to be late.
5 Do you *think / know* I should tell Jan I'm having problems?
6 What *around / about* asking David for help?

Conversation C
7 What do you think I *would / should* do?
8 Well, what *would / do* you do?
9 I don't think you should *tell / to tell* Lily.
10 You *should / ought* to speak to her boyfriend first.

b Which sentences are asking for advice and which are giving advice?

FL asking for and giving advice

Asking for advice	Giving advice
What would you do?	Why don't you …?
What do you think I should do?	If I were you, I would …
Do you think I should …?	I (don't) think you should …
What do you suggest (I do)?	It's (not) a good idea to …
Can you give me some advice?	What about …?
What would you recommend?	You ought to …

9 🔊 **5.11** ❝ *do you* and *would you* in questions ❞
Listen to the questions. Notice how *do you* and *would you* are pronounced. Listen again and repeat.
1 What <u>would you</u> do?
2 What <u>do you</u> think I should do?
3 <u>Do you</u> think I should …?
4 What <u>would you</u> recommend?

10 a Complete the conversation with the words in the box.

| don't | idea | should | suggest |
| think | were | what | would |

A I can't decide what to study at university.
(1) .... do you think I should do?
B It's a good (2) .... to speak to someone who has already graduated from university.
A Like you for example! What do you (3) .... I do?
B I think you (4) .... make a list of subjects you might like to study.
A Well, it's either law or journalism. What (5) .... you do?
B Why (6) .... you imagine being a lawyer or a journalist? Which job makes you happier?
A I think lawyers make more money. So, do you (7) .... I should study law?
B If I (8) .... you, I wouldn't worry about the money. It's more important to enjoy your work.

b In pairs, act out the conversation. Try to speak quickly and pronounce *would you* and *do you* in a similar way to exercise 9.

Speaking

11 In pairs, look at the situations. Take turns asking for and giving advice.

Money
You are trying to save money, but you always spend it going out.

Home
Your flatmate never does any housework, but you don't want to argue with him/her.

Hobbies
You want to do a hobby where you can meet new people and keep fit.

School
You don't do well in your exams because you get so nervous.

Writing bank: page 148

REVIEW UNIT 5

Vocabulary
Collocations with *have, take, do, make*

1 Cross out the nouns that don't go with the verbs.

1 **make:**	an effort	money	advantage
2 **do:**	a nap	exercise	something wrong
3 **take:**	a chance	an excuse	an exam
4 **have:**	fun	an argument	my time

2 a Choose the correct verb to complete the questions.
1. Do your friends listen when you *have / make / do* a problem?
2. Did you *have / do / make* a difficult decision this year?
3. Do you sometimes *do / make / take* mistakes in English?
4. When you're working, how often do you *do / take / make* a break?
5. When was the last time that you *made / took / did* someone a favour?

b In pairs, ask and answer the questions.

Health problems

3 a Match the health problems with the advice.

1	I have a headache.	a	Go to hospital.
2	My foot hurts.	b	Lie down in a dark room.
3	I cut my knee.	c	Go to the dentist.
4	I have toothache.	d	Put it under cold water.
5	I burned my hand.	e	Don't exercise.
6	I broke my finger.	f	Put a plaster on it.

b Put the health problems in order (1 = most serious, 6 = least serious). In pairs, compare your answers.

Suffixes: *-ful* and *-less*

4 Choose the correct adjectives to complete the sentences.
1. They break very easily. Please be *careful / careless* when you wash them.
2. I'll never pass this exam, it's *hopeful / hopeless*!
3. The medicine is *colourful / colourless* – it looks like water.
4. I hurt my knee and it's really *painful / painless*.

5 Complete the sentences with a *-ful/-less* adjective related to the root word in brackets.
1. My mum never remembers dates, she's very .... (forget)
2. The kids are at school so it's very quiet and .... right now. (peace)
3. These people don't have anywhere to live, they're .... (home)
4. Jocelyn is so .... She always offers to do my shopping. (help)
5. You were late home, but you didn't call me. That was .... of you! (thought)
6. I'm really .... for all your help, thank you. (gratitude)

Grammar
should and *must* for advice

6 a Put the words in the correct order to make sentences giving advice.
1. you / meat / day / shouldn't / every / eat
   ....
2. revise / you / exams / the library / should / for / in
   ....
3. think / to / go / you / university / should / I
   ....
4. lies / tell / mustn't / you
   ....

b In pairs, say if you agree with the advice.

will, may, might for predictions

7 Complete the predictions with *will, won't* or *might* and the verbs in the box. In pairs, compare your answers.

live   replace   stop

In the future …
1. we .... damaging the environment.
2. people .... on the moon.
3. robots .... teachers in the classroom.

8 a In pairs, write one prediction about the future for each topic.

1	medicine	4	entertainment
2	the environment	5	education
3	work	6	technology

b Swap predictions with another pair. Order their ideas from most to least likely to happen.

Functional language
Asking for and giving advice

9 a 🔊 5.12 Read the advice. In pairs, guess what the problems were. Listen and check.
1. If I were you, I would ask her to fix it. It looks awful.
2. Why don't you try to buy another one? You might be able to replace it.
3. What about saying you're really sorry? That might help.
4. It's not a good idea to go without a recommendation! I think you should look for a review online.
5. You ought to take him to hospital.

b In pairs, give more advice for each situation.

Looking back

- Which of the problems in this unit do you think is the most serious or difficult? Why?
- Make a prediction about your English learning in the future and compare with your partner.

Ages and changes

6

Grammar G
comparatives, superlatives, *as ... as* present perfect with *ever* and *never*

Vocabulary V
personality adjectives
phrasal verbs
uses of *get*

Functional language FL
giving thanks

Skill
listen for gist

Video
two very different brothers

Writing
a web forum comment

Exams
describing a photo

The big picture: as old as you feel

1 Look at the picture. In pairs, guess the answers to the questions.
   1 What is unusual about this person?
   2 What age do you think most surfers are?
   3 Why does she go surfing?
   4 How is surfing different now from in the past?
   I think she's a lot older than most surfers.

2 🔊 **6.1** Listen and check your answers.

3 In pairs, discuss the questions.
   1 What hobbies, sports or other activities do you do?
   2 When did you start doing them?
   3 Are any of your interests unusual for people your age?
   4 Do you know anyone with unusual interests for their age?
   I started singing in a choir when I was 8 years old.
   My grandmother enjoys skateboarding!

6.1 THE AGE OF RESPONSIBILITY

G comparatives, superlatives, *as ... as*
V personality adjectives

Reading

1 Look at the pictures. In pairs, discuss the questions. Read the text quickly and check your answers.
   1 What do the pictures have in common?
   2 What is the relationship between the people in the pictures?
   3 What responsibilities do they have?
   4 Are they unusual for their age?

TAKING ON BIG RESPONSIBILITIES

THE CHILDMINDER

In many families today, both parents go out and work, so who looks after the children? Very often it is the grandparents who take the kids to school, cook them a meal and take care of them until the parents get home.

CASE STUDY: ALBERTO, 72

I pick up my granddaughters from school and look after them every afternoon. My son and his wife both work, but they can't afford to pay for a childminder. I didn't want to do this when I retired, but I'm glad I can help. The biggest problem is finding a parking space near the school, but I'm a bit shy, so it's a good way to meet other grandparents. It was difficult with the girls at first, but they aren't as silly as they were in the past. In fact, they're very polite now and always say *please* and *thank you*. Olga is my oldest granddaughter and she helps out a lot ... but I still need to be patient!

THE CARER

A carer looks after an elderly or sick person at home, often a relative. We do not know how many hard-working teenage carers there are worldwide, but one of them tells her story.

CASE STUDY: LIBBY, 13

Mum's illness started getting worse a few years ago (she's got multiple sclerosis), and now she needs our help. Dad died when I was younger, but I have an older sister and a brother. I'm as responsible as they are and we share the housework and all take care of Mum. I have to make breakfast for her every morning and clean the kitchen before school. When I get back, I do my homework and then make dinner. I don't have any time to be lazy! I'm definitely more sensible than other people in my class. I'm glad I think of others and I'm not selfish like some people my age!

2 Read the text again. Are the sentences true (T) or false (F)?
   1 Alberto wanted to be a childminder when he retired. ......
   2 His job was easy when the children were younger. ......
   3 He says there are some positive things about picking up his granddaughters. ......
   4 Libby has to look after her mum on her own. ......
   5 She doesn't have enough time to do schoolwork. ......
   6 She thinks the responsibilities have a positive effect. ......

3 In pairs, discuss the questions.
   1 Whose job is more difficult? Why?
   2 Do you know anyone in a similar situation to Alberto and Libby?
   3 Do you look after anyone? What do you do?

   I look after my younger brother. I walk home from school with him.

Vocabulary

4 Match the personality adjectives in the box with their opposites.

V personality adjectives

| impatient | irresponsible | lazy | rude |
| selfish | shy | silly | unkind |

   1 hardworking ....
   2 sensible ....
   3 polite ....
   4 sociable ....
   5 responsible ....
   6 generous ....
   7 kind ....
   8 patient ....

🔊 6.2 Listen, check and repeat.

notice

Many adjectives form opposites with prefixes. The most common prefix is *un-*, e.g. **un**kind   **un**sociable
Some words form opposites with *im-* or *ir-*, e.g. **im**patient   **ir**responsible

5 In pairs, take turns to say a personality adjective and its opposite.

hardworking
lazy

6 In groups, discuss the questions. Use adjectives from the Vocabulary box.
1 How do you describe yourself?
2 How do other people describe you?
3 What qualities are most important for a good friend?
4 What qualities are most important for a good teacher?

My friends think I'm sociable, but actually I'm quite shy.

Grammar

7 Complete the table with the correct adjectives. Use the text to help you.

Adjective	Comparative adjective	Superlative adjective
old	older	(1) the
(2)	sillier	the silliest
sensible	(3)	the most sensible
big	bigger	(4) the
bad	(5)	the worst
(6)	better	the best

8 a Who said the sentences from the text, Alberto or Libby? Who does *they* refer to in each of the sentences?
1 I'**m as responsible as** they are.
2 They **aren't as silly as** they were in the past.

b Look at the words in **bold**. Choose the correct words to complete the meanings.
1 Libby is *more / less / equally* responsible for her mother.
2 Alberto's granddaughters are *more / less / equally* silly now.

G comparatives, superlatives, *as ... as*

Comparatives
I'm **busier than** most other people my age.
Caring for others is **more difficult than** schoolwork!

Superlatives
The oldest child helps out a lot.
I'm **the most responsible** sixteen-year-old that I know!

as ... as
This phone is **as old as** yours is.
I'm **not as patient as** my brother.

→ Grammar reference: page 137

9 🔊 6.3 **ff weak forms in comparatives 𝄙** Listen to the sentences. Notice the pronunciation of *than* and *as*. Listen again and repeat.
1 Is your little sister lazier than you?
2 Yes, she is, but she isn't as lazy as our dad!

10 a Complete the second sentences with the words in brackets so that they mean the same as the first.
1 It's easier to have a small family than a large one. (difficult)
.... to have a large family than a small one.
2 My English course is more difficult than last year. (as)
Last year, my English course ....
3 Living on your own is more stressful than living with your parents. (isn't)
Living with your parents ....
4 Friends aren't as important as relatives. (more)
Relatives ....
5 My teachers are more patient than my parents! (impatient)
My parents ....
6 No one is a better friend than my mum! (best)
My mum ....

b In pairs, read out your sentences. Remember to use the weak forms of *than* and *as*. Say if you agree or disagree.

I agree. Small families are easier because there is less washing up to do!

Speaking

11 In pairs, compare your appearance and personality to one of the people in the box. Take turns to ask and answer questions.

a brother/sister   a parent
a relative   a friend
a classmate

I'm older than my brother, but I'm not as tall as he is.

6.2 TRY SOMETHING NEW

G present perfect with *ever* and *never*
V phrasal verbs

Listening

1 Look at the picture and read about a radio programme. What is it about?

Thursday 19.30–20.00

You won't like it until you've tried it

This week's guest is actor Anna Reed. She tries three new activities for the first time and tells us about her experiences. What did she try and did she enjoy them? Find out on Lifestyle FM.

2 🔊 **6.4** Listen to the radio programme. Tick (✓) the activities Anna is going to try for the first time.
1 eat vegetarian food ☐
2 go to the gym ☐
3 dance ballet ☐
4 do ballroom dancing ☐
5 stay up all night ☐
6 go camping ☐

3 🔊 **6.5** Listen to the second part of the programme. Which activity did Anna enjoy most?

4 In pairs, discuss the questions.
1 Which activity from exercise 2 would you like to try? Why?
2 Do you like trying new things?
3 Is there anything you would like to try for the first time?
4 Is there an activity that you would never try? Why wouldn't you like to try it?

Vocabulary

5 🔊 **6.4 and 6.5** Listen to the whole programme again. Put the sentences in the order you hear them.
a ☐ I'm **looking forward** to trying some nice food!
b ☐ I try to go to the gym and **work out**.
c ☐ We went out and **stayed up** until the morning.
d ☐ I wanted to **take up** a new hobby.
e ☐ Are you going to **give up** meat?
f ☐ I **hang out** with the same friends.
g ☐ I **got on** with my teacher.
h ☐ Do you think you'll **carry on** dancing?
i ☐ I sometimes **run out** of food at home.
j ☐ Do you **eat out** much?

6 Look at the sentences in exercise 5 again. Match the phrasal verbs in the box with the definitions.

V phrasal verbs

carry on	eat out	get on	give up
hang out	look forward to	run out of
stay up	take up	work out

1 continue ....
2 stop doing something ....
3 start a new activity ....
4 do exercise ....
5 have a good relationship ....
6 use all of something ....
7 not go to bed ....
8 spend time together ....
9 be excited about something in the future ....
10 have a meal at a restaurant ....

🔊 **6.6** Listen, check and repeat.

7 In pairs, answer the questions.
1 Where do you hang out with friends?
2 How often do you eat out?
3 Are you looking forward to anything?
4 Who do you get on with best in your family?
5 What food could you never give up?
6 How often do you work out?
7 Do you stay up all night for any special occasions?
8 What new activity would you like to take up?

Grammar

8 a 🔊 **6.7** Match the questions with Anna's answers. Listen and check.
1 Have you ever tried a dance class? ....
2 When did you do that? ....
3 Did you enjoy it? ....
4 Have you tried ballroom dancing? ....

a Yes, I have.
b No, I've never done that.
c I did ballet classes when I was a girl.
d No – I'm not very good at dancing.

b Look at the questions again and answer the questions.
1 Which two questions ask about a general experience in Anna's life?
2 Which tense are they?
3 Which two questions ask about details of a specific event?
4 Which tense are they?

58

G present perfect with *ever* and *never*

General experience
Have you **ever tried** salsa dancing?
Yes, I **have**. I've **done** it twice.
No, I **haven't**. I've **never tried** it.

Specific event
When **did** you **try** it?
I **had** a dance class last year.

→ Grammar reference: page 137

notice

The verb *go* has two past participles: *gone* and *been*.
Charlotte has **been** to San Diego. (she went in 2018 and returned)
Charlotte has **gone** to San Diego. (She went last week and is there now)

9 Complete the conversation with the correct form of the verbs in the box.

be	do	go	like	see

A (1) .... you ever .... rock climbing?
B No, I (2) .... But my sister Teresa (3) ....
A When (4) .... she .... that?
B She (5) .... last year, in the Black Mountains.
A (6) .... she .... it?
B No, she (7) .... scared! What about you? (8) .... you ever .... anything like that?
A Well, I (9) .... never .... rock climbing. But I (10) .... camping a few times.
B (11) .... you ever .... any bears?
A Bears? No. I (12) ....! Are there bears in the mountains?
B Yes, my sister (13) .... a mother bear and her baby cubs last year.
A Wow!

10 a 6.8 **irregular past participles** Listen to the past participles. Notice how the vowels in **bold** are pronounced with a /ʌ/, /əʊ/ or /ə/ sound. Listen again and repeat.

1 begin → beg**u**n
2 know → kn**o**wn
3 eat → eat**e**n

b 6.9 In pairs, say the past participle forms of the verbs in the box and write them in the correct columns. Listen, check and repeat.

do	drink	drive	fly	give
grow	show	swim	write	

/ʌ/	/əʊ/	/ə/
begun	known	eaten

Speaking

11 In pairs, ask and answer the question *Have you ever …?* with the present perfect form of the verbs in **bold**. If your partner answers 'Yes, I have', ask the follow-up questions in the past simple.

1 **stay up** all night?
(Why? What time / go to bed?)
2 **swim** in a river?
(When? How cold?)
3 **eat out**, but **forget** your wallet?
(Which restaurant? How / pay?)
4 **run out** of petrol?
(Where / want to go? What / do?)
5 **write** a poem?
(What / about? Why?)
6 **eat** strange food?
(What / eat? What / taste like?)

Exam practice: page 161

6.3 CELEBRATIONS

V uses of *get*
🔧 listen for gist

a   b

Listening

1 **a** Look at the pictures. Match them with the celebrations.

   1 a wedding ceremony   ....
   2 a graduation ceremony   ....
   3 a birthday celebration   ....
   4 celebrating a birth   ....

   b In pairs, answer the questions.
   1 How old are the people in the pictures?
   2 How do they feel?
   3 Have you ever celebrated any of the events?
   4 What did you do?

🔧 listen for gist

When people speak, it's important to understand the general idea (or gist) quickly.

- Don't worry if you don't understand everything, keep listening.
- Pay attention to words that are repeated or emphasized.
- Think about the tone of voice, e.g. are the speakers happy or sad?
- Notice the tenses of the verbs. Are the speakers talking about the past, present or future?

2 🔊 **6.11** Read the Skill box. Listen to four people talking about important events in their lives. Match four of the events in the box with the speakers.

birth	birthday	exam	driving test
graduation	new home	new job	
retirement	wedding		

   1 Marc   ....   3 Kevin   ....
   2 Irene   ....   4 Sandra   ....

3 🔊 **6.11** Listen again. Are the sentences true (T) or false (F)?
   1 Public transport isn't very good in the area where Marc lives.   ....
   2 He is nervous because he didn't prepare for the test.   ....
   3 Irene thinks the only reason to get married is to have a party.   ....
   4 Her wedding day was one of the most important days of her life.   ....
   5 Kevin is celebrating his birthday.   ....
   6 Lots of people came to the party.   ....
   7 Sandra left home right after she graduated from university.   ....
   8 She thinks living on her own is an important step in her life.   ....

4 In pairs, think of an event you celebrated recently and tell your partner how you celebrated.

   I got a new job last month. I was really happy! I ate out with my friends and family.

Vocabulary

5 a Who said the sentences: Marc (M), Irene (I), Kevin (K) or Sandra (S)?

   a I **got here** at 7.00 this morning to prepare everything. ....
   b She's **getting messages** from lots of people who couldn't come. ....
   c I can't **get the bus** because they only come twice a day. ....
   d We were so happy and excited, but I **got a bit nervous**, too. ....
   e I **got** an OK job after I graduated. ....

b Look at the words in **bold** in the sentences again. Match them with the uses of *get*.

   1 get = arrive ....
   2 get + adjective = become ....
   3 get = buy or obtain ....
   4 get = receive ....
   5 get + transport = use ....

6 Match the words in the box with the correct categories.

> **V uses of *get***
>
> | a coffee | a taxi | a letter | angry | home | emails |
> | married | my driving licence | the train | to work | | |
>
> 1 get = arrive: *here*   / .... / ....
> 2 get + adjective: *nervous*   / .... / ....
> 3 get = buy/obtain: *a job*   / .... / ....
> 4 get = receive: *messages* / .... / ....
> 5 get + transport: *the bus*   / .... / ....
>
> 🔊 **6.12** Listen, check and repeat.

7 In pairs, ask and answer the questions.

   1 When was the last time you got embarrassed?
   2 What's the best way to get to your English class?
   3 What do you usually get for lunch?
   4 How many messages do you get on your phone every day?
   5 How often do you get the train?
   6 What time do you get home at night?
   7 Have you ever got a Valentine's card?
   8 Have you ever got angry with your boss?
   9 Do you think it's important to get a degree?
   10 How easy is it to get a taxi in your city?

Writing

8 Read the email. What special thing did Alberto do as part of his celebration?

To: aliciahalo@starmail.com
From: alberto@yellowmail.com
Subject: Last weekend!

Hi Alicia,

I hope you're well and that you're enjoying your new job. I hear it's been very cold at home.

Well, I've graduated! I got my degree last Friday! Three years of university are over, but I still can't believe it. My parents came from Rio, and they've been sightseeing here in Oxford all week.

Last weekend I had a very special graduation party. I invited all my close friends to dinner – twelve people! I made *feijoada* – I think they liked it. Have you ever cooked for that many people? It was a lot of work, but everyone should celebrate important occasions!

Now I just have to find a job. I don't think I can afford to get my own flat – I'm going to have to share. But if I'm lucky, I can get a car.

Let's catch up soon by Skype! I'm looking forward to hearing from you.

Best wishes,

Alberto

9 Write a similar email to a friend describing an important celebration in your life. Choose one of the events in exercise 2 or think of your own. Use the questions to help you.

   1 What was your celebration? Did you get married/promoted/a new home/a degree?
   2 Who got together for your celebration?
   3 Have you ever done anything like this before?
   4 What are you looking forward to now?

Mediation task: All students, page 127

6.4 THANKS FOR COMING!

giving thanks
two very different brothers

The big picture: two very different brothers

1   Look at the picture of two brothers. In pairs, answer the questions.
    1   Do they look like brothers? Why/Why not?
    2   Do you think they have similar lives?
    3   How often do you think they see each other?

2   📹 6.1 Watch the video and check your answers to exercise 1.

3   📹 6.1 Complete the sentences with *Ivan* or *David*. Watch the video again and check.
    1   .... works as a builder.
    2   .... owns three houses.
    3   .... has worked as a teacher.
    4   .... lives in a van.
    5   .... started a company.
    6   .... moved to London.
    7   .... has been an estate agent.
    8   .... has travelled in South America.
    9   .... is a politician.
    10 .... is very rich.

4   In pairs, compare the brothers using adjectives from the box or your own ideas.

    | generous | hardworking | kind | polite |
    | responsible | sensible | shy | sociable |

    I think David is as hardworking as Ivan.

5   In pairs, discuss the questions.
    1   Do you think the brothers will stay in touch? Why/Why not?
    2   In your opinion, what makes a person successful?
    3   Who's closer to your idea of success, Ivan or David?
    4   Do you have any brothers or sisters?
    5   Are you similar or different to them?

6   📹 6.2 Watch Lou and Rob talking about the video. In pairs, choose the correct words to complete the sentences.
    1   Rob thinks the brothers *see / don't see* each other more often now.
    2   Rob thinks *Ivan / David* is more successful than his brother.
    3   Lou thinks David *is / isn't* as successful as Ivan.
    4   Rob *looks like / doesn't look like* his brother.
    5   Rob and his brother *have / don't have* similar personalities.

7   a   📹 6.2 Watch the video again. Match the phrases giving thanks with the responses.
    1   Thanks for sending it to me.   a   Don't mention it!
    2   I really appreciate it.   b   It was nothing, really.
    3   That's very kind of you.   c   No problem.

    b   In pairs, make a list of different situations when you gave thanks to someone. How did they respond?

Ivan

David

Functional language

8 🔊 **6.14** Look at the pictures. Listen to the conversations and match them with the pictures.

Conversation 1 ....
Conversation 2 ....
Conversation 3 ....
Conversation 4 ....

9 🔊 **6.14** Complete the sentences with the words in the box. Listen again and check.

a lot	grateful	kind	know	need
problem	so	welcome		

1 **A** Where's the sugar?
   B Just over there.
   A Great – thanks ....
   B You're ....
2 **A** Er, excuse me? Hello? Is that your wallet on the table?
   B My wallet? Oh, yes, it is! Thank you .... much!
   A No ....
3 **A** Actually, I have a little something for you – a present.
   B What? That's very .... of you. You didn't .... to do that!
4 **A** We'd like to offer you the position of senior manager with a 50% pay increase.
   B Really? Oh, that's … I don't .... what to say.
   A Will you accept it?
   B Yes, of course! I'm very ...., really.

FL giving thanks

Being polite
Thanks. / Thank you. / Thanks a lot.

For a favour
Thanks for … / Thank you so much. / I really appreciate it.

For a gift
That's very kind of you. / You didn't need to do that.

Formal
I'm very grateful. / I don't know what to say.

Responding to thanks
No problem. / You're welcome.
It's a pleasure. / Don't mention it.
It's nothing, really. / It's the least I can do.

10 a 🔊 **6.15** 💬 **sounding grateful** 💬 Listen to the people giving thanks. Which response sounds more grateful: A or B?

1 I got you a glass of water. A ☐ B ☐
2 I bought you a new hat. A ☐ B ☐
3 The office is over there. A ☐ B ☐
4 The project was a success. A ☐ B ☐

b 🔊 **6.16** Listen and repeat the grateful thanks.

11 In pairs, take turns to respond to the expressions. Remember to sound grateful.

1 I've just finished washing the dishes.
2 Here's your jacket, sir.
3 This watch is very special to me, but I'd like you to have it.
4 I'm very grateful for all your help with my essay.
5 I've made you breakfast in bed!
6 You look really nice this evening.

Speaking

12 a In pairs, choose a situation and prepare a conversation.

> Your friend invites you to lunch and pays for the meal.

> You offer to help your friend with their homework.

> You give a presentation and your boss thinks it was excellent.

> You receive a horrible present from your aunt/uncle.

b Act out the situation to another pair.

✏️ Writing bank: page 149

REVIEW UNIT 6

Vocabulary
Personality adjectives

1 Write the opposite personality adjectives.
   1 hardworking .... 4 responsible ....
   2 patient .... 5 shy ....
   3 rude .... 6 selfish ....

2 a In pairs, write the names of people you know who are:
   1 sociable .... 3 polite ....
   2 generous .... 4 sensible ....

   b Tell your partner how you know the people.

Phrasal verbs

3 a Complete the questions with the phrasal verbs in the box.

   | hang out | look forward to | stay up | take up |

   1 How often do you .... late?
   2 Who do you usually .... with at the weekend?
   3 What new activity would you like to .... ?
   4 What day of the week do you most .... ?

   b In pairs, ask and answer the questions.

Uses of *get*

4 Complete the sentences with the correct form of *get* and the words in the box.

   | nervous | the bus | the job | there |

   1 The interview went really badly. I ....
   2 Dad's car is in the garage so I had to ....
   3 The bus was late so I .... on time.
   4 I .... and I made a few mistakes.

5 In pairs, ask and answer the questions.
   1 How do you get to class?
   2 When was the last time you got a letter?
   3 Is it easy to get a job in your town?

Grammar
Comparatives, superlatives, *as … as*

6 Complete the sentences with the correct comparative or superlative forms of the adjectives in brackets.
   1 Jack doesn't study very hard. He's .... than his brother. (lazy)
   2 No one is a better cook than Dad. He's .... cook in our family. (good)
   3 You need to be happy. Happiness is .... than work. (important)
   4 Pippa is always doing things for other people. She's .... person in the office. (kind)

7 Complete the second sentences so that they mean the same as the first ones. Use *not as … as*.
   1 My sister is more patient than me.
      I'm ....
   2 Windsor Castle is older than Buckingham Palace.
      Buckingham Palace ....
   3 My mum is busier than my dad.
      My dad ....

8 Write four sentences comparing people in your family. Use comparatives, superlatives and (*not*) *as … as*.

Present perfect with *ever* and *never*

9 a Complete the questions for the answers. Use the present perfect form of the verbs in brackets.
   1 A .... a new sport? (ever / take up)
      B Yes, I have. I started doing yoga last year.
   2 A .... someone a cake? (ever / make)
      B No, never. I always buy them.
   3 A .... to another country? (ever / go)
      B Yes, we went to the UK about three years ago.
   4 A .... in a plane? (ever / fly)
      B No, I haven't. But I'm flying to Morocco next year!

   b In pairs, ask and answer the questions from exercise 9a. If your partner answers 'yes', ask a follow-up question in the past simple.

   Have you ever made someone a cake?   Yes, I have.
   Who did you make it for?   I made it for my sister.

Functional language
Giving thanks

10 Read what A says and choose the best response: a or b.
   1 A Hi Mum! These flowers are for you.
      B a I'm very grateful.   b You didn't need to do that.
   2 A That's such a lovely dress!
      B a Thank you.   b I really appreciate it.
   3 A Thanks for the coffee.
      B a No problem.   b It's the least I can do.

11 6.17 In pairs, take turns to respond to the sentences. Listen and compare your answers.
   1 I bought you a small gift.
   2 Your room is here, sir. Just call if you need anything.
   3 Thanks for giving me a lift last night.
   4 I really like your coat.
   5 The food was delicious. Thank you for inviting us.

Looking back

- Are you similar to your family? Compare yourself to a member of your family.
- Have you ever tried a new activity? What was it? Did you enjoy it?

Homelife

7

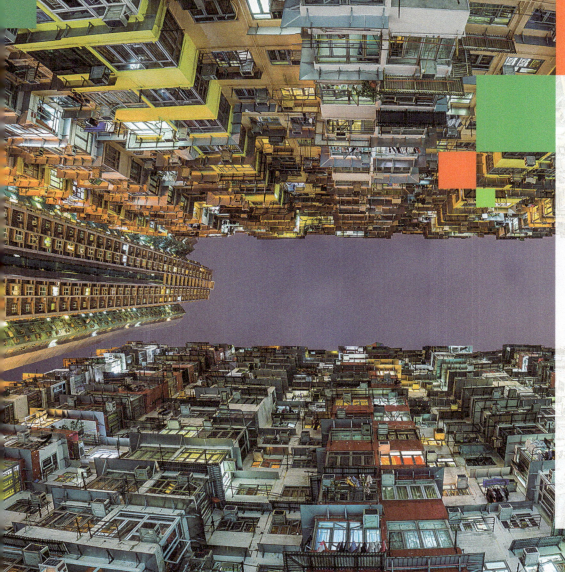

Grammar G
present perfect with *just*, *already*, *yet*
present perfect with *for*, *since*
linkers

Vocabulary V
housework collocations
city features

Functional language FL
telephone language

Skill
scan a text for specific information

Video
sharing your life with cats

Writing
a promotional leaflet

Exams
completing a factual text

The big picture: the monster building

1 Look at the picture. In pairs, guess the answers to the questions.
  1 Where is the building?
  2 How many flats are there?
  3 What is good about living in the building?
  4 What is not good about living in the building?

2 🔊 7.1 Listen and check your answers.

3 In pairs, discuss the questions.
  1 Would you like to live in this building? Why/Why not?
  2 Do you have buildings like this in your country? Do you know anyone who lives in them?
  3 How well do you know your neighbours?
  4 How important are space and privacy to you?

7.1 HAVE YOU TIDIED UP YET?

G present perfect with *just, already, yet*
V housework collocations

Vocabulary

1 In pairs, answer the questions.
   1 Who do you live with?
   2 How much housework do you do?
   3 How important is it to have a clean and tidy house?

2 Look at the picture. In pairs, find the items in the box.

bin	clothes	dishes
dishwasher	floor	kitchen
laundry	pet	plant
rubbish	shelves	table

3 Complete the housework collocations with the words from exercise 2.

V housework collocations

1 water the ……………
2 dust the ……………
3 throw away the ……………
4 load the ……………
5 clear the ……………
6 feed the ……………
7 take out the ……………
8 tidy up the ……………
9 do the ……………
10 wash up the ……………
11 clean the ……………
12 iron the ……………

🔊 7.2 Listen, check and repeat.

4 In pairs, say who does the jobs from the Vocabulary box in your house and how often he/she does them.

I usually water the plants. I water them once or twice a week.

Listening

5 Read the text. Do you think the scientists are correct? Why/Why not?

TIDY ROOMS OR MESSY ROOMS:
which are better for you?

New scientific research says that tidy people are healthier than messy people. In the experiment, the scientists put one group of people in a tidy room and another group in a messy room and then offered them choices. When the scientists offered snacks, the people from the tidy room chose healthy options like fruit, but the group from the messy room chose chocolate bars instead. However, in a different experiment, people in messy environments were more creative and had more interesting ideas than people in tidy places.

🔍 notice

We can also use *do the* + *-ing* to describe common household jobs.

do the ironing, **do the wash**ing up, **do the shop**ping

66

6 🔊 **7.3** Look at the pictures and match the people with their living rooms. Listen to a radio programme and check.

Victor, lawyer

Loretta, artist

7 🔊 **7.3** Listen again. Tick (✓) the actions Victor and Loretta have done, or cross (✗) the jobs they haven't done today.

	Action	Victor	Loretta
1	Make coffee		
2	Tidy up the kitchen		
3	Load the dishwasher		
4	Take out the bins		
5	Iron the clothes		

8 In pairs, discuss the questions.
1 Which living room do you prefer?
2 Are you more like Victor or Loretta?
3 Can a tidy or messy home help you in your job?

Grammar

9 a Look at the sentences from the programme. Who said them: Victor (V) or Loretta (L)?
1 I've **already** loaded the dishwasher. ....
2 Have you had a coffee **yet**? ....
3 I've **just** made some coffee. ....
4 I haven't tidied up the kitchen **yet**. ....

b What tense are the sentences in? Look at the words in **bold** and answer the questions.
1 Which two words do we use to describe an action completed before now?
2 Which of these words means it was very recent?
3 Which word do we use to say an action isn't complete, or to ask if an action is complete?

> **G present perfect with just, already, yet**
>
> just   My sister's **just** called. She'll be here in a few minutes.
> already   I've **already** had lunch, so I'm not hungry.
> yet   I haven't opened the letter **yet** because I'm nervous.
>   Have you called Harry **yet**?

→ Grammar reference: page 138

10 🔊 **7.4** 🗨 **sentence stress** 🗨 Listen to the sentences and underline the stressed words. Listen and repeat.
1 I've just finished the kitchen.
2 I haven't ironed my clothes yet.
3 I've already had three cups.

11 🔊 **7.5** In pairs, add the words *yet*, *just* and *already* to the conversation. Listen, check and repeat.
A Have you finished your work?
B Yes, I have. I've sent the last email.
A Great! Could you help me tidy up the house? I haven't done everything.
B Of course! Have you cleaned the floor?
A Yes, I've cleaned the floor and cleared the table, but I haven't taken out the rubbish.

Speaking

12 a Imagine you are going on holiday tomorrow. In pairs, complete the 'Jobs to do'.

```
       Jobs to do
1  pack a suitcase      ☐
2  ...................  ☐
3  ...................  ☐
4  ...................  ☐
5  ...................  ☐
6  ...................  ☐
```

b Tick (✓) three jobs on your list, but don't show your partner. Ask and answer *Have you ... yet?* questions.

7.2 A CITY FOR EVERYONE

G present perfect with *for*, *since*
V city features

Vocabulary

1 Answer the questions in small groups.
   1 What cities do you know well?
   2 Have you ever lived in a city?
   3 What is the best thing about living in a city?

2 Look at the picture. Match the city features with the words in the box.

V **city features**

> bench   bike lane   cash machine
> fountain   litter bin   pavement
> pedestrian crossing   playground
> roundabout   signpost   traffic jam
> traffic lights

1 ....   7 ....
2 ....   8 ....
3 ....   9 ....
4 ....   10 ....
5 ....   11 ....
6 ....   12 ....

🔊 7.6 Listen, check and repeat.

3 Look out of the window. Which city features can you see? If you can't see any, where are the nearest ones?

I can't see a cash machine. I think the nearest one is on Trinidad Street.

Reading

4 a Look at the picture again. In pairs, answer the questions.
   1 Which country is the city in?
   2 Which side shows the past? How would you describe it?
   3 Which side shows the present? How would you describe it?

   b Read the text quickly and check your answers.

5 a Read the text again. Are the sentences true (T) or false (F)?
   1 In the past, there were no pavements in the centre of Pontevedra. ....
   2 The mayor banned all cars from the city centre. ....
   3 Before the ban, 30 people died in traffic accidents every year. ....
   4 The local shops in Pontevedra are successful. ....
   5 The population of Pontevedra has increased since 1999. ....
   6 Most of the people in Pontevedra have moved from other countries. ....

   b Would you like to live in Pontevedra? Why/Why not?

   Yes, the city is very clean and safe.

THE CITY THAT BANNED CARS

I lived in the Spanish city of Pontevedra from 1990 to 1996. I remember the traffic jams were terrible and the pavements were always full of parked cars and scooters. It was very noisy and dirty ... that's why I left! Now I'm here again, and it's completely different. There are green spaces and children's playgrounds everywhere. And I can't see any cars! I stop a man cycling slowly along a bike lane and ask, 'This is so peaceful. How long has Pontevedra been like this?' 'We haven't had cars here for a long time,' he replies with a smile. This is because when Miguel Anxo Fernandez Lores became mayor of the city in 1999, he decided to ban almost all cars from the centre of the city. Pontevedra has changed a lot since the ban. For many years the traffic was very dangerous, and from 1996 to 2006, 30 people died in accidents, but nobody has died since 2009. There is less pollution, too – CO_2 emissions have gone down 70%. Lores has been mayor for over twenty years, and he is very proud of the change in his city. 'Public space belongs to everyone. When we walk, we are all equal,' he says.
As well as banning cars, the mayor doesn't allow any large shopping malls outside the city centre. This means that everyone does their shopping in the centre. In many cities, local shops have closed down recently, but in Pontevedra, the city's shops have been busy for years.
These are not the only positive results of the changes in Pontevedra. For a long time, people saw the city as dirty and boring, and nobody wanted to live there. But since the ban, central Pontevedra has gained 12,000 new residents. Many of these new people are young families from other parts of Spain, who want their children to live in a cleaner and safer city.

Grammar

6 a Match the halves to make sentences. Check your answers in the text.

1 How long has Pontevedra been ....
2 We haven't had cars here for ....
3 Pontevedra has changed a lot since ....
4 Nobody has died since ....
5 Lores has been mayor for ....

a over twenty years.
b 2009.
c the ban.
d like this?
e a long time.

b Look at the sentences again and answer the questions.

1 What tense are the sentences in?
2 Are the situations finished, or are they still true?
3 Which question word(s) do we use to ask about the duration of a situation?
4 Which word do we use to talk about a period of time?
5 Which word do we use to talk about a fixed point in time?

> **G present perfect with *for*, *since***
>
> **How long has** Lores **been** mayor?
> He**'s been** mayor **for** over twenty years / **since** 1999.
> We **haven't had** cars here **for** a long time / **since** the ban.
>
> → Grammar reference: page 138

> **notice**
>
> We use the past simple to talk about the duration of finished actions in the past.
> **How long did** you **live** in Pontevedra?
> I **lived** in Pontevedra **from** 1990 **to** 1996 / **for** six years.

7 🔊 7.7 ❝ contracted *have/has* ❞ Listen and tick (✓) the sentences you hear. Listen again, check and repeat.

1 a I lived here for three years. ☐
  b I've lived here for three years. ☐
2 a She had a car for six months. ☐
  b She's had a car for six months. ☐
3 a We've worked together for ages. ☐
  b We worked together for ages. ☐

8 a Look at the picture. Which city is it? Read the text quickly and check. Would you like to visit the city?

b Choose the correct words to complete the text.

Seoul in South Korea has had poor air quality ⁽¹⁾*since / for* many years. A lot of the pollution is caused by cars, and ⁽²⁾*from / for* 30 years, one road in Seoul was especially bad. ⁽³⁾*Since / From* 1973 ⁽⁴⁾*to / for* 2003, a 6 km road with four lanes took 170,000 vehicles into the city centre every day. The road was very busy ⁽⁵⁾*from / since* 8.00 a.m. ⁽⁶⁾*from / to* 7.00 p.m. Many people wanted more lanes on the road, but the government decided to remove the road instead, and they opened up the Cheonggyecheon river! It ⁽⁷⁾*was / has been* under the road for many years, but now residents can enjoy it again. It is now a riverside park with 1.5 million trees. ⁽⁸⁾*From / For* nearly twenty years, local people and tourists have enjoyed the river, and since the road disappeared, people ⁽⁹⁾*stopped / have stopped* driving into the city. Now they take the subway!

Speaking

9 Complete the *How long ...?* questions with a verb in the present perfect or past simple tense. Then take turns to ask and answer the questions.

1 Where do you live now?
  How long _have you lived_ there?
2 Where did you live as a child?
  How long _did you live_ there?
3 What's your favourite item of clothing?
  How long _____ it?
4 Which sport are you good at?
  How long _____ it?
5 What pets did you have as a child?
  How long _____ them?
6 Who is your best friend?
  How long _____ him/her?

✓ Exam practice: page 162

7.3 A DIFFERENT KIND OF HOUSE

G linkers
scan a text for specific information

Reading

1 a Look at the pictures and the title of the text. Guess the answers to the questions.
   1 What is the problem?
   2 What is the solution?
   3 Is the solution successful?

   b Read the text quickly and check your answers.

scan a text for specific information

You often need to find information in a text quickly without reading in detail.

Identify the key word(s) you need to look for. Move your eyes quickly through the text until you find the key word.

Read the sentences around it to find the information you need. If you don't find the information, look for the next example of the key word.

2 a Read the Skill box. Scan the text for the underlined key words and answer the questions.
   1 What is the <u>Cubo</u> made of?
   2 What are <u>slums</u>?
   3 Where is <u>Earl Forlales</u> from?
   4 How much <u>prize</u> money did he win?

   b In pairs, underline the key words in the questions. Then scan the text to answer them.
   1 Why did the judges like Cubo so much?
   2 How long does it take to build the Cubo house?
   3 Why are the Cubo houses good for the planet?
   4 How many families will probably have Cubo houses in the next five years?

3 In pairs, answer the questions.
   1 Do you think the Cubo houses are a good solution to the world's housing problems? Why?/Why not?
   2 What other things could Cubo houses be used for?
   3 Would the Cubo houses be a good idea in your country? Why?/Why not?

THE *CUBO* HOUSE: A NEW SOLUTION TO AN OLD PROBLEM

Around the world, millions of people live in poor-quality, crowded housing known as slums. People who live in slums have a low quality of life, and they are more likely to suffer from a variety of health problems. Governments would like to help these people, but building good-quality houses takes a long time and is expensive.

However, one young man has designed a house that may partly solve the problem. Earl Forlales is just 23 years old and from Manila in the Philippines. His house, which he has called *Cubo*, is made from bamboo, and in 2018, it won the first prize in a competition to develop cities of the future.

The judges particularly liked *Cubo* because it is so cheap and quick to build. In fact, Forlales says that the materials for a house can be made in one week, and it takes just four hours to build the house! *Cubo* is environmentally friendly as well. Because bamboo is the fastest-growing plant in the world, these houses are very good for the planet, too!

The prize from the competition is £50,000 and Forlales is using that money to build models of the *Cubo* houses. He then hopes that companies will invest money in his business so he can begin building houses for the poorest people in Manila. He has already chosen an area of land and he plans to build houses for 10,000 families in the Philippines in the next five years. Some of the houses will be connected to each other, so that residents will share bathrooms and kitchens and therefore save money. Forlales hopes that this use of shared space will also help to build communities. Although he will only build *Cubo* in the Philippines at first, he believes the idea could also work in other parts of the world where bamboo grows, such as Africa and South America.

Grammar

4 Look at the sentences from the text. Are the words in **bold** used to contrast information or add extra information?

1. Governments would like to help these people, **but** building good-quality houses takes a long time and is expensive.
2. **However**, one young man has designed a house that may partly solve the problem.
3. The judges particularly liked *Cubo* because it is so cheap **and** quick to build.
4. *Cubo* is environmentally friendly **as well**.
5. These houses are very good for the planet, **too**!
6. This use of shared space will **also** help to build communities.
7. **Although** he will only build *Cubo* in the Philippines at first, he believes the idea could also work in other parts of the world.

G linkers

To add extra information

*The city is dirty **and** it's polluted.*

*It's very noisy **as well**.*

*These houses are very beautiful. They're good for the environment, **too**.*

*Everyone in my house helps with the housework. We **also** share all our food.*

To contrast information

*Living in this city is exciting, **but** it's very expensive.*

*I like living with other people. **However**, I don't like sharing a kitchen.*

***Although** these houses are cheap, they are good quality.*

*These houses are good quality **although** they're cheap.*

→ Grammar reference: page 138

5 Choose the correct linkers to complete the sentences.

1. We have a spare bedroom, *but / and* you can't sleep there because it's full of boxes.
2. I do all the tidying in my house. I do most of the cleaning, *also / too*.
3. *Although / However* I like animals, I don't want to have any pets in my house.
4. My uncle has an amazing house with a huge garden. He has a swimming pool *as well / however*!
5. I want to buy a house. *However, / As well,* I don't earn enough money yet.
6. My flatmates and I share everything. We *as well / also* cook together.
7. There's a small garden in front of my building *but / and* the park is very close.
8. *But / Although* our neighbours are nice, we don't see them very often.

Writing

6 a Look at two unusual houses. Which would you prefer to live in?

The Hobbit House

The Houseboat

b Read about 'The Hobbit House' and complete the gaps with linkers.

This home belongs to Kris Harbour, (1) .... he calls it 'The Hobbit House'. He loves living here because it's peaceful (2) .... beautiful. It's good for the environment, (3) .... When Kris moved here from London, he was worried about getting bored, (4) .... he isn't bored at all. He's too busy finding wood for the fire and cooking food. He (5) .... takes photographs and writes a blog. (6) .... he is happy in his house, it's not perfect. He often finds small animals in the house (7) .... sometimes he gets wet when it rains. (8) ...., he doesn't mind because he loves living in the countryside with no stress.

7 a Make a list of advantages and disadvantages of living in the houseboat.

It's very quiet and peaceful.

b In pairs, compare your lists. Write a paragraph about the houseboat. Use as many linkers as you can.

⇄ Mediation task: All students, page 128

7.4 THANK YOU FOR CALLING
telephone language
sharing your life with cats

The big picture: sharing your life with cats

1 Look at the picture. In pairs, answer the questions.
  1 How many cats can you see?
  2 How many cats live in the house?
  3 Why does the woman have so many cats?

2 **7.1** Watch the video and check. How many places in the house do you see cats?
  There are lots of cats in the kitchen.

3 **7.1** Are the sentences true (T) or false (F)? Watch the video again and check.
  1 Lynea has always had her cat business in the same house.
  2 Teresa, one of Lynea's employees, arrives very early to feed the cats.
  3 Frank started working at the cat house because he loves cats.
  4 A vet only sees the cats once a month.
  5 Lynea gives away the cats as pets.
  6 Lynea loves everything about her business.

4 In pairs, discuss the questions.
  1 Do you think Lynea's work is important? Why/Why not?
  2 Would you like to live in a home like this? Why/Why not?
  3 Have you ever lived with a pet?
  4 What are the good and bad things about having pets?
  5 Which animals make the best pets? Why?

5 **7.2** Watch Rob and Lou talking about the video. Answer the questions.
  1 Who is more positive about Lynea's lifestyle?
  2 Why does Lou think Lynea does this job?
  3 Who has never had a pet?
  4 What are his/her reasons?

6 **7.2** Choose the correct person to complete the sentences. Watch the video again and check.
  1 *Rob / Lou* makes the first call.
  2 The first call ends because *Rob / Lou* can't hear well.
  3 *Rob / Lou* makes the second call.
  4 This call ends because *Rob's / Lou's* battery runs out.
  5 *Rob / Lou* is going to call tomorrow.

Functional language

7 🔊 **7.8** Look at the pictures and listen to the conversations. Where do you think the people are?

8 🔊 **7.8** Look at the sentences. Are they phrases to answer (A), respond (R), end a conversation (E) or deal with a problem (P)? Listen again and check.

1 Thanks for calling. ....
2 I think you have the wrong number. ....
3 Jane speaking, how can I help you? ....
4 I should get going, John. ....
5 Can you speak up? ....
6 Hello, Jessie Carter speaking. ....
7 It's John. Is Fiona there? ....
8 Hi! It's me. ....

FL telephone language

	Home	Office
Answer	Hello?	... speaking. How can I help you?
Respond	Hi. This is / It's ... I just called to ... Is ... there?	My name is ... I'm calling because ... Could I speak to ..., please?
Ending conversation	I should get going. Speak soon.	Thank you for your help. Thanks for calling.
Dealing with problems	I can't hear you very well. Can you speak up a bit? I don't have a very good signal. Could you say that again, please? My battery is running out. I'll call you back. Sorry, I think you have the wrong number.	

9 a 🔊 **7.9** ❝ **sounding polite** ❞ Listen to the sentences. Which sentence sounds more polite: A or B?

1 How can I help you? A ☐ B ☐
2 Could I speak to Selina, please? A ☐ B ☐
3 Could I call you back in a minute? A ☐ B ☐
4 Could you say that again, please? A ☐ B ☐

b 🔊 **7.10** Listen and repeat the polite sentences.

10 a Choose the correct words to complete sentences.

1 Jamie *speaking / calling*. How can I help you?
2 Thank you for your *help / signal*.
3 Can you *say / speak* up a bit, please?
4 Hi, is Núria *here / there*?
5 Can I call *you back / back you* later?

b Match the responses with the sentences. Then in pairs, practise saying them. Remember to sound polite.

a I said, the meeting is at 3.30.
b Yes, of course. Speak soon.
c Hello, could I speak to Alicia, please?
d No problem, thanks for calling.
e Sorry, she's busy at the moment.

Speaking

11 a In groups of three, choose a situation and prepare a telephone conversation.

AT HOME

STUDENT A You haven't spoken to your friend in a long time. You want to meet for a coffee. Call them now to arrange meeting up.

STUDENT B You answer the phone. The call is for your flatmate.

STUDENT C An old friend calls, but you are busy. Find a polite way to end the conversation.

IN THE OFFICE

STUDENT A You try to call a colleague at the office urgently, but you have problems with your phone.

STUDENT B You answer the phone at work. The caller wants to speak to a colleague, but they have problems with their phone.

STUDENT C A colleague calls you at work, but you're very busy. Say you will call back.

b Practise the telephone conversations. Swap roles and practise the other situation.

✎ Writing bank: page 150

REVIEW UNIT 7

Vocabulary
Housework collocations

1 **a** Choose the correct verbs to complete the housework phrases.
   1 load / feed / water the dishwasher
   2 make / do / dust the laundry
   3 clear / throw away / feed the table
   4 throw away / take out / tidy up the bin
   5 clean / wash up / water the plants

   b Put the jobs in order from 1 (jobs you don't mind) to 5 (jobs you hate). In pairs, compare your answers.

2 In pairs, say the last three jobs you did at home and when you did them.
   I washed up the dishes last night.

City features

3 Read the clues and write the city features. The first letters are given for you.
   1 You can get money here. c............... m...............
   2 The road goes in a circle here. r...............
   3 You walk on this. It's next to the road. p...............
   4 Children like to go here after school. p...............
   5 This is where people can cross the road.
      p............... c...............

Grammar
Present perfect with *just, already, yet*

4 Complete the conversations with the present perfect and the words in brackets.
   1 (your neighbours / move / to Frankfurt + yet)
      A *Have your neighbours moved to Frankfurt yet?*
      B Yes, they moved last week.
   2 **A** Does Pippa want to see the film?
      (she / see / it + already)
      B No, ...
   3 (Paulo / start / university + yet)
      A ....?
      B Yes, he started a month ago.
   4 **A** Do you want a coffee?
      (I / have / a drink + just)
      B No thanks, ...
   5 **A** Is dinner ready? I'm hungry!
      (I / not cook / it + yet)
      B No, sorry. ....

5 In pairs, ask and answer questions about the activities in the box. Use the present perfect and *just, already* or *yet*.

   do your homework   go on social media
   have lunch   make coffee   read the news

   Have you had lunch yet?
   Yes, I've just eaten a sandwich.

Present perfect with *for, since*

6 Complete the second sentences so that they mean the same as the first ones. Use the present perfect form of the verbs in brackets and *for* or *since*.
   1 My daughter left home two years ago.
      My daughter .... two years. (not live at home)
   2 I arrived at the hotel last Friday.
      I .... Friday. (be at hotel)
   3 Paul and Marta's wedding was ten years ago.
      Paul and Marta .... ten years. (be married)

7 In pairs, ask and answer the question *How long have you …?* for the activities in the box.

   study English   know your best friend
   have your phone   live in your house

Linkers

8 Choose the correct linkers to complete the text.
   I don't like doing housework, (1)*although / as well* I try to be tidy. I share a flat with two friends (2)*and / but* we all help in different ways. Max cleans the bathroom and tidies up the kitchen, (3)*however / too*. Jake is quite lazy, (4)*and / but* he does load the dishwasher and he (5)*also / too* takes out the rubbish … sometimes.

Functional language
Telephone language

9 🔊 7.11 Put the conversation in the correct order. Listen and check.
   a ☐ **A** Thanks for calling.
   b ☐ **B** I'd like to speak to Kay Lam. I'm calling because of a technical problem.
   c ☐ **A** Ah, OK. I'm sorry, but Kay isn't available at the moment. I'll ask her to call you back.
   d ☐ **B** Hello, this is Laura Waters. Could I speak to Kay Lam, please?
   e ☐ **A** Good afternoon, Tech World, Phoebe speaking. How can I help you?
   f ☐ **B** That's great. Thank you.
   g ☐ **A** Sorry, I can't hear you very well. Could you say that again, please?

10 In pairs, act out a telephone conversation for the situation below.

   You try to call a friend, but someone you don't know answers. You have dialled the wrong number. Say sorry and end the call.

🕑 Looking back

- What housework do you need to do today?
- Think of five useful words or expressions you have learned. Why do you think they are useful?

Technology

8

Grammar G
-ing form and to + infinitive
quantifiers

Vocabulary V
free-time activities
uncountable nouns
transport phrases

Functional language FL
asking for and giving opinions

Skill 🎧
listen for numerical information

Video 📹
a computer-made musical

Writing ✏️
a for-and-against essay

Exams ✓
writing a narrative

The big picture: new uses for old tech

1 Look at the picture. In pairs, guess the answers to the questions.
  1 What devices can you see?
  2 Are they modern or old?
  3 Where are the people?
  4 What do you think they are doing?

2 🔊 8.1 Listen and check your answers.

3 In pairs, discuss the questions.
  1 Did you like the music? Why/Why not?
  2 What devices from your childhood are 'forgotten friends'?
  3 What do you do with devices when you don't want them any more?
  4 What questions would you like to ask the musicians?

8.1 DIGITAL DETOX

G -ing form and to + infinitive
V free-time activities

Vocabulary

1 Look at the pictures. What free-time activities are the people doing? Do you ever do them?

In number 1, they're going window shopping.

2 Match the halves to make free-time activities.

V free-time activities

Sports and games
1 go to ....   a chess / basketball / board games
2 do ....   b yoga / karate / gymnastics
3 keep ....   c hiking / jogging / cycling
4 go ....   d fit
5 play ....   e the gym / the swimming pool

Socializing
6 join ....   a window shopping
7 go ....   b with friends
8 spend ....   c time with family
9 meet ....   d a club
10 meet up ....   e new people

Online hobbies
11 play ....   a a blog
12 surf ....   b online
13 go on ....   c video games
14 write ....   d the net
15 shop ....   e social media

Other
16 play ....   a bread / cakes
17 bake ....   b the piano / the drums
18 do ....   c records / coins
19 learn ....   d photography
20 collect ....   e a language

🔊 **8.2** Listen, check and repeat.

3 In pairs, ask and answer the questions.
1 Which activities did you do last week?
2 Which activities have you never done?
3 Which activities would you like to try?

Listening

4 Read the introduction to a podcast. In pairs, answer the questions.
1 Do you agree that technology is changing how we spend our free time? Why/Why not?
2 What examples of online hobbies replacing traditional hobbies does it mention?
3 Can you think of more examples?
4 Do you think you could do the challenge?

Digital Fingerprint

Technology is changing how we spend our free time. In the past, we met up with friends, but nowadays many people go on social media or chat to friends online. Rather than playing sports outside, younger people are more likely to play video games. Even one of my favourite hobbies – going window shopping – is less popular, as people surf the net and shop online. This week, we challenge two young people to give up their devices and do their hobbies the old-fashioned way.

5 🔊 **8.3** Listen to the podcast and answer the questions.
1 What is Lucas's hobby?
2 Did he enjoy giving up his devices? Why/Why not?
3 What is Anna's hobby?
4 Did she enjoy giving up her devices? Why/Why not?

7 Look at the podcast comments. Complete them with the -ing or to + infinitive form of a verb from the box.

| buy | play | read | spend | sit | take |

NEESHA: Like Anna, I enjoy (1) .... photos, but I don't want (2) .... a lot of money. I can't even afford (3) .... a good camera!

NEIL: I hate (4) .... at the computer. But I love (5) .... video games so prefer to play them on my phone.

UMBERTO: We don't have space in our flat for paper books, and my girlfriend recommended (6) .... an e-reader. And now I love (7) .... with it! I stopped (8) .... paper books a year ago.

Grammar

6 a 🔊 8.3 Choose the correct form of the verbs to complete the sentences from the podcast. Listen again and check.

1 I've always **enjoyed** to learn / learning languages.
2 I **wanted** to try / trying a very different language.
3 I **decided** to learn / learning Chinese.
4 We've **started** to go / going to a language exchange.
5 I **love** to do / doing photography.
6 I **started** taking / to take pictures on my phone.
7 I **spend time** to edit / editing the best ones on my computer.
8 I **managed** to find / finding a shop that sold old-fashioned film.
9 I was really **looking forward to** see / seeing the photos.
10 I **can't afford** to use / using an analogue camera.

b Look at the verbs in **bold** and answer the questions.

1 Which verbs are followed by to + infinitive?
....
....
2 Which verbs are followed by the -ing form?
....
....
3 Which verb can be followed by either to + infinitive or -ing form? ....

G -ing form and to + infinitive

Verbs followed by -ing form

She **enjoys taking** black and white photos.
I **recommend studying** every evening.
I'm **looking forward to seeing** you.

Verbs followed by to + infinitive

I **want to learn** Swahili next.
I **decided to try** photography.
He **would like to buy** a new computer.

→ Grammar reference: page 139

8 🔊 8.4 🎙 **weak form of to** 🎙 Listen to the sentences. Notice how *to* is pronounced. Listen again, check and repeat.

1 I wanted <u>to</u> try a very different language.
2 I decided <u>to</u> learn Chinese.
3 I started <u>to</u> take pictures on my phone.
4 I can't afford <u>to</u> use an analogue camera.

9 a Make sentences with -ing forms or to + infinitive.

1 My friends and I enjoy …   4 I really can't afford …
2 I spend a lot of time …   5 I'm looking forward …
3 Recently, I decided …   6 I don't mind …

b In pairs, compare your answers. Remember to use the weak form of *to*.

Speaking

10 a Ask your classmates questions to find someone for each topic below.

*Do you like playing video games?   No, I don't.
Why not?   I think they're boring.*

b In pairs, compare your answers and tell your partner what you found out.

Alex doesn't like playing video games. He thinks they're boring.

Find someone who …

1 doesn't like playing video games.
2 spends too much time on social media.
3 doesn't mind doing housework.
4 would like to start a new hobby.
5 enjoys going window shopping.
6 decided to learn English recently.
7 wants to keep fit.
8 is looking forward to meeting up with friends.

8.2 GOOD TECH, BAD TECH

G quantifiers
V uncountable nouns

Reading

1 Look at the pictures. What is the connection between them? Read the text and check.

2 Are the sentences true (T) or false (F)? Read the text again and check.
  1 The picture of the bears is about hard work and success. ......
  2 Planes couldn't fly because a drone was too close to an airport. ......
  3 Drones give information about places that are hard to visit. ......
  4 Drones can carry people away from danger in emergencies. ......
  5 Drones need more laws to make them safer to use. ......

Vocabulary

3 a Choose the correct words to complete the sentences. Check your answers in the text.
  1 Scientists explained that the bears *was / were* frightened.
  2 There was also *a / some* news of drones causing problems.
  3 An airport in London was closed because *a / some* drone was flying too close.
  4 *This / These* stories are giving drones a bad name.
  5 The technology *has / have* lots of useful applications.
  6 Scientists can use drones to study *wildlife / wildlives*.

  b Look at the sentences again. Tick (✓) the uncountable nouns. Can you find any more uncountable nouns in the text?
  1 bear ☐   4 wildlife ☐
  2 news ☐   5 story ☐
  3 drone ☐   6 technology ☐

4 Look at the uncountable nouns in the Vocabulary box. Match them with the descriptions.

V uncountable nouns

accommodation	advice	education
employment	information	luggage
news	research	technology	traffic
transport	wildlife

  1 wild animals and plants ....
  2 moving cars on roads ....
  3 recent stories about the world ....
  4 facts about things ....
  5 experiments and studies ....
  6 modern inventions ....
  7 jobs or work ....
  8 lessons at school ....
  9 places to stay or live in ....
  10 planes, buses, trains, etc. ....
  11 suggestions about what to do ....
  12 suitcases and bags ....

🔊 8.5 Listen, check and repeat.

5 a 🔊 8.6 ❝ **word stress** ❞ Listen to the words. Notice the underlined syllables that are stressed. Listen again and repeat.
  1 <u>trans</u>port   4 tech<u>no</u>logy
  2 ad<u>vice</u>   5 edu<u>ca</u>tion
  3 em<u>ploy</u>ment

POSTED BY: MARCUS WATT   **14 MAY**

Drones: toys or tools?

How many readers recognize this photo of a mother bear and her cub? Lots of people saw this cute animal on social media, climbing a difficult mountain to reach its mother. The video's message seemed clear – success is possible if you keep trying. But later some scientists explained that the bears were frightened of the drone that was filming them, and that is why they made the dangerous climb. There was also some news of drones causing problems when an airport in London was closed because a drone was flying too close. Just a few minutes with 'a toy' stopped air traffic at one of the world's busiest airports and affected thousands of passengers. We don't know how much money it cost, but these stories are giving drones a bad name. However, drones are easy to control and they only need a little energy to fly, so the technology has lots of useful applications. Scientists can use drones to study wildlife in places that are difficult for humans to visit, such as Antarctica. And from California to Australia, drones have helped fight forest fires by showing firefighters what is happening from the sky. In emergency situations drones can even deliver food and medical supplies. As we've seen, drones can be good and bad. But are there any laws to control how people use them? The short answer is there are very few laws. Sadly, without regulation, some people will continue to use drones irresponsibly. When cars first appeared, there weren't any rules for the road, but now there is lots of traffic and we understand that rules for drivers are necessary. Drones are no different, so let's make sure they become the safe technology of the twenty-first century.

Share   Like   Comment

b 🔊 **8.7** Say the words in the box and put them in the correct columns. Listen, check and repeat.

| supply | information | photography | pollution | wildlife |

Oo	oO	oOo	oOoo	ooOo
transport	advice	employment	technology	education

6 In pairs, ask and answer the questions.
1 Who do you talk to when you need some advice?
2 Have you had any good news recently?
3 What wildlife is there near where you live?
4 What's the cheapest accommodation in your city?
5 How much luggage do you take on holiday?
6 What's the best type of transport in your city?

Grammar

7 Complete the sentences with the words in the box. Check your answers in the text. Are the nouns in **bold** countable or uncountable?

| few | little | lots (x2) | many | much |

1 How .... **readers** recognize this photo?
2 .... of **people** saw this cute animal.
3 We don't know how .... **money** it cost.
4 Just a .... **minutes** with 'a toy' stopped air traffic.
5 They only need a .... **energy** to fly.
6 Now there is .... of **traffic**.

G quantifiers

Uncountable	Countable
How **much** pollution is there?	How **many** animals did you see?
There's **lots of** pollution.	We saw **lots of** animals.
There's **some** pollution.	We saw **some** animals.
There's **a little** pollution.	We saw **a few** animals.
There isn't **much** pollution.	We didn't see **many** animals.
There's **very little** pollution.	We saw **very few** animals.
There isn't **any** pollution.	We didn't see **any** animals.

→ Grammar reference: page 139

🔍 notice

We use *very few* and *very little* to emphasize a small quantity.
I have **a few** good friends. (positive)
I have **very few** good friends. (negative)

8 Complete the text with correct words. There is sometimes more than one correct answer.

70% of the surface of the planet is oceans, but we know very (1).............. information about them. Scientists want answers to (2).............. questions, such as '(3).............. energy is stored as heat?' and '(4).............. fish are there?'
There are only (5).............. research ships in the ocean, but each ship costs (6).............. of money and needs people to work on it. So, (7).............. scientists are turning to robots, called unmanned surface vehicles or USVs, like the 'saildrone', instead. They don't cost (8).............. money, so you can have (9).............. drones working all over the ocean. They don't use (10).............. fuel because they are 100% solar-powered and can sail for months without stopping.

Speaking

9 In pairs, ask and answer *How many ...?* and *How much ...?* questions about the technology in your lives.
1 photos / you / have / on your phone?
2 apps / you / use / every day?
3 money / your last computer / cost?
4 friends / you / have / on social media?
5 messages / you / send / every day?
6 time / you / spend / watch TV?

How many photos do you have on your phone?
I don't have any photos because I don't have a phone!

✓ Exam practice: page 163

8.3 GETTING AROUND

v transport phrases
⚙ listen for numerical information

Vocabulary

1 a Look at the pictures. Which type of transport do you prefer? Why?

b 🔊 8.8 Listen to four people describe their journeys. Match them with the pictures.

1 .... 2 .... 3 .... 4 ....

2 Match the words with the definitions.

v transport phrases

> be delayed   car park   get in/out   get on/off
> get stuck   give someone a lift   public transport
> queue   reach   return ticket   rush hour
> set off   take   it takes …   season ticket

1 to be late
2 a ticket for both directions of a journey
3 the time of day when traffic is busiest
4 to leave your house and start a journey
5 an area where you can park
6 to wait in a line
7 to arrive
8 to use a type of transport
9 to describe the duration of a journey
10 enter/leave a car
11 enter/leave a bus/train
12 to not be able to move
13 to take someone in your car
14 buses, trains, etc.
15 a ticket for a week, month, year, etc.

🔊 8.9 Listen, check and repeat.

3 In pairs, describe your journey to work/university.

I take the bus to work. It usually takes twenty minutes, but in the rush hour …

Listening

4 a 🔊 **8.10** What are the problems of using electric scooters? Listen to a report and tick (✓) the problems that are mentioned.

1. They cause accidents. ☐
2. They cause pollution. ☐
3. They make lots of noise. ☐
4. It takes a long time to recharge them. ☐
5. They're very expensive. ☐

🔧 listen for numerical information

It's often important to understand dates, times, prices, etc.

years: 2021 = *twenty twenty-one*

money: £12.50 = *twelve pounds fifty* or $10.40 = *ten dollars and forty cents*

decimals: 3.14 = *three point one four*

units come after fractions: 2½ km = *two and a half kilometres*

Some numbers sound similar: 14 = *fourteen*, 40 = *forty*

b 🔊 **8.10** Listen again and complete the notes with the correct numbers.

Light Electric Vehicles in the city

Examples: electric scooters, bicycles, skateboards

No. of LEVs in (1) _____: 12,000

No. of scooters this year: (2) _____

No. of accidents involving LEVs last year: (3) _____

Most accidents happened: on pavement

No. of accidents involving cars last year: (4) _____

Pollution (CO_2) each car makes:
(5) _____ tonnes / year

Name of scooter rider: Adam Theakston

Name of scooter: (6) City Zoom

Maximum speed: (7) _____

Maximum distance: (8) _____

Recharge time: (9) _____

Cost: (10) _____

5 Would you consider using an electric scooter? Why/Why not?

Writing

6 Complete the text with the words from the Vocabulary box on page 80.

How to get around

It's very easy to (1) _____ in traffic if you drive here, especially during the (2) _____ – which is from 7.00–9.00 a.m. Most people use (3) _____ – either the metro or buses.

The bus system goes everywhere and is clean and safe. It's not very fast and (4) _____ about 40 minutes to get to the city centre, but you can see the city while you're travelling. A (5) _____ costs around $2, or you can buy a day ticket for $5 and (6) _____ and off as often as you want.

If you want to (7) _____ your destination quickly, it's probably best to (8) _____ the metro. The problem is that it's very busy and you have to (9) _____ for a long time to buy a ticket.

The most interesting places to visit are in the city centre. As it's not a big city, if you (10) _____ early, you can just walk there. There are lots of good cafés on the way to have breakfast.

7 In pairs, write an information leaflet for visitors to your city. Think about the questions.
- What is the traffic like?
- When is the traffic worst?
- What public transport is there?
- How much does it cost?
- How fast is it?
- Are there any other ways to travel?

🔄 Mediation task: Student A page 129, Student B page 130

8.4 WHAT DO YOU THINK?

FL asking for and giving opinions
🎥 a computer-made musical

The big picture: a computer-made musical

1 Look at the main picture below. In pairs, answer the questions.
   1 What type of building is this?
   2 What can you watch here?
   3 Do you like this type of entertainment? Why/Why not?
   4 What do you think the story is about?
   5 What is different about this show?

2 🎥 8.1 Look at pictures a–c. Match them with the parts of the show. Watch the video and check.
   1 story .... 2 music .... 3 lyrics ....

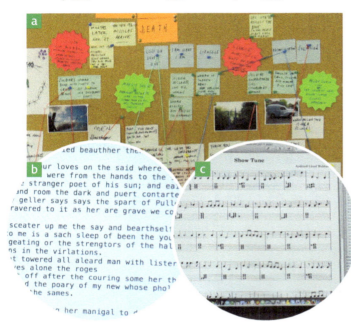

3 🎥 8.1 Are the sentences true (T) or false (F)? Watch the video again and check.
   1 The team have written lots of musicals. ....
   2 They are trying something new. ....
   3 The story is about a soldier who falls in love. ....
   4 The computer software can write the words for songs. ....
   5 The computer always creates good music the first time. ....
   6 The team and the audience are happy with the musical. ....

4 In pairs, discuss the questions.
   1 Why did the team decide to make a musical using computers only?
   2 Can a computer be as creative as a person? Why/Why not?
   3 Would you like to see *Beyond the Fence*? Why/Why not?
   4 What other ways can we use computers to entertain us?

5 🎥 8.2 Watch Lou and Rob talking about the video. Who is more impressed by the musical: Lou or Rob?

6 🎥 8.2 Who gave the opinions: Rob (R) or Lou (L)? Watch the video again and check.
   1 To be honest, I'm not keen on musicals. ....
   2 I don't think you need a machine to tell you people like happy endings! ....
   3 I think that people did most of the work. ....
   4 The way I see it, a computer that can make any music is pretty amazing. ....
   5 They weren't selling the computer part, in my opinion. ....

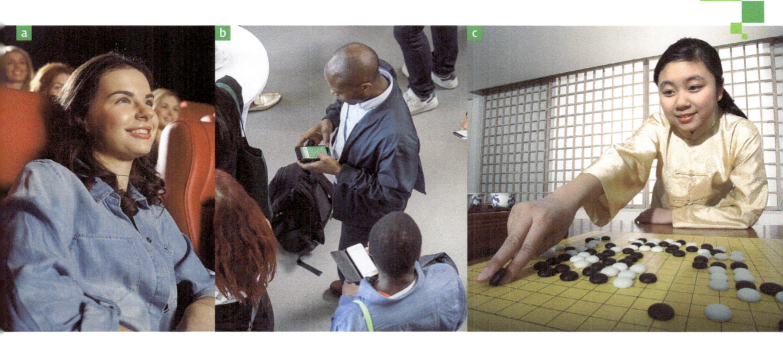

Functional language

7 a 🔊 **8.11** Look at the pictures. Listen and match them with the conversations.

1 .... 2 .... 3 ....

b In which conversation do the friends agree about everything? Agree about most things? Disagree?

8 🔊 **8.11** Complete the sentences with words in the box. Listen again and check.

believe	don't think	feel	honest
opinion	say	way	

1 **A** Do you (1) .... that computers are more intelligent than humans?
   B I'd (2) .... that the people who built the computer are clever, but I (3) .... the computer is 'intelligent'.
2 **A** How do you (4) .... about using mobile phones in public?
   B To be (5) ...., I think that technology has a negative effect on us.
3 **A** I've seen that film. What's your (6) ....?
   B The (7) .... I see it, the story's crazy! I didn't understand it at all.

FL asking for and giving opinions

Asking for opinions	**Giving opinions**
Do you think/believe that ...?	I (don't) think/believe that ...
What do you think about ...?	... in my opinion.
How do you feel about ...?	The way I see it, ...
What's your opinion?	To be honest, ...
What's your point of view?	I'd say that ...

🔍 notice

When we give an opinion with a negative verb, we use *I don't think ...*

I don't think computers **are** very creative.
NOT ~~I think computers aren't very creative.~~

9 a 🔊 **8.12** 🗨 **weak form of *that*** 🗨 Listen to the questions. Notice the pronunciation of *that*. Listen again and repeat.

1 Do you believe <u>that</u> using phones in public is a problem?
2 Do you think <u>that</u> films use too many special effects?
3 Do you believe <u>that</u> technology changes too quickly?
4 Do you think <u>that</u> computers can be intelligent?

b In pairs, ask and answer the questions. Remember to use the weak form of *that*.

Do you believe that using phones in public is a problem?
The way I see it, it's a personal choice. I don't think it's a problem.

Speaking

10 a Look at the topics and think about your opinions. In pairs, take turns asking and giving opinions about the topics.

Do you think we ate healthier food in the past?
Yes, I'd say we eat more junk food today. What's your opinion?

- food and eating habits
- social media
- phones and technology
- today's fashions
- movies or music
- travelling by plane

b Did you have similar opinions to your partner?

REVIEW UNIT 8

Vocabulary
Free-time activities

1 Complete the sentences with the correct verbs. There are two verbs you don't need.

> collect   join   keep   learn
> play   shop   surf

1. What do you do to .... fit?
2. I hardly ever go to the supermarket these days. I prefer to .... online.
3. It was snowing so we decided to stay at home and .... board games.
4. What kind of coins did he ....?
5. I'd really like to .... an African language.

2 Imagine you have three hours of free time. Look at the activities in the box. Which would you most like to do? Compare your answers with a partner.

> go to the gym   meet up with friends
> play video games   go hiking   spend time with family
> go window shopping   go on social media

Uncountable nouns

3 a 🔊 8.13 Listen and match the uncountable nouns in the box with the people (1–6).

> advice   education   employment
> research   technology   wildlife

1. ....   3. ....   5. ....
2. ....   4. ....   6. ....

b Write an example sentence for four of the nouns.

Can you give me some advice about winter clothes, please?

Transport phrases

4 a Choose the correct words to complete the questions.
1. Has your flight ever *been delayed / got stuck*?
2. Did you give someone a *journey / lift* this morning?
3. How long does it *last / take* to get to class?
4. How often do you use public *traffic / transport*?

b In pairs, ask and answer the questions.

Grammar
-ing form and to + infinitive

5 a Complete the sentences with the correct form of the verbs in brackets.
1. I enjoy .... photos with my phone. (take)
2. I don't mind .... the kitchen. (clean)
3. I want .... to play the guitar. (learn)
4. I've decided .... more exercise. (do)
5. I'd like .... in another country. (live)

b In pairs, say if the sentences are true for you.

Quantifiers

6 Choose the correct words to complete the conversation.

A The Van Gogh Museum was so busy. We had to wait a long time at the entrance.
B Really? How (1)*many / much* people were in the queue?
A Hundreds! It was worth waiting though. We saw (2)*lots / few* of his famous paintings.
B What else did you do in Amsterdam?
A We hired bikes and cycled along the canals.
B Is it safe to do that? How (3)*many / much* traffic is there in the city centre?
A Away from the main areas, there are (4)*some / any* quieter streets. There are (5)*a few / a little* cars, but it's not dangerous.
B It sounds lovely, but I think I'd prefer to cycle in the Dutch countryside, so that I could see (6)*much / lots* of flowers in the fields.
A Yes, that's a nice idea. We didn't see (7)*a few / many* tulips, except in the flower market, of course!

7 a Complete the questions with *much* or *many*.
In one day …
1. how .... exercise do you do?
2. how .... hours do you sleep?
3. how .... cups of coffee do you drink?
4. how .... time do you spend on social media?
5. how .... emails do you send?

b In pairs, ask and answer the questions.

Functional language
Asking for and giving opinions

8 a Complete the questions with the words in the box. There are two words that you don't need.

> believe   feel   opinion   point   say   think

1. Do you .... that the planet is getting warmer?
2. What's your .... of electric cars?
3. How do you .... about zoos?
4. What do you .... about studying online?

b In groups of three, discuss the questions. Use the phrases in the box to give your opinions.

> I (don't) think/believe that …   … in my opinion.
> The way I see it, …   To be honest, …   I'd say that …

🕒 Looking back

- Think of three things you learned to say about new technology.
- Has technology changed how you spend your free time? How?

Healthy lifestyles 9

Grammar
too, too much/many, (not) enough
first conditional
adverbs of manner

Vocabulary
food
sports

Functional language
warnings and promises

Skill
find information in a text

Video
growing cities

Writing
an invitation

Exams
listening to a monologue

The big picture: a world record attempt

1 Look at the picture. In pairs, guess the answers to the questions.
  1 Where are the people?
  2 How many people are there?
  3 What are they doing?
  4 Was it a successful day?

2 🔊 9.1 Listen to the interview and check your answers.

3 In pairs, discuss the questions.
  1 Have you ever done yoga? Would you like to try it?
  2 What are some benefits of yoga?
  3 What are some other ways to stay fit and healthy?
  4 Do you think people are healthier today than they were a hundred years ago? Why/Why not?

9.1 HAVE YOU EATEN ENOUGH?

G too, too much/many, (not) enough
V food

Vocabulary

1 Look at the pictures. In pairs, answer the questions.
   1 Which countries do you think they're from?
   2 Which ingredients do they contain? Use the words in the Vocabulary box to help you.
   3 Which would you prefer to eat? Why?

2 a Put the words in the Vocabulary box in the correct columns.

   b Add two words to each column.

   V food

beef	chicken	cod	cucumbers	garlic
herbs	lamb	lettuce	oil	olives
onions	peas	peppers	prawns	salmon
spices	sweetcorn	tuna	turkey	vinegar

Meat	Fish and seafood	Vegetables	Other
beef			

   🔊 9.2 Listen, check and repeat.

3 In pairs, answer the questions.
   1 What are some typical dishes in your country?
   2 What ingredients do they contain?
   3 What type of food do you enjoy most?
   4 What ingredients does it contain?

Reading

4 Read the text and match the pictures to the people.
   1 Nelly ....   3 Erika ....
   2 Nikos ....   4 Vijay ....

5 Complete the summaries with the words in the box.

   | busy | fish | healthy | main |
   | meat | slowly | small | spices |

   1 Nelly thinks people in the UK are .... and don't have a .... diet.
   2 In Greece, people have their .... meal at lunchtime and eat ....
   3 .... is very popular in Japan, but people eat .... portions of food.
   4 In India, people don't eat much ...., but they use lots of ....

6 In pairs, discuss the questions.
   1 Which country has the healthiest diet, in your opinion?
   2 Which country is your diet most similar to?
   3 What other tips can you give to eat healthily?

Nelly's world

Posted: 8 July   Nelly Williams, *London*

A new diet?

Life is so busy these days that it often feels like we don't have enough time to cook a proper meal. We eat too many snacks and we don't eat enough fruit and vegetables. If I have time, I'll cook steak and chips … but apparently it isn't healthy enough because we eat too much red meat now! Maybe I need a new diet! Can you tell me what people eat in your country and how healthy it is?

💬 Reply   ⇄ Share   👍 Like   ⊕ Follow

Nikos Samara, *Athens*

In Greece, we use a lot of olives, garlic, lemon and herbs in our food – all healthy ingredients. But the important thing about Greece is *when* and *how* we eat. I know in other countries people often eat a big meal in the evening, but this is too late! And I've also noticed that too many people eat very quickly, or even eat a sandwich while they're walking in the street! In Greece, everyone comes together in the middle of the day and we have our main meal. We eat slowly and talk to each other!

Posted 3.16

Grammar

7 a Look at the sentences from the text. Do they refer to: more than is good (+), less than is good (–) or the correct amount (✓)?
1 We don't have **enough** time. ....
2 We eat **too many** snacks. ....
3 It isn't healthy **enough**. ....
4 We eat **too much** red meat. ....
5 We certainly eat **enough** fish. ....
6 Some food may be **too spicy** for you. ....

b Look at the words in **bold**. Choose the correct options to complete the rules.
1 We use *enough* before / after nouns, but before / after adjectives.
2 We use *too much* before *countable* / *uncountable* nouns.
3 We use *too many* before *countable* / *uncountable* nouns.
4 We use *too* before / after adjectives.

G too, too much/many, (not) enough

	Countable nouns	Uncountable nouns	Adjectives
+	We've ordered **too many** chips.	He puts **too much sugar** in his coffee.	It's **too hot** in here.
–	There aren't **enough** plates on the table.	There isn't **enough** milk.	My soup is **not hot enough**.
✓	Do we have **enough** spoons?	We have **enough time**.	It's already **sweet enough**.

→ Grammar reference: page 140

🔍 notice

We usually use *not enough*, but we can also use *too few* and *too little*.
There is **too little** time. = There isn't **enough** time.
There are **too few** students. = There aren't **enough** students.

8 a 🔊 9.3 🎙 /uː/, /ʌ/ and /ʊ/ sounds 🎙 Listen to the words. Notice the /uː/, /ʌ/ and /ʊ/ sounds.
1 too /uː/   2 much /ʌ/   3 sugar /ʊ/

b 🔊 9.4 Say the words in the box and put them in the correct columns. Listen, check and repeat.

cup   enough   few   put   should   tuna

/uː/	/ʌ/	/ʊ/
too	much	sugar

9 Add (*not*) *enough*, *too*, *too much* or *too many* to the sentences to make them true for you. In pairs, compare your sentences.
1 There is salt in my diet.
2 Fish is expensive.
3 There are restaurants in this town.
4 We eat red meat.
5 I drink coffee.
6 It is easy to buy healthy food.

Speaking

10 In groups, discuss your opinions of the topics below, using (*not*) *enough*, *too*, *too much* or *too many*. Say if you agree or disagree. Give your classmates advice when you can.

time to study English   students in this class
homework   price of clothes
cost of houses in this city   number of job opportunities
cafés near here   places to buy fresh food

HOME   ABOUT   **BLOG**   CONTACT

Erika Kitagawa, *Osaka*

Maybe you should try eating like a Japanese person! Many Japanese people live long lives, and this is probably because of our diet. We certainly eat enough fish – 65 kg per person per year! The two most popular fish in Japan are tuna and salmon. But it's not just about what we eat, it's *how much* we eat. I've been to other countries and I think people eat too much food! In Japan, many people practise *Hara hachi bun me*. This means we eat until we're 80% full and then we stop. So we don't get too full!

Posted 3.50

Vijay Chopra, *Bangalore*

In India, we don't eat very much meat. We occasionally eat chicken or lamb and there's always good fish on the coast, but most people just eat vegetables. People sometimes call India 'The land of spices' because we produce and use more spices than any other country. And spices are very good for you. Of course, some food may be too spicy for you, so you should be careful!

Posted 4.28

9.2 WIN, LOSE OR DRAW
G first conditional
V sports

Listening

1 a Look at the pictures. Match them with the sports in the box.

| race walking | synchronized swimming |
| tug of war | ultimate |

b In pairs, discuss the questions.
1 Have you ever played or watched a game of tug of war or ultimate?
2 Have you ever done or watched race walking or synchronized swimming?
3 Which of these sports would you like to try? Why?

2 a In pairs, discuss the questions.
1 How do you think these sports are played or done?
2 Which do you think are Olympic sports?

b 🔊 9.5 Listen to a radio report about these four sports and check your answers to exercise 2a.

3 🔊 9.5 Are the sentences true (T) or false (F)? Listen again and check.
1 Race walking has been an Olympic sport for over a hundred years. ......
2 There are no rules in race walking. ......
3 People play tug of war in teams. ......
4 Tug of war is a very quick game. ......
5 In ultimate, you can run when you catch the disc. ......
6 A team wins ultimate when they score 14 points. ......
7 Synchronized swimming is a relaxing sport to do. ......
8 Sandra will definitely go to the next Olympics. ......

Vocabulary

4 Complete the sentences with words in the box.

V sports

| beat | cheat | come | draw | lose | score |
| take part in | train | warm up | win | | |

1 I was very slow in the race, but I didn't .... last.
2 He's no good at tennis. He's going to .... the match.
3 You must .... before you play sport, or you can injure yourself.
4 No one can .... our team. We're the best team in the world!
5 I think we're going to .... The score is still 2–2.
6 She's very serious about karate. She has to .... three times a week.
7 Don't ....! Touching the ball with your hand is against the rules.
8 I want to .... our city's marathon next year.
9 We usually .... more than 100 points every game.
10 We didn't .... the competition, but it was fun.

🔊 9.6 Listen, check and repeat.

5 a Choose the correct words to complete the questions.
1 Have you ever *scored / won* an important goal or point?
2 Do you know anyone who has *cheated / beat* at a sport?
3 Have you ever *scored / come first* in a race? How did you feel?
4 Do you think it's more important to *win / beat* a game, or to *take part in / warm up* it?
5 Do you always *train / warm up* before you do exercise?

b In pairs, ask and answer the questions.

88

Grammar

6 🔊 **9.7** Match the halves to make sentences from the report. Listen and check.

1 **If** I **say** the word 'Olympics',
2 I**'ll be** very surprised
3 **If** you **come** with me,
4 It **will be** in the next Olympic games
5 **If** we **don't work** really hard this year,

a **if** the Olympic Committee **agree**.
b **if** I **come** first, but I hope I do well.
c we **won't qualify** for the Olympics.
d you**'ll** probably think of athletics.
e I**'ll show** you how to play!

7 Look at the words in **bold** in the sentences in exercise 6. Answer the questions.

1 What is the tense of the verbs after *if*?
2 What is the tense of the verbs in the other clauses?

3 Are the sentences about things that will definitely happen in the future?

G first conditional

*My family **will be** so proud of me if I **score** a goal.*
*If I **score** a goal, my family **will be** so proud of me.*
*If I **don't warm up** before the race, my legs **will hurt**.*
*My legs **will hurt** if I **don't warm up** before the race.*

→ Grammar reference: page 140

8 🔊 **9.8** 🗣 **intonation in clauses** 🗣 Listen to the sentences. Tick (✓) to show if the intonation goes up (↗) or down (↘) at the end the clauses. Listen again, check and repeat.

1 If you come with me, I'll show you how to play.
   ↗☐ ↘☐   ↗☐ ↘☐

2 I'll show you how to play if you come with me.
   ↗☐ ↘☐   ↗☐ ↘☐

9 a Complete the sentences with the correct form of the verbs in brackets.

1 If our national football team _____ the next World Cup, I _____ surprised. (win / be)
2 You _____ cold if you _____ outside without a coat. (get / go)
3 If our teacher _____ us homework, I _____ it at the weekend. (give / do)
4 If it _____, I _____ home after this class. (not rain / walk)
5 I _____ dinner tonight if there _____ enough food in the fridge. (cook / be)
6 I _____ to bed early tonight if there _____ any good programmes on TV. (go / not be)

b Change the sentences so they are true for you. In pairs, compare your answers. Remember to use the correct intonation in the clauses.

Speaking

10 a 🔊 **9.9** Listen to two people playing a game with sentences. What word do they begin each sentence with?

b 🔊 **9.9** Listen again. What are the rules of the sentence game?

11 In pairs, choose a starting sentence and play the game. Try to keep talking for as long as possible.

If I go out tonight …
If it rains tomorrow …
If I want to keep fit …
If I find some money in the street …
If my teacher gives us homework …

9.3 RELAX, BE HAPPY!

G adverbs of manner
find information in a text

Reading

1 Look at the pictures of factors for a healthy lifestyle. In pairs, order them from most important (1) to least important (6). Can you think of any other things you should include?

a healthy diet ....

sleeping well ....

exercise ....

socializing ....

relaxing ....

being outside ....

2 Read the article quickly and compare. Does the writer have similar ideas to you about a healthy lifestyle?

find information in a text

We often have to find information in a long text.
- Read the text quickly to understand the main idea in each paragraph.
- Identify the information you need to find and think about which paragraph contains this information.
- Read the paragraph carefully to find the information you are looking for.

3 Read the Skill box. Then match the headings to the paragraphs.
   a A good night's sleep
   b Don't get fit, get happy!
   c A long and happy life
   d A new idea?
   e What makes *you* happy?
   f Smiles beat sneezes

4 a Read the questions. Which paragraphs have the information you need?
   1 Which chemical stops you sleeping well? ....
   2 What benefits does happiness have on your heart? ....
   3 When did Aristotle give his advice? ....
   4 How does the writer stay happy? ....
   5 Where can you find fitness advice? ....
   6 How many people were infected with a cold virus? ....
   7 What are the benefits of sleeping well? ....
   8 How much longer do happy people live? ....

   b Read the paragraphs you identified to answer the questions. Did you choose the correct paragraphs?

5 In pairs, discuss the questions.
   1 Do you agree with the article? Why/Why not?
   2 What makes you happy?
   3 Do you have any more tips for a healthy life?

HAPPY PEOPLE

1 ....

We all want to be healthy. If you open a magazine or surf the web, you'll find lots of advice from experts telling you to exercise regularly or follow a special diet, but is this really the most important thing for our health? I see people who work hard on exercise machines at the gym and eat healthily (but miserably!), and they all look bored or stressed. Well, I'm pleased to say that lots of new research shows that happiness is just as important for your health.

2 ....

For a start, happy people are 50% more likely to sleep well. After a night sleeping peacefully, they are more active and productive, and they can concentrate easily. However, if you feel worried and stressed, your body produces a chemical called cortisol, which makes it harder for you to sleep. Doctors say that people who sleep badly at night have more health problems.

Grammar

6 a Look at the words in **bold** from the text. Which is an adjective and which is an adverb?
1. We all want to be **healthy**.
2. You need to follow special diets to eat **healthily**.

b Match the adverbs in the text with the adjectives.

1	regular	*regularly*	6 peaceful	....
2	hard	....	7 bad	....
3	miserable	....	8 loud	....
4	good	....	9 slow	....
5	easy	....	10 fast	....

c Answer the questions.
1. Which letters do most adverbs end in? ....
2. Which adverbs in the text are irregular? ...., ..., ...
3. Do the adverbs describe *how* or *why* an action happens? ....
4. Do the adverbs come *before* or *after* the verbs? ....

G adverbs of manner

Adjectives	Adverbs
He's a **bad** driver.	He drives **badly**.
This traffic is **slow**.	This traffic is moving **slowly**.
She's a **good** singer.	She sings **well**.
That's a **fast** train.	That train is going really **fast**.
It was a really **hard** ball.	He threw the ball really **hard**.

→ Grammar reference: page 140

7 Choose the correct words to complete the sentences. Which sentences do you agree with?
1. Singing is a really *good / well* way to get happy. It doesn't matter if you can't sing *good / well*.
2. If you go to bed early, you will be able to work *hard / hardly* and think *clear / clearly* in the morning.
3. Happiness is a *serious / seriously* subject, but people don't treat it *serious / seriously*.

Writing

8 Complete the text with the adverbs in the box.

angrily	badly	calmly	completely
differently	properly	slowly	well

A few months ago, I was feeling unhappy. At work, I didn't get on (1) .... with my colleagues. I was getting stressed and reacting (2) .... when my colleagues asked me to do things. At home, I was eating really (3) .... and I wasn't sleeping (4) .... Then last year, I bought a camera and it has changed my life (5) .... Now, I spend a lot of time outside taking photos. Every evening, I walk around town (6) .... and take photos of interesting buildings and trees. I didn't notice how beautiful the world was before I started taking photos! It has made me see things (7) ...., and I don't get so stressed about small things any more. Now, when a colleague asks me to do something, I answer them (8) .... I know there is a world outside of work!

9 Write a paragraph about something that has made you happy. Include adverbs of manner.

---

3 ....

Happiness is also good for your body. In one experiment, scientists spent two weeks measuring how happy 300 adults felt. Then they tried to infect these people with a cold virus. The results were very interesting. Many of the unhappy people caught a cold and were soon sneezing loudly, but the happy people had better immune systems and didn't get ill.

4 ....

Perhaps the most amazing news is that happy people actually live for longer. In another study, scientists looked at old essays that people wrote when they were teenagers. They found that the people who had lots of positive ideas in their writing lived around ten years longer! Perhaps this is because happiness is good for your heart. Doctors have found that happy people have lower blood pressure and their hearts beat more slowly.

5 ....

So, the message seems to be clear: we should all be trying to make ourselves as happy as possible. But this isn't anything new. Over 2,000 years ago, the Greek philosopher Aristotle said, 'Happiness is the meaning and the purpose of life, the whole aim and end of human existence.' So, don't listen to the people who tell you to eat nothing but lettuce and go to the gym every day. Focus on being happy instead.

6 ....

The final question, is how to be happy? Well, everybody is different. For me, it involves spending time with friends and family, having fun and enjoying nature. I don't want to live my life fast, I want to sit back with the people I love and laugh … and maybe – just maybe – have a piece of chocolate cake now and again! Remember, you know yourself better than anyone else. Follow your own best advice.

9.4 LOOK OUT!
warnings and promises
growing cities

The big picture: growing cities

1 Look at the picture. In pairs, guess the answers to the questions.
   1 What food are they growing?
   2 Where are they growing the food?
   3 Why are they growing the food like this?

2 ▶ 9.1 Watch the video and check. In pairs, answer the questions.
   1 Why did Dan and Andrew go on a trip?
   2 Was the trip successful?
   3 Did you find anything surprising?

3 ▶ 9.1 Match the cities with the problems and the solutions. Watch the video again and check.

City	Problem	Solution
1 Omaha	no space to grow food	grow food on rooftops
2 Detroit	plants grown aren't for people	grow food on disused land
3 New York	no access to fresh food	grow food locally

4 In pairs, discuss the questions.
   1 How easy is it to buy fresh food where you live?
   2 Is the food you eat grown locally?
   3 What are the advantages of eating locally grown food?
   4 Where could you grow food in your city?
   5 Would you like to grow your own food? Why/Why not?

5 ▶ 9.2 Watch Rob and Lou talking about the video. Complete the advantages Lou mentions of buying locally grown food.
   1 Buying local food protects the ....
   2 .... stays in the local community.
   3 There are more .... for local people.
   4 Locally grown food .... much better.

6 a ▶ 9.2 Who says the sentences: Rob (R) or Lou (L)? Watch the video again and check.
   1 If we continue buying food from around the world, it will cause more pollution. ....
   2 You'd better start looking at the food labels. ....
   3 I'll check where the food is grown next time. ....
   4 I swear I won't buy any more frozen pizzas. ....

b Which sentences are warnings and which are promises?

©Brooklyn Grange Rooftop Farm.

Functional language

7 🔊 9.13 Look at the pictures. In pairs, guess the answers to the questions. Listen and check.
1 What are the people talking about?
2 Who is giving a warning?
3 Who is making a promise?

8 🔊 9.13 Complete the sentences with the words in the box. Listen again and check. Write W for warning and P for promise.

| believe | better | don't | if |
| out | promise | should | word |

1 But .... do it again. ....
2 .... I catch you speeding again, I'll have to give you a ticket. ....
3 .... me, I won't do it again. ....
4 Look ....! Be careful! ....
5 You .... never go so close to the water. ....
6 I .... I'll keep it a secret. ....
7 You'd .... not tell Mike. ....
8 I won't! You have my ....! ....

FL warnings and promises

Giving warnings	Making promises
If you (don't) …, I will / won't …	I will / won't …
You shouldn't … or …	I promise I will / won't …
You'd better (not) …	I swear I will / won't …
Don't …!	Believe me, …
Look out! / Watch out! / Be careful!	You have my word.

9 🔊 9.14 **omission of /t/ sounds** Listen to the sentences. Notice how the /t/ sounds in brackets aren't pronounced when there is a consonant sound before and after them. Listen again, check and repeat.
1 I'm jus(t) going to give you a warning this time.
2 But don'(t) do it again.
3 Who was that tex(t) message from?
4 I can'(t) tell you.

10 🔊 9.15 Match the halves to make warnings and promises. Where could you omit the /t/ sounds? Listen, check and repeat.
1 Don't sit down!   a or you'll have an accident.
2 If you break that,   b I won't let you have it again.
3 I'm just going now.   c The chair is broken.
4 You shouldn't drive so fast d You have my word.

Speaking

11 a In pairs, choose a situation. Prepare a conversation where you give warnings and make promises.

AT UNIVERSITY
Student A: You are a student. You haven't worked very hard until now. Convince your tutor that you are going to work harder in the future.

Student B: You are a tutor. Warn your student that he/she must start working harder.

AT THE DOCTOR'S
Student A: You are at the doctor's. You have not had healthy habits until now. Tell your doctor that you are going to be much healthier in the future.

Student B: You are a doctor. Warn your patient that he/she must change to a healthier lifestyle.

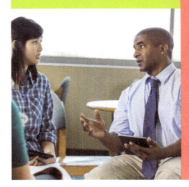

b Act out your conversation to another pair. Repeat the activity with the other situation.

Writing bank: page 152

REVIEW UNIT 9

Vocabulary
Food

1 Look at the types of food. Write the names in the correct categories.

1 Meat ....
2 Fish and seafood ....
3 Vegetables ....
4 Other ....

Sports

2 Choose the correct verbs to complete the sentences.
   1 I didn't *win / beat*, but I *made / came* second.
   2 You can't *score / draw* points like that – it's *beating / cheating*!
   3 We *beat / won* them easily and they were really angry when they *came / lost*.

3 In pairs, ask and answer the questions.
   1 What was the last sports event you watched?
   2 What was the score?
   3 Did your favourite team/player win?

Grammar
too, too much/many, (not) enough

4 a Choose the correct words to complete the sentences.
   1 I eat *too many / too much* chocolate.
   2 My room isn't *enough big / big enough*.
   3 I have *too many / too much* clothes.
   4 It's *too / enough* hot in this room today.

   b In pairs, say if the sentences are true for you. If not, change them so that they are true.

First conditional

5 🔊 9.16 Listen to the conversation. Are the sentences true (T) or false (F)?
   1 If Jack completes the full marathon, he'll run 26 miles. ....
   2 Jack won't finish the race if he doesn't train more. ....
   3 Jack will run more slowly if Mia trains with him. ....
   4 If Mia doesn't go swimming, she can run with Jack. ....

6 Complete the sentences so they are true for you. In pairs, compare your answers.
   1 If I pass my exams, I ....
   2 My parents will be very happy if I ....
   3 If I have some free time this week, I ....
   4 I'll feel very tired tomorrow if I ....

Adverbs of manner

7 Complete the sentences with adverbs formed from the adjectives in brackets.
   1 She took the box and put it .... on the table. (careful)
   2 Tell her to be quiet. She's talking really .... (loud)
   3 We enjoy tennis, but we play it quite .... (bad)
   4 Slow down! You're driving too .... (fast)
   5 You can .... travel there in a day. (easy)
   6 The trees were moving .... in the wind. (gentle)

8 a Complete the questions with adverbs formed from the adjectives in the box.

   | good | hard | regular |

   1 What sport do you play .... ?
   2 Do you speak English .... ?
   3 Do you work .... every day?

   b In pairs, ask and answer the questions.

Functional language
Warnings and promises

9 🔊 9.17 Match the halves to make two warnings and two promises. Listen and check.
   1 If you don't listen carefully,   a It's dangerous.
   2 Don't do that!   b You have my word.
   3 I won't say anything to Rita.   c I'll make you dinner.
   4 If you help me with my   d you won't know
     homework,   what to do.

10 In pairs, think of a warning and a promise you could make in each situation.

You're **cooking dinner** for a friend, but she phones to say that she is going to a party instead.

You need help with your **English homework**, but your teacher is too busy.

🕘 Looking back

• What was the most interesting part of this unit? Why?
• What promises could you make to a) your teacher? b) your best friend?

Money and shopping

10

Grammar
second conditional
so and *such*
indefinite pronouns

Vocabulary
money nouns
money verbs

Functional language
shopping

Skill
identify reasons and results

Video
second-hand markets

Writing
a complaint

Exams
writing an article

The big picture: a small business

1 Look at the picture. In pairs, discuss the questions.
  1 What kind of business is this?
  2 Where is the business?
  3 How is the customer paying?
  4 How did the owner start the business?

2 🔊 10.1 Listen and check your answers.

3 In pairs, discuss the questions.
  1 What do you spend your money on?
  2 Do you save money every month?
  3 What are you saving up to buy?
  4 If you got a loan for a small business, what kind of business would you start?
  If I got a loan, I'd start …

10.1 MONEY PROBLEMS

G second conditional
V money nouns

Listening

1 Look at the pictures. In pairs, discuss the questions.
  1 Where are the people?
  2 What are they doing?
  3 What problems could they have?

2 🔊 10.2 Listen to the conversations and match them with the pictures.

Conversation 1 .... Conversation 3 ....
Conversation 2 .... Conversation 4 ....

3 🔊 10.2 Listen again and answer the questions.

Conversation 1
1 How many hats does the woman buy?
2 How does she pay for them?

Conversation 2
3 What did the woman buy last week?
4 Why doesn't she want it?

Conversation 3
5 How many yen does the man want to change?
6 How many dollars does he get?

Conversation 4
7 What does the man want to buy?
8 What is his job?

Vocabulary

4 Match the words in the box with the definitions.

V **money nouns**

account	bargain	bills	coins	
currency	discount	fee	loan	notes
receipt	refund	rent	salary	tax

1 a lower price than normal ....
2 money that goes to the government ....
3 a very good price for something ....
4 money made of paper ....
5 money made of metal ....
6 a ticket you get when you pay ....
7 the type of money used in a country ....
8 the price of a service ....
9 a shop returns money you spent ....
10 money you earn from your work ....
11 money you borrow from a bank ....
12 money you pay each month to live in a house ....
13 where you keep your money at a bank ....
14 money you pay for electricity, etc. ....

🔊 10.3 Listen, check and repeat.

5 In pairs, ask and answer the questions. If you say 'yes', explain what happened. Use the words from the Vocabulary box.

Have you ever …
1 bought something at a market?
2 got a refund for something?
3 changed money?
4 borrowed money from the bank?
5 lost the receipt for something you wanted to take back to a shop?
6 got a very good price for something that you really wanted to buy?

My aunt bought me a T-shirt for my birthday, but I didn't like it. Luckily, she gave me the receipt, so I took it to the shop and got a refund.

Grammar

6 a Match the halves to make sentences from the conversations in exercise 2.

1 If I were you,
2 If you had the receipt,
3 If I didn't have my wallet,
4 If you earned more money,

a I'd be annoyed.
b we'd lend you £130,000.
c I'd give you a refund.
d I'd get this one.

b Look at the sentences again and answer the questions.
1 What are the sentences about?
   real possibilities / hypothetical situations
2 What tense are the verbs after *if*? ....
3 Which modal verb do we use in the second half of the sentence? ....
4 What is unusual about the verb *be* in the first sentence?
....
5 Are the sentences correct if we put the second half first? yes / no

---

G second conditional

*What **would** you **do if** you **had** a better salary?*
*If I **had** a better salary, I'**d buy** a new car.*
*I'**d buy** a new car **if** I **had** a better salary.*
*If Sarah **wasn't/weren't** so busy, she'**d help** you.*
*Sarah **would help** you **if** she **wasn't/weren't** so busy.*

→ Grammar reference: page 141

🔍 notice

We often use *If I were you, …* to give advice.
***If I were you**, I'd get this one. It looks warm.*
*I wouldn't sit there **if I were you**. The seat is wet.*

---

7 a Complete the sentences so they are true for you.
1 If we didn't pay tax to the government, …
2 I'd ask for a refund if …
3 If we didn't use notes or coins, …
4 If I found a bargain in an online shop, …
5 I'd ask for a discount if …

b In pairs, compare your answers. Did you have similar ideas?

8 🔊 10.4 ❝ *would you* ❞ Listen and notice how *would you* is pronounced in the questions. Listen again and repeat.
1 What <u>would you</u> do if you had more money?
2 <u>Would you</u> buy a new car?

Speaking

9 Look at the situations. In pairs, ask and answer *What would you do if …?* questions. Ask follow up questions. Remember to pronounce *would you* correctly.

What would you do if you found a wallet in the street with $5,000 in it?
I'd open it and see if there was an ID card.
Would you give it to the police?
No, I wouldn't. I'd contact the owner.

WHAT WOULD YOU DO IF …

- your boss offered to double your salary to work in Alaska?
- you found a wallet in the street with $5,000 in it?
- you discovered $100,000 in your bank account?
- you had to pay for dinner, but didn't have your wallet?

10.2 MAKING MONEY

G *so* and *such*
V money verbs

Reading

1 Look at the pictures and the title of the article. Tick (✓) what you think it is about. Read the text quickly and check.

   a How to cut grass well
   b A boy who found a lot of money
   c A successful business
   d Why gardens are expensive

2 Are the sentences true (T) or false (F)? Read the text again and check.

   1 Emil worked on a golf course when he was young. ....
   2 He was more interested in his job than his friends. ....
   3 When he was 16, he was the boss of other people. ....
   4 He wasn't very successful at university. ....
   5 He still owns the company now. ....

3 In pairs, discuss the questions.

   1 How would you describe Emil? Why?
   2 Do you know anyone who runs a business? Is it successful?
   3 Do you have any ideas for a business?

Vocabulary

4 a Complete the sentences about money with the words in the box.

   b In pairs, say if you agree or disagree with the sentences.

V money verbs

borrow	can afford	charge	cost
earn	get paid	lend	owe	own
pay back	save	spend	waste	(be) worth

1 Never .... more money than you ....
2 If you want to be happy, never .... people money and never .... money from people either.
3 The most important things in life don't .... very much, but they are .... everything.
4 You might think you .... a house, but really, you just .... the bank money.
5 You should use 10% of your salary every month to .... your debts. If you don't have any debts, then .... 10%.
6 If you work hard to .... money, it's OK to .... it buying anything you want.
7 It's crazy that banks .... you a fee to take your money when you .... each month.

🔊 10.5 Listen, check and repeat.

WHERE THERE'S GRASS, THERE'S MONEY

EMIL MOTYCKA, from Colorado in the USA, started earning money when he was in the first year of primary school. His family home was so close to a golf course that he often found golf balls on his way home from school. He took the balls home, cleaned them and then sold them back to the golfers. He charged a dollar per ball, which was pretty good considering they cost him nothing!

A few years later, he realized he could make more money cutting grass in people's gardens. His first customers were his aunt and uncle. But he didn't have all the tools he needed, so when it was time to tidy up the edges, he used some scissors! He was so serious about this job that he even spent his weekends working while his friends were out having fun. When he was 13, he borrowed $8,000 to buy a professional lawnmower – with this machine he could work twice as fast. In fact, it was such a success that he paid back the loan in just two years!

By the time he was 16, Emil owned a business that was growing fast – he had several vans and he was even paying employees (who were a lot older than him) to cut the grass, but he knew it would be difficult to continue when he started at university. He decided to sell some of the equipment and make the business smaller, so he could concentrate on his studies.

But he didn't imagine he'd get such bad news. Although Emil and his family were saving money for his education, they couldn't afford to pay all the course fees. There was only one option – he had to start the business again. This time he asked the bank to lend him more money to buy other lawnmowing companies, so he would have more customers quickly.

After five years of studying and running a large business, Emil graduated from university, but it was such an impressive achievement that he was invited to the White House to meet the president. However, a few years ago, Emil had to make a tough decision. His company was worth a lot of money, but he wanted to find new challenges. In the end, he sold the business and started to work for a water conservation company.

5 In pairs, ask and answer the questions.
1 What would you like to buy, that you can't afford?
2 What do you spend most of your money on?
3 Who would you ask if you needed to borrow money?
4 How can you earn a lot of money but do very little?
5 What's something that's always worth spending money on?
6 What type of work do you never get paid for doing?

Grammar

6 a Complete the sentences with *so* or *such*. Check your answers in the text.
1 His family home was .... close to a golf course that he often found golf balls.
2 He was .... serious about this job that he even spent his weekends working.
3 It was .... a success that he paid back the loan in just two years!
4 He didn't imagine he'd get .... bad news.
5 It was .... an impressive achievement that he was invited to the White House.
6 So, why has Emil had .... great results?

b Look at the sentences again. Complete the rules with the words in the box.

| so | such | such a/an |

1 We use .... before adjectives.
2 We use .... before singular nouns.
3 We use .... before plural and uncountable nouns.

G *so* and *such*

so + adjective
This website is **so interesting**.
Our weekend was **so relaxing**.
The computers in that shop are **so cheap**!

such + (adjective +) noun
His idea was **such a success**.
We had **such a relaxing time**.
There are **such good discounts** here.

→ Grammar reference: page 141

notice

So and *such* are often followed by a clause with *that* which expresses a result.

He was **so** intelligent / **such** a good student **that** he graduated a year early.

7 🔊 10.6 **emphasis with *so* and *such***
Listen to the sentences and notice how *so* and *such* are emphasised. Listen again and repeat.
1 His family home was <u>so</u> close to a golf course that he often found golf balls.
2 It was <u>such</u> a success that he paid back the loan in just two years!
3 He didn't imagine he'd get <u>such</u> bad news.

Speaking

8 a Complete the sentences so they are true for you.
1 Yesterday I was so .... that I ....
2 I have such a .... tomorrow that I ....
3 The party was so .... that ....
4 My parents are such .... that ....
5 My rent is so .... that ....
6 The shops around here are so .... that ....

b In pairs, start conversations with the phrases. Your partner will ask questions and express his/her opinion.

Yesterday, I was so tired that I almost fell asleep in class.
Really? Did you go out the night before?
No, but I had an exam, so I stayed up revising.

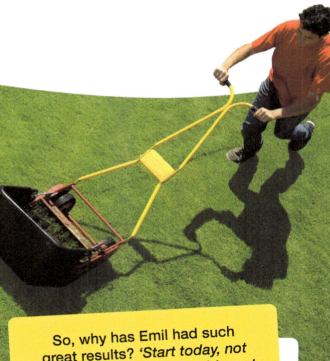

So, why has Emil had such great results? 'Start today, not tomorrow,' he says, 'The biggest failure you can have in life is not trying at all.'

So if you have an idea for a business, give it a try ... today!

Exam practice: page 165

10.3 MONEY FOR NOTHING

G indefinite pronouns
🔧 identify reasons and results

Listening

1 Read the text about Universal Basic Income (UBI). Tick (✓) the best definition.

Everyone …
a who has a job earns the same salary.
b receives the same amount of money from the government.
c who doesn't have a job receives the same money.

2 🔊 10.7 Listen to an interview about UBI. Tick (✓) the topics that are discussed. Who is more positive about UBI: Mara or the presenter?

1 Problems with the benefits system.
2 How much money we need to live.
3 If people would work with 'free money'.
4 Why prices are increasing quickly.
5 If it's fair to give money to rich people.
6 Machines taking people's jobs.

Basically, what is Universal Basic Income (UBI)?

Some people can't work. And some people who work don't earn enough money to live on. So, in many countries the government pays benefits to people to help them live. It's a complicated system and many people say it's not fair. But imagine if the government gave you, me … and everyone in the country a fixed amount of money every month – enough to buy food, pay for the rent and cover the bills. UBI, or Universal Basic Income is an exciting idea, but could it ever become a reality?

🔧 identify reasons and results

It's often important to understand why things happen or the consequences of actions.

Reasons can be emphasized:

Some people can't work, so the government pays them benefits.

Or results can be emphasized:

The government pays some people benefits because they can't work.

It's important to listen for phrases that introduce reasons and results.

Introduce reasons: *because …, as …*

Introduce results: *So …, That's why …, As a result, …*

3 🔊 10.7 Read the Skill box. Then listen again and choose the correct options to answer the questions.

1 Why can getting benefits be a difficult process?
a There are lots of forms to complete.
b People don't really need the help.
c Governments don't want to help people.

2 Why is UBI a fairer system?
a It helps people who have jobs.
b It helps everyone who needs it.
c It helps people who lost their jobs.

3 Which is a consequence of 'free money', according to the presenter?
a People would only work in the mornings.
b The prices of food and rent would increase.
c People wouldn't work at all.

4 How would UBI help the economy?
a People would be more creative and productive.
b People could leave school earlier.
c People would get up earlier.

5 Which is a consequence of machines doing more jobs?
a Computers will provide education.
b There will be more jobs for people.
c People will need to train for different jobs.

4 In pairs, discuss the questions.

1 Are you in favour of UBI? Why/Why not?
2 If your country had UBI, how much money should each person receive?
3 If you received this amount of money, how would it change your life?

Grammar

5 a Look at the words in **bold** in the sentences from the interview. Do the words refer to things, people or places?

1. We have **someone** with us today who can help.
2. **Everybody** would get help.
3. **No one** would be left out.
4. We wouldn't do **anything**.
5. You might do **something** more interesting.
6. **Everywhere** you look, machines are doing more jobs.
7. **Anyone** could lose their job because of a change in technology.
8. Do you know **anywhere** that has UBI?

b Answer the questions with the prefixes *every*, *some*, *any* and *no*.

1. Which do we use to talk about all of a group?
   ....
2. Which do we use to talk about none of a group?
   ....
3. Which two do we use to talk about a member of a group? .... and ....
4. Which do we usually use in questions and negatives?
   ....

G indefinite pronouns

People *Everyone/Everybody* knows that the shops are open.
Places *Nowhere* is better than my parents' house.
Things I have *something* to give you.
I don't have *anything* to wear.
Do you know *anything* about science?

→ Grammar reference: page 141

notice

Not any ... and *no ...* have the same meaning.
There is**n't anything** in my account. = There**'s nothing** in my account.
NOT ~~There's not nothing in my account.~~

6 Complete the sentences. In pairs, compare your answers.

1. Everyone in the class ....
2. Nobody in the class ....
3. I don't know anyone who ....
4. I would like to meet someone who ....

Writing

7 Complete the advert with the correct indefinite pronouns.

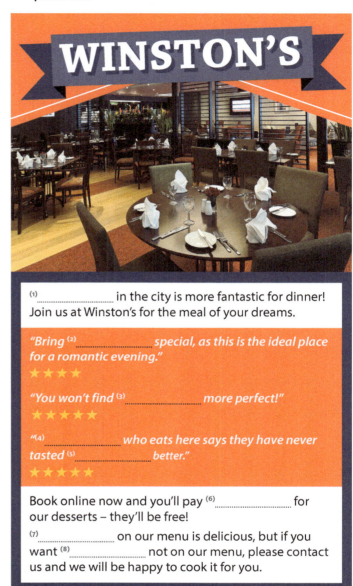

WINSTON'S

(1) .... in the city is more fantastic for dinner! Join us at Winston's for the meal of your dreams.

"Bring (2) .... special, as this is the ideal place for a romantic evening."
★★★★

"You won't find (3) .... more perfect!"
★★★★★

"(4) .... who eats here says they have never tasted (5) .... better."
★★★★★

Book online now and you'll pay (6) .... for our desserts – they'll be free!

(7) .... on our menu is delicious, but if you want (8) .... not on our menu, please contact us and we will be happy to cook it for you.

8 In pairs, choose a product and write an advert for it. Include as many indefinite pronouns as you can.

Italian leather wallet   Multitool   Underwater phone

Mediation task: All students, page 128

10.4 WHAT A BARGAIN!

FL shopping
second-hand markets

The big picture: second-hand markets

1 Look at the picture of Anna at a market. In pairs, answer the questions.
   1 What type of market is it?
   2 What products can you see?
   3 Can you see any prices?
   4 Have you ever been to a market like this?
   5 What did you buy?

2 a 10.1 Watch the video and match the items Anna looks at with the correct markets. Some items can go in both columns.

| book | camera | handbag | hat | jacket |
| jewellery | sunglasses | teddy bear | toy bus |

Fleadonia	Two Markets

b Which items did Anna buy?

3 10.1 Are the sentences true (T) or false (F)? Watch the video again and check.
   1 Anna is from Sweden, but she lives in Barcelona. ....
   2 At Fleadonia, people only sell things they have made. ....
   3 The market is for local people to sell things. ....
   4 Anna paid €10 for the camera. ....
   5 At Two Markets, everything costs less than €1. ....
   6 The main purpose of Two Markets is to sell fashionable clothes. ....

4 In pairs, discuss the questions.
   1 Which market do you prefer? Why?
   2 What are the good things and bad things about buying second-hand items?
   3 Have you ever bought second-hand clothes? What did you buy?
   4 Do you ever try to negotiate a lower price when you buy something?
   5 Where do you do this? Are you successful?

5 10.2 Watch Rob and Lou talking about the video. Tick (✓) the reasons Rob likes markets.
   1 You can find a bargain. ☐
   2 You can return items easily. ☐
   3 It's better for the environment. ☐
   4 The products are better quality. ☐
   5 The atmosphere is better. ☐

6 10.2 Choose the correct words to complete the sentences. Watch the video again and check.
   1 Lou bought a T-shirt in a *market / shop*.
   2 She took it back because it *was the wrong size / didn't look good on her*.
   3 When she returned the T-shirt, she got *a refund / a different colour*.
   4 The original price of Rob's sunglasses was *£7 / £10*.
   5 Rob paid *£5 / £7* for his sunglasses.
   6 Rob sometimes asks for a discount if he buys *more than one item / food and drink*.

Functional language

7 🔊 **10.8** Look at the pictures. Listen to conversations 1–3 and match them with the pictures. In which conversation were the customers satisfied?

Conversation 1 .... Conversation 3 ....
Conversation 2 ....

8 a 🔊 **10.8** Complete the sentences with the words in the box. Listen again and check.

| discount | manager | order | price |
| refund | return | sold | wrong |

1 I'm afraid we've .... out.
2 We can .... it for you.
3 Could you offer me a ....?
4 That's the best .... we can offer.
5 I'd like to .... this dress, please.
6 Is there anything .... with it?
7 Unfortunately, I can't give you a ....
8 Can I speak to the ...., please?

b Who says the sentences above: the customer or the shop assistant?

FL shopping

Buying an item
I'm looking for ... / Do you have ...   I'm afraid we've sold out.
Do you deliver?   We can order it for you.

Negotiating a price
Is it in the sale?   Sorry, but that's the best price we can offer.
Could you offer me a discount?   I can offer you a ...% discount
... are selling the same one for ...   We can match the price.

Returning an item
I'd like to return this ...   Is there anything wrong with it?
Can I exchange it for ...?   You can exchange it for something else.
I'd like a refund please.   Unfortunately, I can't give you a refund.
It doesn't fit me / suit me / work.   Do you have the receipt / card you paid with?
Can I speak to the manager, please?

9 🔊 **10.9** 66 **sounding sorry** 99 Listen to the phrases. Notice how the shop assistants sound sorry when they give bad news. Listen again and repeat.
1 I'm afraid we've sold out.
2 Sorry, but that's the best price we can offer.
3 Unfortunately, I can't give you a refund.

10 a 🔊 **10.10** Choose phrases from the Functional language box to complete the conversations. Listen and check.

1 A ....?
   B Yes, we do. Where do you live?
2 A Excuse me. I'm looking for this T-shirt in a medium.
   B ....
3 A ....?
   B Yes, there is. The keyboard doesn't work.
4 A ....?
   B If you buy two, I can give you a 10% discount.
5 A ....?
   B No, I'm sorry. I've lost it. Is that a problem?

b In pairs, practise the conversations.

Speaking

11 a In pairs, choose a situation. Decide who is the customer and shop assistant. Have a conversation.

b Swap partners. Choose a different situation and have another conversation.

Customer: You want to buy some new shoes for a wedding on Sunday.
Shop assistant: The shoes are sold out. You can order them for Monday.

Customer: You want a better price for a new phone that costs £120.
Shop assistant: You can only offer a lower price if it is available at a different shop.

Customer: You received a handbag as a gift and want to return it because you don't like it.
Shop assistant: You can give a refund if the customer has the receipt, but you prefer to exchange for another item.

📝 Writing bank: page 153

REVIEW UNIT 10

Vocabulary
Money nouns

1 Answer the questions with the words in the box. Sometimes, more than one answer is possible.

bills	coins	notes	receipt
rent	salary	tax	

1 What is usually paid into your bank account every month?
2 What do you have to pay regularly?
3 What do you receive when you buy something?
4 What do you pay to the government?

2 In pairs, ask and answer the questions. If the answer is yes, explain what happened.

Have you ever …
1 found a bargain?
2 asked for a discount?
3 asked for a refund?
4 opened a bank account?

Money verbs

3 Complete the text with the words in the box.

borrow	lend	own	pay	save

I'd really like to (1) .... a house one day, so I'm trying to (2) .... as much as possible. My parents will (3) .... me some money, but I'll have to (4) .... most of it from the bank and (5) .... it back over the next 25 years.

4 a Choose the correct words to complete the sentences about money.
1 I get *earned* / *paid* once a week.
2 I never *waste* / *worth* money on things I don't need.
3 I *save* / *charge* more money than I *cost* / *spend*.

b In pairs, say if the sentences are true for you. If not, change them so that they are true.

Grammar
Second conditional

5 a Complete the sentences using the second conditional and the verbs in brackets.
1 If I .... more money, I .... a new laptop. (earn / buy)
2 I .... working if I .... a lot of money. (not stop / win)
3 I .... to another country if I .... a good job there. (move / get)
4 If I .... a $20 note in the street, I .... it quickly. (find / spend)

b In pairs, say if the sentences are true for you. If not, change them so that they are true.

so and *such*

6 Choose the correct words to complete 1–3. Then match the halves to make sentences.
1 The film was *such* / *so* boring that ....
2 He was *such* / *so* a rich man that ....
3 It was *such* / *so* an exciting book that ....
a I read it in a day.
b I fell asleep.
c he could afford to give money away.

Indefinite pronouns

7 Complete the sentences with the correct indefinite pronoun.

anything	anywhere	everybody
nothing	anyone	something

1 There's .... inside that box, it's empty.
2 Listen. I have .... important to say.
3 She doesn't have .... to stay.
4 Is there .... who can help you?
5 .... in this class is learning English.
6 Are you doing .... this weekend?

Functional language
Shopping

8 🔊 10.11 Put the conversation between a customer (C) and a shop assistant (S) in the correct order. Listen and check.
a ☐ C It doesn't fit. Do you have a medium?
b ☐ S Do you have the receipt?
c ☐ C I'd like to return this jumper.
d ☐ C No, sorry, I don't. It was a gift.
e ☐ S Ah, OK. Unfortunately, I can't give you a refund, but you can exchange it for something else.
f ☐ S I'm afraid we've sold out. Would you like me to order it for you?
g ☐ C No, thanks. I'd prefer a refund, please.
h ☐ S Is there anything wrong with it?

9 In pairs, choose a product. Decide who is the customer and shop assistant and have a conversation. Try to get the best price you can. Swap roles and choose another product.

Looking back

- Think of five useful words or expressions you have learned. Why do you think they are useful?
- Think of five things you would do if you could.

A global market

11

Grammar G
passives
used to
past perfect

Vocabulary V
describing clothes
verbs and dependent prepositions

Functional language FL
asking for and giving permission

Skill
identify a sequence of events

Video
how to work and travel full time

Writing
a report

Exams
listening to a radio interview

The big picture: global trade

1 Look at the picture. In pairs, discuss the questions.
   1 Where is the ship? Where is it going?
   2 How many containers is it carrying?
   3 Why do ships like this go from one country to another?
   4 What are the good and bad things about global trade?

2 🔊 11.1 Listen and check your answers.

3 In pairs, discuss the questions.
   1 Are there any big ports in your country? Where are they?
   2 Which products does your country make or grow?
   3 Which products does it import from other countries?
   4 Do you think people should try to buy local products? Why/Why not?
   5 Do you think global trade is good or bad for the world? Why?

105

11.1 ETHICAL FASHION

G passives
V describing clothes

Vocabulary

1 **a** Look at the pictures. In pairs, write a list of the clothes you can see.

b 🔊 11.2 Describe the clothes with the words in the Vocabulary box. Listen and compare.

2 Put the words in the box in the correct columns.

V describing clothes

casual	cotton	denim	fur
leather	loose	old-fashioned	
patterned	plain	silk	smart
stylish	synthetic	tight	wool

Styles	Materials

🔊 11.3 Listen, check and repeat.

🔍 notice

Most materials can be used as adjectives, e.g.: *The belt is made of **leather**. It's a **leather** belt.*

But some materials have different words as adjectives, e.g.: *The scarf is made of **wool**. It's a **woollen** scarf.*

3 In pairs, discuss the questions with the words in the Vocabulary box.
1 Which clothes in the pictures do you like? Why?
2 Which clothes in the pictures don't you like? Why?
3 What are you wearing today?
4 What do you wear for a special occasion?

▶ HOW ETHICAL IS YOUR WARDROBE?

What do you think about when you buy clothes? Is it stylish? Is it good quality? How much does it cost? Does it suit me? But perhaps you should ask more questions:

- **Where was it made?** Some factories treat their workers badly and don't pay them enough money to live on.
- **What is it made from?** Some materials are bad for the environment or for animals.
- **Do I really need it?** Buying new clothes and throwing old clothes away creates more waste.

Today, I interview people in a shopping centre to find out how ethical they are.

Listening

4 Look at the title of a new podcast. What does it mean? Read the introduction to the podcast and check.

5 🔊 11.4 Listen to the podcast and tick (✓) the correct answers.

	spends a lot of money on clothes		ethical shopper	
	yes	no	yes	no
1 Ellie	☐	☐	☐	☐
2 Diego	☐	☐	☐	☐
3 Rick	☐	☐	☐	☐

6 🔊 11.4 Complete the sentences with the correct names: *Ellie*, *Diego* or *Rick*. Listen again and check.
1 .... buys new clothes at low prices.
2 .... thinks about where clothes are made.
3 .... doesn't buy any new clothes.
4 .... has a jacket made from wool.
5 .... thinks it's important to look fashionable.
6 .... doesn't like to throw away clothes.

7 Which three factors are most important to you when you buy clothes?

| brand | colour | country | material |
| price | quality | style | |

Grammar

8 a Match the words in the box with the pronouns in **bold** in the sentences.

| Diego's T-shirt | factory workers |
| Rick's jumper | Rick's shoes |

Passive form		Active form
1 **They** aren't allowed to take breaks.	→	The bosses don't allow **them** to take breaks.
2 **They** were given to me by a friend.	→	A friend gave **them** to me.
3 **It** was made by my mum.	→	My mum made **it**.
4 What's **it** made from?	→	What do they make **it** from?

b Look at the sentences again. Answer the questions.
1 Are the pronouns in **bold** the subjects or the objects of the sentences?
2 Did the speakers in the podcast use the passive or the active form? Why?
3 Which sentences are in the present? Which are in the past?
4 Which verb do we use with the past participle of the main verb in passive sentences?
5 Which preposition do we use in passive sentences to include the people who did the action?

G passives

Present
The clothes **are made** in Mexico (by workers).
These watches **aren't sold** in the USA (by shops).
Is that shirt **designed** by Ralph Lauren?

Past
This picture **was painted** by Picasso.
These oranges **weren't grown** in Spain (by farmers).
When **were** the factories **opened** (by the company)?

→ Grammar reference: page 142

9 a Complete the sentences with the present passive form of the verbs in brackets.
1 Everyone .... to marry before the age of 30. (expect)
2 Babies .... three names when they are born. (give)
3 Many new houses .... each year. (build)
4 Children .... to weddings. (not invite)
5 A lot of sugar .... in food. (use)
6 People under the age of 18 .... to ride a motorcycle. (not allow)

b Change the sentences so they are true for where you live.

10 In pairs, ask *When was the last time you …?* with the past passive form of the verbs.
1 bite / by an animal
2 pay / for doing a job
3 teach / a useful word in English
4 tell / an interesting story
5 ask / a difficult question
6 give / a disappointing present

Speaking

11 In pairs, take turns to ask and answer the questions about the clothes you are wearing today. Who is the most ethical shopper?

- Where and when was it/were they bought?
- How was it/were they chosen? (price, style, etc.)
- Where was it/were they made?
- What is it/are they made of?
- Who was it/were they designed by?

11.2 A GLOBAL WORKFORCE

G used to
V verbs and dependent prepositions

Reading

1 Look at the pictures. In pairs, discuss how the world of work has changed over the last 80 years.

2 Read the article quickly. Which of your ideas from exercise 1 does it mention?

3 In pairs, complete the table with the phrases in the box.

find work in different countries
have different types of jobs
speak to colleagues in person
use technology to communicate
work at just one company
work locally

	Past		Present
1	.... Careers	4	....
2	.... Workforce	5	....
3	.... Communication	6	....

4 In pairs, discuss the questions.
 1 Do you know anyone who has moved to another country for work?
 2 Why did he/she make this decision?
 3 Do you know anyone who works from home?
 4 Is he/she happy with the situation? Why/Why not?
 5 How many jobs do you think you will have in your career?
 6 Would you prefer to always work for the same company? Why/Why not?

THE CHANGING FACE OF THE WORKPLACE

How do modern jobs compare with the past? How did we use to work? We look at three big changes and get young people's views on them.

PORTFOLIO CAREERS

In the past, there used to be a clear career path. People left school and got a job. Then they worked for the same company until they retired 50 years later. Nowadays, people develop 'portfolio careers', which means they combine several different jobs in one career.

Edward, 26: *My dad retired last year. He worked for the same company all his life. He always tells me to get a 'job for life', but I don't agree with him. I teach photography two days a week, I design websites for two days, and I work on my own projects on the other day! I have less job security, but at least I don't get bored! My dad worries about me, but he forgets that the world is different now.*

GLOBALIZATION

In the past, companies used to choose the best people they could find in the local area. But these days, they can employ people from anywhere in the world. More people are working outside their home country than ever before. This means that job seekers can search for jobs anywhere in the world and apply for jobs that are right for them.

Carrie, 27: *I'm from Australia, but I succeeded in finding a great job in Tokyo, Japan. At first, I suffered from homesickness because I missed my family and friends and things are so different here. In Australia, we used to leave the office at 5.00 p.m. every day, but here we sometimes work until 8.00! It's just a different work culture, so I can't complain about it. I'm hoping for a holiday soon, though!*

REMOTE WORKING

Working from home didn't use to be possible. These days, thanks to email and the internet, many people can now work without travelling to the office. These 'remote workers' can choose when and where they work. A recent survey showed that 70% of professionals around the world work at least one day a week remotely.

Rohit, 32: *I work for Automattic, a company which specializes in blogging software. I'm one of 918 remote workers from 69 different countries. I have a great relationship with my co-workers, even if I don't see them in person. The best thing is I don't have to pay for transport or wait for the bus every day – my office is in my home!*

Vocabulary

5 Find the verbs in the text. Which prepositions follow the verbs: *about*, *for*, *from*, *in* or *with*?

V verbs and dependent prepositions

1 agree	....	7 search	....
2 apply	....	8 specialize	....
3 compare	....	9 succeed	....
4 complain	....	10 suffer	....
5 hope	....	11 wait	....
6 pay	....	12 worry	....

🔊 **11.5** Listen, check and repeat.

6 a Complete the sentences with the correct form of the verbs in the box and the correct preposition.

agree	apply	not complain	pay
search	not suffer	wait	worry

1 I .... my parents about most things.
2 I spend a lot of time .... clothes before I buy them.
3 I .... the future of our planet.
4 I usually .... dinner when I go out with friends.
5 I .... nerves before I take an exam.
6 I hate .... packages to arrive.
7 I .... my problems to my friends.
8 I'm going to .... a new job soon.

b In pairs, say if the sentences are true for you.

I hardly ever agree with my parents!

Grammar

7 a Read the sentences from the text and match them with the descriptions.

1 In the past, there **used to be** a clear career path. ......
2 My dad **retired** last year. ......
3 In Australia, we **used to leave** the office at 5.00 p.m. every day. ......

a a repeated action in the past
b a situation that was true in the past
c an action that happened once in the past

b Look at the verbs in **bold** in the sentences and answer the questions.

1 Are sentences 1 and 3 correct if we use the past simple?
2 Is sentence 2 correct if we use *used to* and the infinitive?
3 Can you find an example of *used to* in a question in the text?
4 Can you find an example of *used to* in a negative sentence in the text?

G used to

	Situations	Actions
+	I **used to be** very shy when I was younger.	I **used to start** work at 7.00 a.m. in London.
–	I **didn't use to have** a car when I lived in L.A.	I **didn't use to drive** to work, but now I have to.
?	**Did** there **use to be** an office here?	**Did** you **use to work** with Helen?
Y/N	Yes, there **did**. / No, there **didn't**.	Yes, I **did**. / No, I **didn't**.

→ Grammar reference: page 142

8 🔊 **11.6** 💬 *used to and use to* 💬 Listen to the sentences. Do the words in **bold** sound the same or different? Listen again, check and repeat.

1 I **used to** wake up really early.
2 We didn't **use to** know each other.
3 Did she **use to** work remotely?

9 a Rewrite the questions with *used to* where it is correct.

1 Which jobs were you interested in when you were younger?
2 Did you help with the housework as a teenager?
3 How many emails did you send last week?
4 How did you travel to school?
5 Which year did you leave school?
6 Did you work in the summer holidays?

b In pairs, ask and answer the questions. Use *used to* where possible and give more information.

Which jobs did you use to be interested in when you were younger?
I used to want to be an astronaut. I used to read lots of books about space. I even went to a space camp once.

Speaking

10 Look at the different topics. In pairs, compare life today with 50 years ago.

People used to use buses and taxis, but now there is a metro.

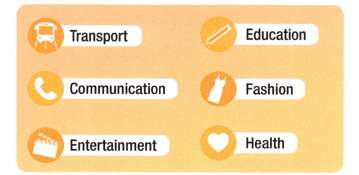

✅ Exam practice: page 166

11.3 IMMIGRATION STORIES

G past perfect
F identify a sequence of events

Grammar

1 In pairs, discuss the questions.
   1 Have you ever lived or worked in a different country?
   2 Do you know any immigrants?
   3 Who is the most famous immigrant in your country?

2 Read the text about a very successful immigrant. In pairs, guess who she is.

> She was born in Barbados in 1988. She loved reggae music and started performing with three school friends. An American music producer invited her to the USA after he had seen the group sing. In 2007, she became famous around the world because her song 'Umbrella' had been so successful. Although she is still making music, she also has other interests. She has appeared in films such as *Ocean's 8* and *Guava Island*. She helps design trainers for sports company, Puma. And after her cosmetics company had made over $500 million, she was named the richest female singer in the world!

3 a Read the sentences from the text. Which action happened first: a or b?
   1 a An American music producer **invited** her to the USA after
     b he **had seen** the group sing.
   2 a She **became** famous around the world because
     b her song 'Umbrella' **had been** so successful.
   3 a After her cosmetics company **had made** over $500 million,
     b she **was named** the richest female singer in the world!

   b Look at the verbs in bold and answer the questions.
   1 Which tense are the actions that happened first?
     past simple / past perfect
   2 Which tense are the actions that happened later?
     past simple / past perfect
   3 How do we form the past perfect? .... +
     ....

   G past perfect

   + He was very tired because **he had started** his journey at 4.00 a.m.
   – **She hadn't been** on a plane before, so she was very nervous.
   ? **Had you studied** English before you started the class?
   Y/N Yes, I had. / No, I hadn't.

   → Grammar reference: page 142

4 Complete the sentences with the past perfect or past simple forms of the verbs in brackets.
   1 My phone .... of battery because I .... it. (run out / not charge)
   2 By the time I .... at the station, the train .... (arrive / leave)
   3 She .... well, so she .... really tired. (not sleep / be)
   4 .... you .... at the gym when I .... you yesterday? (be / see)

Reading

5 Read the article about other successful immigrants. Answer the questions with Haute Rogue (H), TransferWise (T) or both companies (B).
   Which company's owner(s) ...
   1 came from a former Soviet Union country? ....
   2 started the company to help people save money? ....
   3 moved to the USA? ....
   4 faced many challenges when they were young? ....
   5 used to have very few clothes? ....

Company: Haute Rogue
Country of origin: Belarus
Story: Anna Metselitsa is the founder of the clothing company, Haute Rogue. Today, it sells clothes in more than 800 shops in North America. This is especially impressive because Metselitsa arrived in the USA in 2007 with just $300. She grew up in Minsk, in the former Soviet Union and she didn't have an easy childhood. When she was a teenager, she dreamed of becoming a fashion designer, but she only had one pair of jeans, which she had to fix many times. She moved to the USA after she had finished a degree in Economics and for seven years, she worked as a waiter in New York and saved money. Eventually in 2014, her dream came true and she opened Haute Rogue. The first years of the business were very hard for Metselitsa. She worked most nights promoting her new company on social media, but two years after it had opened, Haute Rogue received its first big order, from fashion giant, Forever 21. Since then, the company has grown and grown. Metselitsa explains her success very simply: 'I didn't give up,' she says.

11.3

🔧 identify a sequence of events

Events aren't often described in the order in which they happened, but you can identify the sequence of events.

- Notice time expressions (*in the morning, last week, in 2012*).
- Notice sequencers (*next, after that, before, finally*).
- Notice use of tenses (past simple, past continuous, past perfect).

6 a Read the text about Anna Metselitsa again and look at the highlighted words. Order the events 1–8.

- a [1] grow up in Minsk
- b [ ] get an order from Forever 21
- c [ ] work as a waiter
- d [ ] dream of being a fashion designer
- e [ ] move to the USA
- f [ ] do a degree in Economics
- g [ ] start Haute Rogue
- h [8] sell clothes in 800 shops

b Read the text about Kristo Käärmann and Taavet Hinrikus again and order the events 1–8.

- a [ ] realize people want a transfer service
- b [ ] grow up in the old Soviet Union
- c [ ] transfer $3 billion of customers' money
- d [ ] Estonia becomes independent
- e [ ] Käärmann moves to London
- f [ ] set up TransferWise
- g [ ] company is worth $3.5 billion
- h [ ] transfer money between their accounts

7 In pairs, discuss the questions.
1. Had you heard of the companies before?
2. Which story is more impressive? Why?
3. Do you think their backgrounds helped them to become successful?
4. Do you have an idea for a business?

Writing

8 Complete the newspaper story with the past perfect forms of the verbs in the box.

| be | expire | leave | refuse | see |

Company: TransferWise
Country of origin: Estonia
Story: Set up in 2011, the money transfer service, TransferWise, is currently valued at over $3.5 billion. The company was started by two childhood friends from Estonia, Kristo Käärmann and Taavet Hinrikus. The story began after Käärmann had emigrated to England and his salary was paid in British pounds. Meanwhile, Hinrikus was being paid in euros, but he needed pounds for his business trips to London. They found it was cheaper to transfer money into each other's bank accounts than pay fees at a currency exchange. They soon realized that other people wanted a similar service and so they set up TransferWise. The company was immediately successful and by 2015, it had transferred more than $3 billion of customers' money around the world. Hinrikus believes their success was partly because their early lives hadn't been easy. They grew up in the old Soviet Union before Estonia had become independent. 'If you wanted something, you had to build it yourself,' he says. 'That has given people an attitude of not being afraid of rolling up their sleeves and getting their hands dirty.'

Syrian refugee, Hassan al-Kontar arrived in Canada yesterday after he ⁽¹⁾ .... trapped in an airport in Kuala Lumpur for more than seven months. He is now living in the small town of Whistler with Laurie Cooper, who organized a campaign to bring him to Canada after she ⁽²⁾ .... his videos on Twitter. Hassan explained that he ⁽³⁾ .... Syria in 2006 to avoid fighting in the civil war. He then travelled to the United Arab Emirates and worked for seven years. However, he was sent to Malaysia when officials discovered his Syrian passport ⁽⁴⁾ .... When his visa for Malaysia ran out, he went to the airport and tried to travel to Ecuador and Cambodia, but was refused entry. After Malaysian authorities ⁽⁵⁾ .... to let him leave the airport, he began sending videos to the world explaining his situation.

9 a Complete the sentences with verbs in the past perfect. In pairs, compare your sentences.
1. Maria arrived at the airport late because she ....
2. She felt very excited because she ....
3. After she .... , she bought a map.
4. When she got there, she realized that she ....
5. She thought she .... , so she took out her camera.

b In pairs, write a short story about Maria using some of the sentences you have written.

🔁 **Mediation task:** All students, page 131

11.4 OF COURSE YOU CAN!

asking for and giving permission
how to work and travel full time

The big picture: how to work and travel full time

1 Look at the picture of two people who travel full time. In pairs, guess the answers to the questions.
   1 Where do they live?
   2 How do they travel?
   3 How do they make money?
   4 Do they enjoy their lives?

2 ▶ 11.1 Watch the video and check your answers to exercise 1. What types of landscapes did Bee and Theo travel to?

3 ▶ 11.1 Match the ways Theo and Bee make money in the box with the sentences. Watch the video again and check.

| podcast | shop | stock photography | website |

   1 It's the first thing people see about you.
   2 People can buy your images and you don't have to do anything.
   3 So many people wanted to buy prints all the time.
   4 We wanted to interview people who were living alternative lifestyles.

4 In pairs, discuss the questions.
   1 Would you like to have a similar life to Bee or Theo? Why/Why not?
   2 What skills do Bee and Theo need to do their work?
   3 Which jobs involve travelling a lot?
   4 Would you like to travel more for your work? Why/Why not?

5 ▶ 11.2 Watch Lou and Rob talking about the video. Tick (✓) the reasons why Rob doesn't think travelling and working is a good idea.
   1 You miss friends and family. ☐
   2 You can't talk to colleagues in an office. ☐
   3 It's expensive at the start. ☐
   4 Not everybody has the correct skills. ☐
   5 You can't visit the places you travel to. ☐

6 ▶ 11.2 Watch the video again and match the requests with the responses.
   1 Can I press play? ....
   2 Would it be OK if I call someone first? ....
   3 Would you mind if I just get a drink? ....
   4 Do you think I could speak to him? ....
   a Sure. Go right ahead.
   b The video is ready. You can call afterwards.
   c I suppose it's OK.
   d Of course!

Functional language

7 🔊 **11.8** Look at the pictures and listen to the conversations. Answer the questions.

In which conversation does the person …
1 give permission happily? ....
2 give permission weakly? ....
3 refuse permission? ....

8 🔊 **11.8** Complete the conversations with the words in the box. Listen again and check.

| may | once | please | suppose |

A Could I have some, (1) ....?
B But you said you didn't want any.
A I know, but it looks so good! And it's so hot today.
B Well, all right, but just this (2) ....!
A Thank you! Oh, (3) .... I use your spoon?
B I (4) .... so … but don't take too much.

| afraid | rather | sorry | think | would |

A Excuse me, do you (5) .... I could get off here?
B I'm (6) ...., but we aren't at a bus stop, so I can't open the doors.
A But we aren't going anywhere! We haven't moved for ages.
B I'm (7) .... it's not safe to get off here. We'll be there soon. Don't worry.
A Well, (8) .... it be OK if I waited here?
B I'd (9) .... you didn't, sir. It might be dangerous when we start moving again.

| course | course not | mind |

A Wow, it's really hot in here. Can I open the window, please?
B Yes, of (10) .... Go right ahead.
A It's stuck. It won't open. Do you (11) .... if I put on the air conditioning?
B No, of (12) ....
A Ahh – that's better. Thanks.

FL asking for and giving permission

Asking for permission
Can/Could/May I … (please)?
Do you think I could …?
Would it be OK if I …?
Do you mind if I …?

Giving permission
Yes, of course (you can).
Go right ahead.
No problem (at all).
No, of course not! / I don't mind at all.

Giving permission weakly
I guess/suppose so.
I guess/suppose it's OK.
All right. Just this once, though.

Refusing permission
I'm sorry, but …
I'm afraid …
I'd rather you didn't (because) …

🔍 notice

When someone asks permission with *Do you mind …?* we give permission by answering *no*, e.g. *Do you mind if I put on the air conditioning? No, of course not.*

9 a 🔊 **11.9** 🗨 **sounding polite** 🗨 Listen to the requests. Which version sounds more polite: A or B?

1 Could I have some, please? A ☐ B ☐
2 Excuse me, do you think I could get off here? A ☐ B ☐
3 Do you mind if I put on the air conditioning? A ☐ B ☐

b 🔊 **11.10** Listen and repeat the polite requests.

Speaking

10 In pairs, take it in turns to ask permission to do these things. Remember to sound polite. Your partner will respond with an expression from the Functional language box.

leave English class early today	take your shoes off
return your homework late	borrow some money
call your partner at home tonight	open the window
turn the lights off	take a photo of your partner

Writing bank: page 154

REVIEW UNIT 11

Vocabulary
Describing clothes

1 Look at the pictures. Are the sentences true (T) or false (F)? Correct the false sentences.

Helen is wearing …
1 stylish clothes.
2 a woollen scarf.
3 plain loose trousers.

Juan is wearing …
4 a tight cotton shirt.
5 blue denim jeans.
6 smart shoes.

2 In pairs, describe what another student in the class is wearing. Your partner has to guess who the person is.

Verbs and dependent prepositions

3 a Complete 1–4 with the prepositions in the box.

| about | for | from | in |

1 What do you worry _____ the most?
2 Do you suffer _____ colds in winter?
3 Did you succeed _____ passing your exams?
4 Have you ever applied _____ a job?

b In pairs, ask and answer the questions.

Grammar
Passives

4 Complete the sentences about jeans with the correct form of the verb *to be*.

> This style of trousers (1)_____ invented by Jacob W. Davis and Levi Strauss in the 1870s.
>
> They (2)_____ originally created for workers and sailors, but now they (3)_____ worn by everybody.
>
> In the 1950s, jeans (4)_____ allowed in some places because they were a symbol of youth rebellion and some people didn't like them, but now millions of pairs (5)_____ worn by people all over the world.
>
> Today, they (6)_____ still usually made from denim, a thick strong cotton cloth.

used to

5 a Complete the questions with the correct form of *used to* and the verbs in brackets.

1 What sports _____ at school? (play)
2 _____ vegetables when you were a child? (like)
3 What primary school _____ to? (go)
4 When you were very young, _____ English? (speak)

b In pairs, ask and answer the questions.

Past perfect

6 Complete Kat's description of yesterday evening with the past simple or past perfect forms of the verbs in brackets.

By the time I (1)_____ (finish) work the last bus (2)_____ (leave), so I (3)_____ (not get) home until 7.30 p.m. The house was a mess because no one (4)_____ (tidy) up, so I (5)_____ (do) some housework and then I (6)_____ (watch) my favourite programme on TV. My housemate Jen (7)_____ (cook) dinner for us both and after we (8)_____ (eat), I (9)_____ (wash up) the dishes. Feeling quite tired, I (10)_____ (go) upstairs and after I (11)_____ (check) a few emails, I (12)_____ (decide) to have a relaxing bath.

7 In pairs, describe to each other what you did yesterday evening. Try to use the past perfect at least three times in your description.

I felt quite tired because I'd woken up very early.

Functional language
Asking for and giving permission

8 🔊 11.11 Complete the conversations with the words in the box. Listen and check.

| afraid | ahead | can | mind | once |
| problem | rather | right | sorry | would |

1 A Do you (1)_____ if I sit here?
  B I'm (2)_____ that seat is taken.
  A Really? But nobody is sitting in it.
  B I'm (3)_____, but my friend's sitting there. She's just gone to buy a drink.
2 A (4)_____ I have an ice cream?
  B Why? Are you hungry?
  A Not really.
  B I'd (5)_____ you didn't because it's nearly dinner time.
  A But they look so delicious!
  B All (6)_____. Just this (7)_____.
3 A (8)_____ it be OK if I used your laptop?
  B How long do you need it for?
  A Only a few minutes, I just want to check my emails.
  B No (9)_____ at all. Go right (10)_____.

9 In pairs, ask for permission to do the things.
1 borrow your partner's phone
2 turn on the air conditioning
3 arrive late for class

🕐 Looking back

- Think of two things you used to do in the past that you don't do now.
- In pairs, talk about the last piece of clothing you bought. Where was it made?

Entertain me!

12

Grammar G
reported speech
uses of the -ing form and infinitive

Vocabulary V
entertainment
music
gradable and extreme adjectives

Functional language FL
giving instructions

Skill
identify attitude and opinion

Video
pottery challenge

Writing
a review

Exams
understanding details in short texts

The big picture: a big impression

1 Look at the picture. In pairs, answer the questions.
   1 What kind of entertainment is it?
   2 What are the people doing?
   3 What are some reasons people go to this show?
   4 Do you think it's expensive?

2 12.1 Listen and check your answers.

3 In pairs, discuss the questions.
   1 Is there any free entertainment where you live?
   2 What was the last art show you went to? Did you enjoy it?
   3 What other types of entertainment do you enjoy?
   4 Are there any types of entertainment that you don't like at all?

12.1 WHAT'S ON?

G reported speech
V entertainment

Vocabulary

1. Look at the pictures. In pairs, describe what you see with the words in the Vocabulary box.

2. Put the words in the box in the correct columns. Which words can go in more than one column?

V entertainment

album	audience	author	band	channel
chapter	concert	episode	exhibition	
gallery	novel	orchestra	painting	play
screen	sculpture	series	stage	

Art	Literature	Music	Theatre	TV

🔊 12.2 Listen, check and repeat.

3. Choose the correct words to make questions. In pairs, ask and answer the questions.
   1. Which TV *channel / episode / series* are you watching? Which *channel / episode / series* of it is the best?
   2. What's the longest *author / chapter / novel* you have ever read? How many *authors / chapters / novels* does it have?
   3. What are the most famous art *galleries / exhibitions / paintings* in your country? Have they had any good *galleries / exhibitions / paintings* recently?
   4. What's your favourite *album / band / concert*? What's the name of their latest *album / band / concert*?
   5. When was the last time you watched *an audience / a play / a stage* at the theatre? Were there any famous actors on the *audience / play / stage*?

Listening

4. 🔊 12.3 Listen to the conversations and match them with four of the pictures in exercise 1.
   1 .... 2 .... 3 .... 4 ....

5. 🔊 12.3 Complete the sentences with the correct words. Listen again and check.

   Conversation 1
   1. **Simon told his friend** the play was very ....
   2. **He said that** the play was running for .... weeks.

   Conversation 2
   3. **Ruth said** she would probably watch a .... series.
   4. **Lee told Ruth that** they had just bought a new ....

   Conversation 3
   5. **Ned told his friend** he had got back from .... yesterday.
   6. **He said that** he couldn't speak ....

   Conversation 4
   7. **Charlie told his friend that** he was going to a concert on ....
   8. **He said** he had heard one of their songs on the ....

Grammar

6. Look at the words in **bold** in the sentences in exercise 5 and answer the questions.
   1. Which verbs do we use to report what someone said?
   2. Which verb do we use to say who the person was speaking to?
   3. Is it always necessary to use *that* with these verbs?

116

7 🔊 12.4 Listen carefully to the extracts from the conversations and complete the sentences with the correct verbs.
1 Well, the play _____ very funny.
2 It _____ for three weeks – until the 31st.
3 Nothing much. I _____ probably _____ a comedy series on TV.
4 We _____ just _____ a new TV.
5 I'm tired. I _____ back from Moscow yesterday.
6 I _____ Russian, but I bought a book anyway.
7 I _____ a concert on Saturday.
8 I bought their album because I _____ one of their songs on the radio.

8 Compare the verbs in exercise 7 with the reported speech sentence verbs in exercise 5. Complete the table.

Direct speech	→	Reported speech
1 present simple	→	
2 present continuous	→	
3 past simple	→	
4 present perfect	→	
5 past perfect	→	
6 am going to	→	
7 will	→	
8 can	→	

G reported speech

	You **said/told me** (that) …
'I **have** the tickets.' →	you **had** the tickets.
'I**'m reading** a good book.' →	you **were reading** a good book.
'I **bought** the album last week.' →	you **had bought** the album the week before.
'I **haven't seen** the play yet.' →	you **hadn't seen** the play yet.
'I **hadn't met** her before today.' →	you **hadn't met** her before that day.
'I**'m going to visit** a gallery.' →	you **were going to visit** a gallery.
'I**'ll go** to the cinema with you.' →	you **would go** to the cinema with us.
'We **can't see** the match here.' →	we **couldn't see** the match there.

→ Grammar reference: page 143

notice

In reported speech, pronouns, possessive adjectives and time expressions also change:
'**My** brother loves **you**!' → He said that **his** brother loved **me**.
'I was **here yesterday**.' → She said she had been **there the day before**.

9 🔊 12.5 ❝ **weak form of *that*** ❞ Listen to the sentences. Notice how *that* is pronounced. Listen again and repeat.
1 He said that the play was running for three weeks.
2 Charlie told his friend that he was going to a concert.

10 Read what the people are saying. In pairs, ask and answer *What did … say?* using reported speech. Remember to use the weak form of *that*.

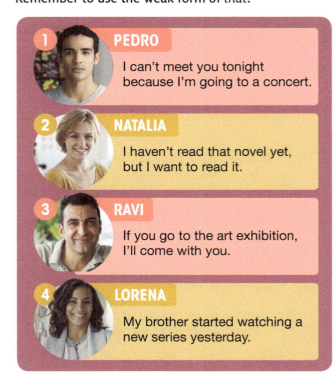

1 **PEDRO** — I can't meet you tonight because I'm going to a concert.
2 **NATALIA** — I haven't read that novel yet, but I want to read it.
3 **RAVI** — If you go to the art exhibition, I'll come with you.
4 **LORENA** — My brother started watching a new series yesterday.

Speaking

11 a In pairs, ask and answer the questions. Make notes of your partner's answers.

Have you ever acted or sung on stage?
Yes, I've been in a play before.
- Have you ever acted or sung on stage?
- What did you watch on TV yesterday?
- What are you going to do at the weekend?
- What was the first album you bought?
- Can you play a musical instrument?
- What books are you reading at the moment?

b Tell the class what you partner said using reported speech.

Maria said that she had been in a play.

12.2 STREET MUSIC

G uses of the *-ing* form and infinitive
V music

Vocabulary

1 Put the words in the box in the correct columns. Write two more examples in each column.

V music

amplifier   cello   classical   country
double bass   drums   electronic
flute   folk   headphones   keyboard
microphone   pop   rap   reggae
rock   trumpet   violin

Types of music	Instruments / equipment

🔊 12.6 Listen, check and repeat.

2 🔊 12.7 Listen to the music. Write the instruments or types of music you hear.

1 ....   4 ....
2 ....   5 ....
3 ....   6 ....

Reading

3 Look at the pictures. In pairs, answer the questions.
  1 What instruments and equipment can you see?
  2 What types of music are the musicians performing?
  3 Where are the musicians performing?
  4 Are there any musicians like this where you live?
  5 Do you enjoy listening to this type of musician?

4 Read the text. Tick (✓) the best title.
  a Busking: advantages and disadvantages ☐
  b Busking helps musicians and local communities ☐
  c The long history of busking ☐

5 Read the text again. Are the sentences true (T) or false (F)?
  1 Busking is a very old form of entertainment. ....
  2 Everyone likes buskers to perform in towns. ....
  3 Buskers encourage people to visit town centres. ....
  4 It's impossible to make much money busking. ....
  5 It's illegal to pay buskers money. ....
  6 Some famous musicians started off busking. ....

6 Should you give money to buskers? Why/Why not?

STREET MUSIC has been a part of town culture ever since there were towns. In the days before recorded music, people used to travel to towns and fairs to listen to street musicians, or buskers, because they were the only performers available for poor people. Today, however, some people don't like having buskers in their town, so they are trying to stop them from performing. They complain that they make too much noise, make the town look untidy, and get in the way of people when they are shopping. But before they complain, they might be surprised to read that buskers actually help the local economy.

'The problem is that our local shopping streets are losing business to the big out-of-town shopping centres', says Emily, a 42-year-old shop owner. 'It's important to encourage shoppers back into town, and buskers help by providing entertainment for everyone – local people and visitors.' She adds, 'And it's free ... unless you choose to give them money, of course!' And Ted, 25, who's a street musician had this to say: 'Busking doesn't have a professional image, but it is actually a real career. I make enough money to live on and my music reaches thousands of people every day!'

He's right. Busking is a business. In fact, in one busy street in Melbourne, Australia, musicians have to do auditions, where they show how well they can play before they can perform there. And now that people are carrying less cash, buskers in some cities even have contactless card readers to accept payment with a credit card!

Playing in the street has also been a path to success in the music industry for some stars. Passenger, Sheryl Crow, Ed Sheeran, Miley Cyrus, James Arthur ... even U2 started off playing in their local towns. Benjamin Clementine, winner of 2015's Mercury Prize, was homeless for several years in Paris before he was discovered by an agent. His guitar was broken, and his keyboard was very cheap, but that didn't stop him breaking into the music industry. So, next time you see a busker, listen with respect – they may be one step from being on MTV!

Grammar

7 a Choose the correct form of the verb to complete the sentences. Check your answers in the text.
1. People used to travel to towns and fairs *to listen / listening* to street musicians.
2. It's important *to encourage / encouraging* shoppers back into town.
3. Buskers help by *to provide / providing* entertainment for everyone.
4. *To play / Playing* in the street has also been a path to success in the music industry.

b Look at the correct options again and complete the rules with: *-ing form* or *infinitive*.
1. We use the .... to express a purpose.
2. We use the .... after prepositions.
3. We use the .... after adjectives.
4. We use the .... as the subject or object of a sentence.

c Can you find another example of each of the rules in the text?

G uses of the *-ing* form and infinitive

After prepositions	I'm interested **in learning** the guitar.
Subject of a sentence	**Listening** to buskers is great.
Object of a sentence	I love **listening** to buskers.
After adjective	He's **brave to sing** in public.
To express purpose	I started busking **to make** money.

→ Grammar reference: page 143

8 a Complete the sentences with the *-ing* or infinitive forms of the verbs in brackets.
1. I *usually / hardly ever* go to the city centre .... (shop)
2. I *sometimes / never* stop in the street .... people money. (give)
3. I'm *interested / not interested* in .... to speak Chinese. (learn)
4. I *would / wouldn't* be happy .... for money if I needed it. (ask)
5. I usually use *cards / cash* .... for things these days. (pay)
6. .... at the weekend is *a bad idea / sometimes necessary*. (study)
7. I'm *quite good / terrible* at .... tennis. (play)
8. .... in public *is / isn't* my idea of fun! (speak)

b Choose options to make the sentences true for you. In pairs, take turns telling your partner and ask follow-up questions.

I hardly ever go to the city centre to shop.
Where do you usually do your shopping?

Speaking

9 Complete the questionnaire and choose the answers that are most true for you.

HOME	ABOUT	QUESTIONNAIRE

1. I listen to music to help me …
   a study.
   b relax.
   c do exercise.
   d (other)

2. I've always found it difficult to …
   a remember songs.
   b sing in tune.
   c dance well.
   d (other)

3. I'm keen on learning more about …
   a classical music.
   b reggae.
   c folk music.
   d (other)

4. If I could learn any instrument, I'd learn …
   a the piano.
   b the guitar.
   c the trumpet.
   d (other)

5. Imagining myself singing in public makes me …
   a excited and happy.
   b nervous.
   c want to run away and hide!
   d (other)

6. The last time I went out to listen to music was …
   a last week.
   b earlier this year.
   c more than a year ago.
   d never.

7. My perfect musical evening would be …
   a singing in a karaoke bar.
   b listening to loud music at home.
   c going to a classical concert.
   d (other)

8. For me, the best way of buying music is …
   a on vinyl.
   b on CD.
   c streaming it online.
   d downloading it.

10 In pairs, compare your answers. Then tell the class how similar you are.

We both listen to music to help us relax.
I've always found it difficult to sing in tune, but Antonio finds it difficult to dance!

12.3 NEW WAYS TO HAVE FUN

V gradable and extreme adjectives
identify attitude and opinion

Listening

1 Look at the pictures. Match them with the types of games the people are playing.
   1 an escape room ....
   2 geocaching ....
   3 a board game ....

2 🔊 12.8 In pairs, guess what you have to do to play the games. Listen to three conversations and check.

identify attitude and opinion

To understand people's attitudes and opinions it's important to listen to what they say **and** how they say it.
- Pay attention to the tone of voice. Does it sound enthusiastic, bored, angry or sad?
- Think about the words that are emphasized, e.g. 'I would *love* a drink!' means the speaker is really thirsty and not just accepting an offer.
- Listen for words and expressions that show people's emotions, e.g. 'I don't believe it!' shows the speaker is surprised.

3 a 🔊 12.8 Read the Skill box. Then listen again and choose the correct options to answer the questions.

Conversation 1
1 How does Marina feel about trying an escape room?
   a She's frightened.   c She's excited.
   b She's not interested.
2 How does she feel about the next available date?
   a She's disappointed.   c She's angry.
   b She's excited.

Conversation 2
3 How does the man feel about his friend going geocaching?
   a He's pleased.   c He's angry.
   b He's envious.
4 How does the woman feel about geocaching?
   a She's confused.   c She's not interested.
   b She's curious.

Conversation 3
5 How does Matt feel about playing Forbidden Island?
   a He's impatient.   c He's relaxed.
   b He's bored.
6 What does Erin think about the rules of the game?
   a She doesn't understand.
   b She understands completely.
   c She isn't 100% sure.

b 🔊 12.9 Listen to the extracts from the conversations and check your answers. In pairs, explain why you chose your answers.

4 In pairs, discuss the questions.
   1 What do all the games have in common?
   2 Have you ever played any of the games?
   3 Which game would you like to play most? Why?

Vocabulary

5 a Read the extracts from the conversations. What are they talking about?
   1 A That sounds **awesome**! I can't wait to go!
     B Yeah! They're really **good** … although they're quite expensive.
   2 A That's quite **interesting**.
     B I think it's absolutely **fascinating**. And it's great fun, too!
   3 A Some of them are really difficult to find because they're very **small**.
     B That's absolutely **tiny**!

b Look at the adjectives in **bold** in the sentences and answer the questions.
   1 Which adjectives are gradable (we can make them weaker or stronger with modifiers like *quite*, *very*, *really*, etc.)?
   ....
   2 Which adjectives are extreme (we can't use modifiers, but we can use *absolutely* for emphasis)?
   ....

12.3

6 Match the extreme adjectives in the box with the gradable adjectives.

V gradable and extreme adjectives

awesome	awful	boiling	delicious
exhausted	fantastic	fascinating	
freezing	furious	huge	starving
terrible	terrifying	tiny	

	Gradable	Extreme
1	angry	....
2	bad	.... / ....
3	big	....
4	cold	....
5	frightening	....
6	good	.... / ....
7	hot	....
8	hungry	....
9	interesting	....
10	small	....
11	tasty	....
12	tired	....

🔊 **12.10** Listen, check and repeat.

7 🔊 **12.11** Look at the pictures and complete the conversations with words from the Vocabulary box. Listen and check.

1 Mmm! Those pancakes look very .... They're absolutely ....!

2 Are you ....? I'm absolutely ....!

3 My brother was .... and his wife was quite ...., too.

4 You can't go running. It's absolutely .... today! It's quite ...., but I'll be OK.

8 🔊 **12.12** 📢 **emphasis of extreme adjectives** 📢
Listen to the sentences and notice how the words in **bold** are emphasized. Listen again and repeat.
1 They're **absolutely delicious**!
2 I'm **absolutely exhausted**!
3 It's **absolutely freezing** today!

9 a In pairs, prepare short conversations about the things in the box using gradable and extreme adjectives.

| the weather | how you feel | a new phone |
| a book | your teacher | a film |

b In pairs, act out your conversations. Remember to emphasize the extreme adjectives.

Writing

10 Complete the reviews with the extreme adjectives in the box. Then give each review a star rating.

| fantastic | fascinating | freezing |
| furious | huge | terrible | tiny |

Exploding kittens is a (1) .... game! I bought it two weeks ago and my friends and I have played it almost every night – we love it! The only problem is that the writing on the cards is absolutely (2) .... I couldn't read it at first. But you quickly learn what each card does in the game. ☆☆☆☆☆

I enjoyed reading *The Life of Mozart*. The first part of the book about his childhood is (3) ...., but I have to say the rest of the book was sometimes a bit boring, especially the politics of Vienna. The main problem with this book is that it's absolutely (4) .... – 958 pages. I couldn't finish it … but maybe you will. ☆☆☆☆☆

We went to see the play *Two Gentlemen of Verona* last night at the Guildhall, unfortunately it was absolutely (5) .... They had the windows open (in winter!), so it was (6) .... in the theatre, the seats were uncomfortable and the actors forgot their lines several times. I'm absolutely (7) .... that I paid £85 for the tickets. A waste of time! ☆☆☆☆☆

11 a Write a short review of a type of entertainment. Try and use as many extreme adjectives as you can.

b Swap reviews with a classmate. Would you like to do the activity? Why/Why not?

⇄ Mediation task: All students, page 131

12.4 DON'T FORGET!
FL giving instructions
pottery challenge

The big picture: pottery challenge

1 Look at the picture. In pairs, answer the questions.
   1 What is the potter making?
   2 What other things can you make from clay?
   3 What skills do you need to make good pottery?
   4 Have you ever tried to make pottery? Would you like to try it? Why/Why not?

2 **12.1** Watch the video. Are the sentences true (T) or false (F)?
   1 The potters have to make tiles in the competition. ....
   2 The tiles are all one colour. ....
   3 The final designs are all similar. ....

3 **12.1** Choose the correct words to complete the sentences. Watch the video again and check.
   1 The potters have *90 minutes / 3 hours* for the contest.
   2 They *can / mustn't* write their names on the tiles.
   3 *Some / None* of the potters are nervous.
   4 The judges like the designs that are *easy / difficult* to do.
   5 They think some designs show an exciting use of *colour / clay*.
   6 The winner *knows / doesn't know* why he has won the contest.

4 Look at the picture of the winning tiles. In pairs, discuss the questions.
   1 Do you agree they are the best? Why/Why not?
   2 Why do you think the judges chose them?
   3 Would a pottery contest be popular where you live?
   4 What kind of contest would you like to take part in?

5 **12.2** Watch Sophia and Sam talking about the video. What do they think about the winning tiles? Which tiles do they prefer?

6 **12.2** Order the instructions for making pottery. Watch the video again and check.
   a ☐ Cover the clay in glaze.
   b ☐ Create your design on the clay.
   c ☐ Put the clay in the kiln again.
   d ☐ Bake the clay in the kiln.
   e ☐ Shape the clay.
   f ☐ Think of an idea and draw a design.

12.4

Functional language

7 🔊 **12.13** Look at the picture. What is the person doing? Listen to the conversation and check.

8 a 🔊 **12.13** In pairs, complete the conversation with the phrases in the box. Listen again and check.

change the wheel	get the spare wheel
lift up the car (x2)	lower the car
stop at a mechanic's	tighten the nuts all the way
you're on level ground	

Craig Hi Mum.
Mum What's wrong?
Craig Nothing. It's just I've got a flat tyre.
Mum Are you OK?
Craig Yeah, I'm fine. But I don't know how to change the tyre.
Mum OK, **first of all**, (1) .... from the back of the car.
Craig Yes, I've done that.
Mum Have you got your tools? You need a spanner to undo the bolts and the jack to lift up the car.
Craig Yes, I have them.
Mum OK, **before you** (2) ...., **make sure** (3) .... You can't do it on a hill.
Craig It's OK. The road is flat.
Mum So, **then you** (4) .... and undo the bolts with the spanner.
Craig OK.
Mum **After that, you** (5) .... But **be careful not to** (6) ....
Craig Right.
Mum **The last thing you do is** (7) .... so it's on the ground and then you tighten the bolts, OK?
Craig OK.
Mum And **don't forget to** (8) .... to check everything is OK.
Craig OK, Mum, I will – thanks!

b Look at the phrases in **bold**. Which ones do we use to order actions? Which do we use to say what is important?

FL giving instructions

Ordering actions
First (of all), you ...
The first thing you do is ...
Before you ..., you ...
After you've ..., you ...
Next/Then/After that, you ...
Finally, ...
The last thing you do is ...

Saying what's important
Make sure ...
It's important to ...
Be careful not to ....
Don't forget to ...

9 🔊 **12.14** 🗨 **intonation in sequences** 🗨 Listen to the instructions. Notice how the intonation goes up ↗ on the first two sentences and goes down ↘ on the last sentence. Listen again and repeat.

1 First, you put the coffee in the machine.
2 Then, you add the water here.
3 Finally, you press this button to switch it on.

10 a In pairs, use the expressions from the Functional language box to write instructions for sending a selfie from your phone.

1 open camera app (use selfie camera, not normal one)
2 take photo (don't put finger on camera lens)
3 press share button, choose app, e.g. WhatsApp, Messenger, etc.
4 choose the person to send it to
5 press send

b Practise saying the instructions. Remember to use the correct intonation in sequences.

The first thing you do is open the camera app on your phone. Don't forget ...

Speaking

11 a Choose an activity from the list or think of your own. Prepare to explain how to do the activity.

cook spaghetti

do a yoga exercise

iron a shirt

make coffee

start a car

use a printer

use your phone to get directions

get money from a cash machine

b In pairs, give your partner instructions for the activity.

Writing bank: page 155

REVIEW UNIT 12

Vocabulary
Entertainment

1 Cross out the words that don't belong in the groups.
  1 author   chapter   episode   novel
  2 album   band   concert   exhibition
  3 stage   channel   series   screen
  4 gallery   audience   painting   sculpture

2 In pairs, ask and answer the questions.
  1 When was the last time you saw some live entertainment?
  2 What was it?
  3 Where was it?
  4 Did you enjoy it?

Music

3 Put the letters in the correct order to make music words.
  1 LLSAICSCA ......
  2 LFTEU   ......
  3 LLECO   ......
  4 GAGEER   ......
  5 PTTERUM   ......
  6 LKFO   ......
  7 KORC   ......
  8 MDSRU   ......

4 In pairs, ask and answer the questions.
  1 Can you play an instrument? If so, what?
  2 What's your favourite type of music?
  3 Are there any types of music that you hate?

Gradable and extreme adjectives

5 Replace the phrases in **bold** with the extreme adjectives in the box. There is one adjective you don't need.

   awful   boiling   delicious   exhausted
   fascinating   furious   huge

  1 It was a **really interesting** programme. You should watch it.
  2 I'm **very angry** with Juan – he just walked out of the meeting.
  3 Can you open a window? It's **so hot** in here.
  4 That's a **very big** piece of cake, Pippa. Can you eat it all?
  5 Thanks for dinner, Marco. It was **such** a **tasty** meal.
  6 I'm **really tired** tonight. I think I'll go to bed.

6 Complete the sentences so they are true for you.
  1 I was furious when ....
  2 The most delicious thing I've ever eaten is ....
  3 In my opinion, ... is awesome.
  4 I think .... is terrible. I don't recommend it.

Grammar
Reported speech

7 🔊 12.15 Listen and use reported speech to say what Tetsu and Mia said.
  1 Mia said   *that she hadn't eaten lunch yet.*
  2 Tetsu told me   ....
  3 Mia said   ....
  4 Tetsu said   ....
  5 Mia told me   ....
  6 Tetsu told me   ....

Uses of *-ing* form and infinitive

8 a Complete the questions with the *-ing* or infinitive forms of the verbs in brackets.
  1 Do you think that .... (speak) English is more difficult than .... (write) it?
  2 Which school subject did you find the most difficult ....? (learn)
  3 Are you good at ....? (cook)
  4 What activities are you bad at ....? (do)

  b In pairs, ask and answer the questions.

Functional language
Giving instructions

9 🔊 12.16 Put the instructions in the correct order 1–6. Listen and check. What are the instructions for?
  a ☐ After you've added the liquid, you turn the switch to the programme you want to use.
  b ☐ Make sure you shut the door correctly.
  c ☐ Then you need to add washing liquid. Open the drawer and pour it in.
  d ☐ Finally, press the 'on' button and the machine will start.
  e ☐ Of course, the first thing you do is put your clothes in the machine.
  f ☐ Be careful to choose a programme with the correct temperature.

10 In pairs, read the situation below and write a set of instructions. Remember to think about what is important.

> Ana wants to buy something online with a credit card. She has never shopped online before.

⏱ Looking back

- What's your favourite type of entertainment?
- Have you ever given instructions to someone?

MEDIATION

1.3 Talk about specific information: Student A

1 Read the text. Answer Student B's questions and explain the scuba diving hand signals.

SCUBA DIVING HAND SIGNALS

When you go scuba diving, you can't talk to the other divers, but it's important to be able to communicate. That's why people need to learn special hand signals before they go diving.

1 **Look:** Hold up two fingers and point to your eyes. Then point to the thing that you want the other person to look at.

2 **Stay together:** Make your hands into balls and put them together with the first finger on each hand sticking out. It's important not to get separated from other divers.

3 **I'm cold:** Cross your arms across your body and move your hands up and down over your upper arms. When divers start to get cold, it's important to end the dive.

4 **Not OK:** Hold out your hand with your fingers separated and twist it left and right. After you make this signal, point at the problem. For example, point to your ear if your ear hurts.

2 Ask Student B to describe the skydiving hand signals and match them to the pictures.

What's the hand signal for 'open parachute'?
1 open parachute ....
2 make legs straighter ....
3 relax ....
4 bend your legs ....

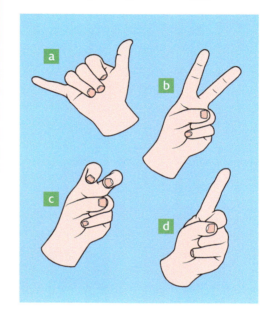

3.3 Talk about a text: Student A

1 Read the text. Explain the history of the Peace symbol to Student B. He/She will take notes.

The peace symbol

People all over the world know the peace symbol. However, it was first used in the UK as the symbol of a group called CND (Campaign for Nuclear Disarmament).

A British designer called Gerald Holtom created the symbol in 1958. He explained that he used the letters N and D from semaphore – a way of communicating using flags. The straight line down the middle is the letter D. In semaphore, this is created by holding one flag straight up in the air and the other straight down. The other lines are made by the letter N, where you hold both flags down and slightly away from your legs.

Holtom also said that the circle represented the world and that the lines in the circle showed a person holding hands out at the sides and feeling sad.

2 Listen to Student B. Make notes about the Bluetooth symbol.

MEDIATION

1.3 Talk about specific information: Student B

1 Ask Student A to describe the scuba diving hand signals and match them with the pictures.

   What's the hand signal for 'I'm cold'?
   1 I'm cold ....
   2 not OK ....
   3 stay together ....
   4 look ....

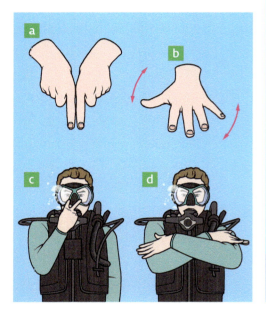

2 Read the text. Answer Student A's questions and explain the skydiving hand signals.

SKYDIVING HAND SIGNALS

When you jump out of a plane 4,000 metres in the air, it's too noisy to talk because of the wind. So, it's important to learn the signals that the instructor uses to make sure you stay safe.

1 **Make legs straighter:** It's important to be in a stable position when you're falling. If your instructor holds out the first two fingers straight with a space between them, this means you need to make your legs straighter.

2 **Bend your legs:** If your legs are too straight, you need to bend them. This is similar to the signal for straighter legs. Your instructor holds out the first two fingers, but they bend the tops of their fingers down.

3 **Relax:** It sounds difficult, but you need to relax your body when you're falling. If the instructor makes a hand signal with the thumb and the little finger sticking out, this is to tell you to relax.

4 **Open parachute:** This is the most important signal. When your instructor makes his hand into a ball and points with the first finger, it's time to open your parachute!

3.3 Talk about a text: Student B

1 Listen to Student A. Make notes about the peace symbol.

....
....
....
....
....

2 Read the text. Explain the history of the Bluetooth symbol to Student A. He/She will take notes.

The Meaning of Bluetooth

If you have an electronic device, you'll probably recognize the Bluetooth symbol. It's a way to connect devices without using a cable. But why do we call it 'Bluetooth'? And what does the symbol mean?

In 1996, technology companies met in Sweden to decide on a name for a new way of connecting mobile phones. Someone at the meeting liked reading history books and suggested the word Bluetooth – the name of a Danish king from over 1,000 years ago. The king's name was Harald Gormson, but people called him 'Harald Bluetooth'. Did he really have blue teeth? Nobody knows for sure.

The technology companies used an ancient form of writing from the time when King Bluetooth was alive to create the symbol. The left side of the symbol is the letter H, for Harald, and the right side is the letter B, for Bluetooth.

So, next time you use Bluetooth to connect to a device, think about the history behind it!

MEDIATION

2.3 Write about specific information: All students

1 Read the text. In pairs, write down the key things to remember about surviving in a desert.

Surviving in the desert

In the desert, there are three main problems: it's very hot in the day, it's very cold at night, and there isn't much water. So, you need to deal with these problems to survive. The first thing to take care of is the heat. Your body needs to keep cool, so cover your head with a hat or piece of clothing. Don't try to walk in the middle of the day – it's too hot. When the sun is hottest, you should find a tree and stay in the shade. But don't try to walk at night either because it can get very cold. When it begins to get dark, find a place to rest and keep warm. Water is extremely important in the desert. Drink small amounts slowly. If you have any food, only eat a little at a time or you will become thirsty. People may be looking for you, so make it easier for them to find you by writing a big message on the ground that could be seen from a rescue plane. And most importantly, stay calm. When people panic, they make bad choices.

How to survive in the desert
- Wear a hat or cover your head
- ....
- ....
- ....
- ....
- ....
- ....

5.3 Help a friend: All students

1 Your friend Helena has started university, but she doesn't understand the advice on the university website. Look at the words she has highlighted. What do they mean?

2 In pairs, write an email to Helena to explain what she should do.

UNIVERSITY HEALTH CENTRE

The University Health Centre provides advice for students about diet, lifestyle, and dealing with stress. You can make an appointment with an adviser or speak to someone on the phone. Please complete a form to make an appointment.

VISITING A DOCTOR
When you start university, you should register with a medical centre. This is important if you take medicine regularly for a health issue. You can then make appointments to see your doctor. The nearest medical centres are Park Lane Health Centre and Elm Tree Medical Centre. Please contact the University Health Centre if you need help registering. If you are not registered with a doctor and you need medical help now, you should contact City Heights Hospital.

URGENT MEDICAL ATTENTION
For urgent medical treatment, you should go to the City Heights Hospital or call the national health advice line on 111.

6.3 Discuss a story: All students

1 🔊 6.13 Look at the picture. What is happening? Listen and check.

2 🔊 6.13 Listen again and answer the questions. In pairs, compare your answers.
   1 Who is Ethan?
   2 How does he feel?
   3 Who is Sally?
   4 How does she feel?
   5 Who is Mr Suárez?
   6 What kind of person is he?

3 In pairs, discuss the questions.
   1 Did the story remind you of your life? Why/Why not?
   2 Which character in the story is most like you?
   3 Can you remember a time you felt like the characters in the story?

MEDIATION

7.3 Work in a group: All students

1   In groups of three, complete the table. Student A leads the discussion, Student B takes notes and Student C is the spokesperson.

    Student A
    Maria, what's an advantage of living in the city?
    Student B/C
    In the city, you're close to shops, universities, doctors, etc.

2   Tell the class which is better: living in the city or the countryside. Use the notes to explain your answer.
    Student C
    We think that living in the … is better because …

	Living in the city	Living in the countryside
Advantages		
Disadvantages		

9.3 Take notes: All students

1   Look at the picture of someone who is stressed. In pairs, think of ways to reduce stress.

2   🔊 9.12 Listen to a presentation about reducing stress and make notes. In pairs, compare your notes. Did you write down the same things?

	Idea	Reasons
1		
2		
3		
4		
5		

10.3 Rewrite a text: All students

1   Look at the picture and read the article. Use a dictionary to check the meaning of any words you don't know.

HOW TO GET THE BEST PRICES ON ONLINE AUCTIONS

1   Do some research before you bid. Make sure the item you want is fairly priced.
2   Decide the maximum amount you want to spend before you bid.
3   Most people bid in multiples of ten, so you are more likely to win if you bid one dollar more than a multiple of ten.
4   Don't place a bid until just before the auction ends. If you bid earlier, it brings attention to the item for sale.
5   Look for auctions that end in the middle of the night because there will be less competition.

2   In pairs, continue the new version of the text with examples and explanations, so it is easier to understand.

How to get the best prices on online auctions

1   Do some research before you try to buy something in an online auction. For example, you could look at shops' websites to see how much the same product costs new or second-hand. Then you will know if the item you want to buy is a good price or not.

MEDIATION

4.3 Simplify a text: Student A

1. Read the reviews and highlight the important information.

2. Tell Student B the important information. Listen to him/her tell you about two more reviews.

3. In pairs, decide which cultural event you want to go to this weekend.

Art exhibition: Paintings from the Highlands

This exhibition has some interesting works by Scottish painters. It's a great way to learn about life in the Scottish Highlands. The paintings show the beautiful scenery of Scotland, but they also tell you about the traditional life of Scottish farmers. Unfortunately, the exhibition is quite small and there are only 30 paintings on display, but I still recommend going. The exhibition is open every day from 9.00 to 17.00 until the end of the month. It costs £5.50 per person, but there is a 20% discount for students.

Film: *Vanuatu*

This documentary is about the island of Vanuatu in the South Pacific and its plan to stop using plastic. Vanuatu is a small island with beautiful beaches. However, when the beaches started to become covered in plastic rubbish, two people living on the island began a campaign to clean up the beaches and stop using plastic bags in the island's shops. It's quite a long film, but it's very interesting and it will make you think about how to protect the environment. It's on at the City Cinema at 5.40 p.m., 8.00 p.m. and 10.30 p.m. Tickets cost £10.50.

8.3 Explain a diagram: Student A

1. Look at the graph that shows the results of a survey question. Explain it to Student B.

2. Listen to Student B and complete the information on the chart.

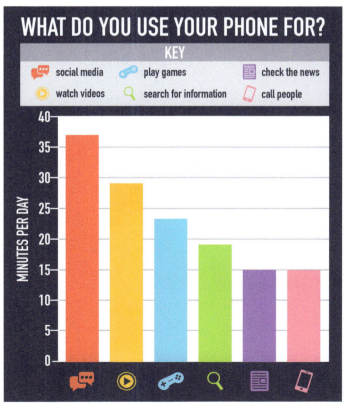

MEDIATION

4.3 Simplify a text: Student B

1. Read the reviews and **highlight** the important information.

2. Tell Student A the important information. Listen to him/her tell you about two more reviews.

3. In pairs, decide which cultural event you want to do this weekend.

Play: *Prince Panji*

Prince Panji is a love story about a famous Indonesian prince and princess and is told using traditional Indonesian shadow puppet theatre. The puppets that are used in the show are amazing. The performers hold them behind a white screen to create shadows and they also sing and provide the voices for the characters. This is a great opportunity to see a traditional type of entertainment from another country. All performances are in Indonesian, but you can read an English translation of the script and songs. It's on at the Park Theatre at 2.00 p.m. on Sunday and tickets are £25 per person.

Museum talk: Life in Ancient Egypt

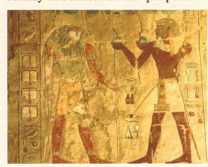

The City Museum is holding a series of talks about Ancient Egypt this month. Professor Farida Ahmed from the University of Cairo looks at what life was like for normal people living in Ancient Egypt – What work did they do? What clothes did they wear? What food did they eat? You might find the answers quite surprising! The talks are free, but the room where the talks take place is quite small, so if you're interested you should reserve places as soon as possible. The talks are at 3.00 p.m. on Saturday and Sunday and last approximately two hours.

8.3 Explain a diagram: Student B

1. Listen to Student A and complete the information on the graph.

2. Look at the chart that shows the results of a survey question. Explain it to Student A.

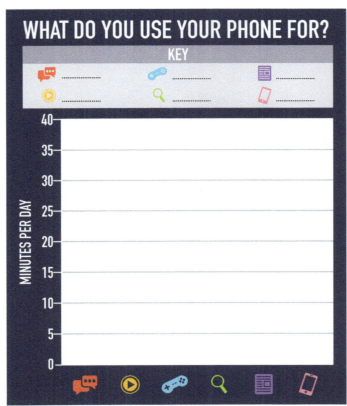

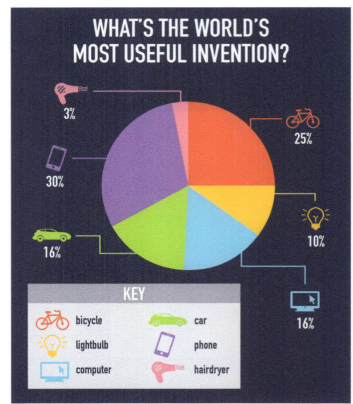

MEDIATION

11.3 Summarize a text: All students

1 Look at the picture and read the article.

2 Write a one-paragraph summary of the article. Make sure you include a sentence to introduce the topic and a sentence for each main idea.

3 In pairs, compare your summaries. Are they clear? Do they include all the key information?

Corporate Social Responsibility

These days, most companies have a CSR (Corporate Social Responsibility) policy. **This means they try to behave in a responsible way and help the planet and society … as well as making money.**

There are several ways that a company can do this. One way is to try to be environmentally friendly. This means making sure that the environment isn't polluted by factories and that recycled materials are used in products. Companies can also encourage staff to travel less for work.

Responsible companies should also treat all employees well and only work with suppliers that do the same. This means checking that workers of other companies they do business with have good working conditions and are paid fairly.

Some companies also help people more directly. They can donate money or products to charity. For example, the shoe company TOMS gives a pair of shoes to poor children every time someone buys a pair. Companies can also donate money or allow staff to use their work time to do charity work.

Although these actions might affect a company's profits, they can increase sales. Customers are more likely to want to buy products from companies that behave in the right way. In fact, according to one survey, 75% of shoppers said they would not buy from a company that did not behave ethically.

12.3 Work together: All students

1 You are trapped on an island and you must survive until you are rescued. You can choose five items to help you. In pairs, explain your reasons for choosing items and agree on which five items to use.

GRAMMAR REFERENCE UNIT 1

1.1 Present simple and adverbs and expressions of frequency

We use the present simple to talk about facts and regular routines and habits:
We live in San Francisco.
My wife takes the bus every day.

+	I/You/We/They He/She/It	speak speaks	English.
−	I/You/We/They He/She/It	don't doesn't	speak	French.
?	Do I/you/we/they Does he/she/it		speak	Spanish?
Y/N	Yes, I/you/we/they do. Yes, he/she/it does.	No, I/you/we/they don't. No, he/she/it doesn't.		

We use adverbs and expressions of frequency with the present simple to talk about routines and habits:
How often do you see your friends?
I usually see them every week.

Adverbs of frequency come before most main verbs:
John usually has a coffee at 11.00.
But they come after the verb *to be*:
I'm sometimes late. NOT *I sometimes am late.*

always — almost always — usually — often — sometimes — occasionally — hardly ever — never

Expressions of frequency can come at the start or end of sentences:
Once a week, I call my parents.
I call my parents once a week.

▶ 1.1

1.2 Present simple and present continuous

We use the present continuous to talk about things that are temporary or happening now:
I'm staying with my brother for a week.
Kim is wearing a beautiful scarf today.

+	I'm You're/We're/They're He's/She's/It's	having lunch.
−	I'm not You/We/They aren't He/She/It isn't	sitting here.
?	Am I Are you/we/they Is he/she/it	working today?
Y/N	Yes, I am. Yes, you/we/they are. Yes, he/she/it is.	No, I'm not. No, you/we/they aren't. No, he/she/it isn't.

We don't usually use state verbs (*be, like, love, hate, need, have, know, want, believe, understand*) with the present continuous:
I believe her story. NOT *I'm believing her story.*
Do you know the answer? NOT *Are you knowing the answer?*

▶ 1.2

1.1 a Complete the sentences with the present simple form of the verbs in brackets.
1 Where _____ you _____? (live)
2 My sister _____ a lot of sport. (do)
3 My friends _____ very hard. (not work)
4 Our boss always _____ to be funny. (try)
5 How often _____ Martin _____ TV? (watch)
6 Sheila _____ dancing every weekend. (go)

b Put the words in the correct order to make sentences.
1 don't / usually / lot / watch / of / we / TV / a
_____
2 my / every / talk / to / day / parents / I
_____
3 late / he / occasionally / class / for / is
_____
4 often / bus / you / how / take / the / do ?
_____
5 feel / weekend / I / lonely / at / never / the
_____
6 bed / always / to / almost / goes / she / late
_____

1.2 a Tick (✓) the correct sentences. Correct the sentences that are not correct.
1 I usually play football on Sundays. ☐
2 We are often chatting online in the evening. ☐
3 I'm not understanding the words of English songs. ☐
4 I'm learning French at the moment. ☐
5 We eat dinner right now. ☐
6 I'm not really liking sport. ☐

b Complete the conversation with the correct form of the verbs in brackets.

Tim Where (1) _____ you _____? (go)
May I (2) _____ (go) to my yoga class. I always (3) _____ (do) yoga on Mondays.
Tim What time (4) _____ the class _____? (start)
May It (5) _____ (start) at 6.00 p.m. and (6) _____ (finish) at 7.30. (7) _____ you _____ (want) to come?
Tim No, thanks. I (8) _____ (do) my homework right now. I (9) _____ (prefer) to finish it, so I can go out tonight.
May OK, see you later.

2.1 Past simple

We use the past simple to talk about completed actions and situations in the past:
I decided to go a different way.
They didn't have any water to drink.
To make questions and negative forms, we use *did/didn't* followed by the main verb in the infinitive form:
Did she have a mobile phone? NOT *Did she had a mobile phone?*
They didn't stay on the path. NOT *They didn't stayed on the path.*

+	You		watched bought	a TV show. a shirt.
−	We	didn't	watch buy	a TV show. a shirt.
?	Did	they	watch buy	a TV show? a shirt?
Y/N	Yes, they did.		No, they didn't.	

The past simple forms of irregular verbs don't end in *-ed* (see page 168 for a list of common irregular verbs):
buy → bought, lose → lost, see → saw, think → thought ▶ 2.1

2.2 Past continuous and past simple

We use the past continuous to talk about an action in progress at a specific time in the past:
Two years ago, Kit was living in Barcelona.
They were waiting for me when I arrived.

+	He You	was were	waiting for a bus.
−	I We	wasn't weren't	eating lunch.
?	Was Were	she they	driving to work?
Y/N	Yes, she was. Yes, they were.	No, she wasn't. No, they weren't.	

We use the past simple to describe a series of completed actions:
I woke up, I opened the tent and I saw a gorilla.

I woke up.   I opened the tent.   I saw a gorilla.

We use the past continuous with the past simple to show that an action was in progress at the time of another completed action. We usually use *while* + past continuous, or *when* + past simple:
I heard a strange noise while I was sitting in the tent.
I was sitting in the tent when I heard a strange noise.
I was sitting in the tent.

I heard a strange noise. ▶ 2.2

UNIT 2   GRAMMAR REFERENCE

2.1 Read the text about the adventurer Bear Grylls. Look at the verbs in **bold**. Find and correct five mistakes.

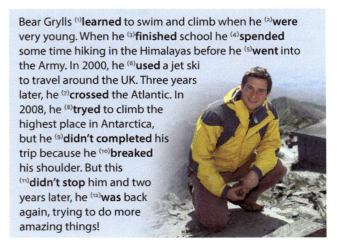

Bear Grylls (1)**learned** to swim and climb when he (2)**were** very young. When he (3)**finished** school he (4)**spended** some time hiking in the Himalayas before he (5)**went** into the Army. In 2000, he (6)**used** a jet ski to travel around the UK. Three years later, he (7)**crossed** the Atlantic. In 2008, he (8)**tryed** to climb the highest place in Antarctica, but he (9)**didn't completed** his trip because he (10)**breaked** his shoulder. But this (11)**didn't stop** him and two years later, he (12)**was** back again, trying to do more amazing things!

2.2 a João had a party last night. Use the verbs in the box to complete sentences about what the people were or weren't doing.

| choose | dance | eat | play | read | use |

1 João and Alice .... a laptop.
2 David .... a cake.
3 Leo .... some music.
4 Paulo and Amy .... cards.
5 Jon and Emily .... together.
6 Simon .... a magazine.

b Complete the text using the past simple or the past continuous forms of the verbs in brackets.

It was a beautiful day. The sun (1)................ (shine) and the sky was blue. We (2)................ (cycle) in the countryside when we (3)................ (hear) some dogs. But they were far away so we (4)................ (not think) any more about it and (5)................ (continue) on our ride. While we (6)................ (come) round a corner in the road, an enormous white dog (7)................ (jump) out in front of us. Three other dogs (8)................ (follow) him. They were wild dogs and we were scared. We (9)................ (shout) loudly and eventually they (10)................ (run) away.

GRAMMAR REFERENCE UNIT 3

3.1 Questions review

We use question words to ask for information:
What are you studying? *I'm studying Spanish.*
Where did he go? *He went to the shops.*
We don't use question words when we ask for a Yes/No answer:
Is he coming to the party? *Yes, he is.*
Do you work here? *No, I don't.*

Question word	Auxiliary verb	Subject	Main verb
Where	does	Jackie	work?
-	Can	you	speak Spanish?
Why	are	you	wearing that?
-	Did	I	see you yesterday?
What	was	Jin	doing this morning?

Questions with the verb *be* don't use an auxiliary verb. The subject comes after the verb *be*:
Is she an engineer? NOT ~~Does she be an engineer?~~
Where were you yesterday? NOT ~~Where you were yesterday?~~
Prepositions usually come at the end of questions:
Who was she talking to? NOT ~~To who was she talking?~~
What is she worried about? NOT ~~About what is she worried?~~

3.2 Relative clauses

We use relative clauses to say which person, thing, place or time we are talking about:
That's the man who I met yesterday.
I remember the day when Jeff and Anya got married.
Relative clauses begin with relative pronouns:

Relative pronoun	who/that	which/that	where	when
Refers to	people	things	places	times

She's the engineer who/that designed the new system.
This is the computer which/that I decided to buy.
Is this the town where your grandparents met?
We can't find a time when everyone is free.

3.3 Articles: *a/an*, *the*, no article

We use *a* (before consonants) or *an* (before vowel sounds) with singular nouns to talk about things for the first time:
I bought a new laptop and an e-reader last month.
We use *the* to talk about things we have already mentioned:
The new laptop is great and really fast.
We use *the* for things where only one exists or it's clear which one we mean:
You can only buy this phone on the internet.
We use no article in some common phrases with places:
He's going to bed/work/school/university/hospital/jail.
When we talk about things in general, we use a plural or uncountable noun and no article:
I like paintings and sculptures.
Milk comes from cows.
To talk about specific things, we use *the* with plural or uncountable nouns:
The paintings in the Louvre are amazing.
The milk from Ireland tastes great.

3.1 a Put the words in the correct order to make questions.

1 musical / instrument / you / play / can / a ?
2 lunch / go / do / where / you / for ?
3 to / music / listening / what / you / are ?
4 subjects / in / interested / he / which / was ?
5 last / what / you / night / did / do ?

b Write questions for the answers.
1 ....
I live in New York City.
2 ....
No, I'm not. I'm single.
3 ....
I'm reading a book about Mahatma Gandhi.
4 ....
I went to the cinema last night.

3.2 a Complete the sentences with the relative pronouns: *who*, *which*, *where* and *when*. Which ones can you change for *that*?

1 Do you know a place .... we can eat?
2 I know someone .... works in those offices.
3 Is there a time .... we can get together?
4 It's a machine .... cleans the carpet.

b Use the sentences to write relative clauses. Remember to remove any unnecessary pronouns.
1 This is the photo. I took it on holiday last year.
2 These are the people. We met them at the hotel.
3 That was the night. We arrived at the hotel.

3.3 Complete the sentences with *a/an*, *the* or – (no article).

1 **A** Where's your dad?
   B He's in .... kitchen.
2 Did you have .... interesting trip?
3 **A** Shall we go for .... walk?
   B Why not – that's .... great idea!
4 Paul's .... waiter. He works in Café Luxe near .... shopping centre.
5 I always drink .... coffee in the morning, but .... coffee you bought was horrible!

UNIT 4 GRAMMAR REFERENCE

4.1 *going to* and present continuous for plans and arrangements

We use *be + going to + infinitive* to talk about future plans:
I'm going to invite all my friends to my party next week.
If the main verb is *go*, we usually omit *to go*:
Jack's going (to go) swimming this afternoon.

+	I'm	going to	stay at home.
−	You aren't He isn't	going to	meet up with friends.
?	Am I Is she	going to	work tonight?
Y/N	Yes, I am. Yes, you are. Yes, he is.	No, I'm not. No, you aren't. No, he isn't.	

We can also use the present continuous for arrangements (where there is a fixed place or time):
I'm seeing Leanne this evening.
Where are you meeting her?
At the cinema. We're watching a film at 8.30.

▶ 4.1

4.2 *must(n't)* and *(don't) have to*

We use *must* + infinitive or *have to* + infinitive to talk about obligations and rules:
Pippa has to wear a uniform at work.
She must be at the office by 8.00 a.m.
When we ask questions about rules, we usually use *have to* + infinitive:
Do you have to lock the doors at night?
We use *mustn't* to say that an action is against the rules, or that it is important NOT to do something:
You mustn't use your phone in class.
We use *don't have to* + infinitive to say that it isn't necessary to do something (but you can if you want):
You don't have to wear a suit and tie in the office.

Have to	We She	have to has to	finish the report.
	Do Does	you she	have to	study Maths?
Don't have to	They He	don't doesn't	have to	wear a uniform.
Must	I	must	arrive at 8.00.
Mustn't	We	mustn't	eat too much sugar.

▶ 4.2

4.1
a Complete the conversations with *be going to* and the verbs in the box.

do	find	go	not go out	stop

1. **A** What .... you .... tonight?
   B I .... I'm too tired!
2. **A** Are you and Kris trying to be healthy?
   B Yes, we .... eating chocolate and do more exercise.
3. **A** .... Marta .... to university next year?
   B No, I think she .... a job.

b Which sentence is correct: a, b or both?

1. a I'm going to the theatre tonight.
   b I go to the theatre tonight.
2. a Jay is going to stay with Tim at the moment.
   b Jay is staying with Tim at the moment.
3. a Are you going to come with us tomorrow?
   b Are you coming with us tomorrow?
4. a They're moving to Edinburgh next year.
   b They're going to move to Edinburgh next year.

4.2
a Complete the sentences using *must*, *have to*, *don't have to* and *mustn't*. Sometimes more than one answer is possible.

1. You really .... study more if you want to pass the exam.
2. There's a free concert at the park tonight. You .... pay.
3. I .... call my mum this evening. It's her birthday!
4. There's a public holiday on Monday, so we .... work.

b Look at the sign and make sentences with *must*, *have to*, *don't have to* and *mustn't* and the verbs in brackets.

1. Adults .... $5.00 to enter. (pay)
2. Children .... to go swimming. (pay)
3. You .... around the pool. (run)
4. You .... a shower before you swim. (have)
5. You .... any food in the pool. (eat)

GRAMMAR REFERENCE UNIT 5

5.1 *should* and *must* for advice

We use *should/shouldn't* + infinitive to ask for and give advice:
What should I do?
You should eat more vegetables. They're good for you.
You shouldn't go to that restaurant. The food is horrible.

We can use *I think/don't think* + *should* to make advice sound less direct and more polite:
I think she should study Maths at university.
I don't think you should buy that phone.

Although we often use *must/mustn't* to talk about rules (see 4.2), we can also use it to give strong advice:
You must take an umbrella. It's going to rain.
You mustn't take the bus. It's too slow.

?	What	should	I	do?
+	You I think you You	should should must	tell	the truth.
–	You I don't think you You	shouldn't should mustn't	call	him.

▶ 5.1

5.2 *will, may, might* for predictions

We use *will* + infinitive to ask about and make predictions about the future:
Will the bus be late this morning?
It will be late. There's lots of traffic.
It won't be late. It's always on time.

We can use *definitely* after *will* and before *won't* to show that we are very sure about a prediction:
Anna called me. She'll definitely come tomorrow.
She definitely won't bring her children. They're with her parents.

We can use *probably* after *will* and before *won't* to show that we aren't sure about a prediction:
She'll probably come tomorrow. It depends on the trains.
She probably won't bring the children. They're very young.

We can also use *may/may not* or *might/might not* to say we are unsure about a prediction:
She may/might come tomorrow.
She may/might not bring the children.

100%	She'll definitely come to the party.
	She'll come to the party.
	She'll probably come to the party.
	She may/might come to the party.
	She may/might not come to the party.
	She probably won't come to the party.
	She won't come to the party.
0%	She definitely won't come to the party.

▶ 5.2

5.1a Do the sentences give strong advice (S), direct advice (D) or indirect advice (I)?

1 You should cook more often. It was absolutely delicious! ....
2 I think you should book a table. It's usually very busy at that restaurant. ....
3 I don't think you should tell Pippa about the party. Dan didn't invite her. ....
4 You must be more patient with Jo. He doesn't always understand. ....

b Read the questions and give advice using the phrases in the box and the type of advice in brackets.

> find a different course   not tell him
> ~~not buy it~~   go to Scotland

1 **A** Do you like this bag?
  B Yes, but it's really expensive. *I don't think you should buy it.* (indirect advice)
2 **A** Does Geraint know about the party?
  B No, but it's a secret. .... (strong advice)
3 **A** I'm not enjoying English classes. What should I do?
  B .... (indirect advice)
4 **A** Where's a good place for a walking holiday?
  B .... It's so beautiful there. (direct advice)

5.2 a Put the words in the correct order to make or ask about predictions.

1 rain / probably / tonight / will / it
....
2 bank / 6.00 p.m. / close / not / the / might / until
....
3 be / there / year / exam / will / an / this ?
....
4 may / they / a / later / barbecue / have
....
5 finish / by / my / won't / Friday / I / homework
....

b Complete the text using *will, won't, might* or *might not*.

> Dario and Lina are 6 years old. They (1) .... leave school for at least ten years. What (2) .... the world be like then? (3) .... their university courses be online? What languages (4) .... they need to know? Of course, they (5) .... want to continue their studies. They (6) .... want to do something else instead. But what jobs (7) .... be available? The same ones as today? We (8) .... just have to wait and see.

136

UNIT 6 GRAMMAR REFERENCE

6.1 Comparatives, superlatives, *as ... as*

We use comparative adjectives + *than* to compare two people or things.
English is easier than Japanese.
We use *the* + superlative adjectives to say that someone or something is more than all the others in a group:
Debbie is the most cheerful person I know.
For short adjectives, we usually add *-er* and *-est*:
old → older → oldest
But we add *-r* and *-st* to short adjectives ending in *-e*:
safe → safer → safest
We double the final consonant and add *-er* and *-est* to short adjectives ending in consonant + vowel + consonant:
hot → hotter → hottest
For adjectives ending in *-y*, we remove the *-y* and add *-er* and *-iest*:
busy → busier → busiest
Before longer adjectives, we use *more* and *most*:
beautiful → more beautiful → most beautiful
We can use *as ... as* to say that two people or things are the same: *My phone was as expensive as my computer.*
And we use *not as ... as* to say that two people or things are different to each other:
Their new house isn't as big as their old one. (= it's less big) ▶ 6.1

6.2 Present perfect with *ever* and *never*

We use the present perfect to talk about experiences. We often use *ever* with questions to emphasize that we're asking about an experience in our lives: *Have you (ever) tried sashimi? Yes, I have. I've tried lots of Japanese food.*
I haven't tried sashimi, but I'd like to.
We use *never* + positive form of the present perfect to emphasize that we haven't had an experience in our lives:
Sara has never tried Japanese food.
We form the present perfect with *have* + past participle of the main verb. Some past participles are irregular (see page 168).

+	I He	've 's		baked	bread.
−	We She	haven't hasn't		seen	that film.
	They He	've 's	never	been	to China.
?	Have Has	you she	ever	ridden	a bike?
Y/N	Yes, you have.			No, you haven't.	

The verb *go* has two past participles, *been* and *gone*:
He's been to London. (= He went to London at some time in the past, but he's not there now.)
He's gone to London. (= He went to London at some time in the past and he's still there now.)
We use the present perfect to ask an initial question about past experiences:
What's the most interesting country you've ever visited?
Thailand. Bangkok is great. I've been there twice.
But we use the past simple to ask for or give more information about specific events:
When did you go to Bangkok?   I went with my dad in 2019. ▶ 6.2

6.1 a Look at the table about three Australian cities. Complete the sentences with the comparative or superlative forms of the adjectives in brackets.

	Sydney	Melbourne	Perth
Population	4 million	3.5 million	1.5 million
Average temperature	26°	27.2°	31°
Rainfall per year	1,200 mm	650 mm	790 mm
Average house price	$815,000	$650,000	$470,000

1 The population of Melbourne is .... the population of Perth, but Sydney has .... population. (big)
2 Melbourne is .... Sydney, but Perth is .... city. (hot)
3 Melbourne is .... city, but Perth is .... Sydney. (dry)
4 .... houses are in Sydney, but houses in Melbourne are .... than in Perth. (expensive)

b Look at the table again. Complete the sentences using *not as ... as* and the adjectives in the box.

cheap   large   warm   wet

1 Houses in Melbourne .... they are in Perth.
2 Perth .... Sydney, where most of the rain falls in March.
3 The population of Perth .... the population of Melbourne.
4 Melbourne and Sydney .... Perth, which has hot, dry summers.

6.2 Complete the conversation using the correct present perfect or past simple forms of the verbs in brackets, or short answers.

A I (1) .... (always / want) to try kite-surfing.
B Really? I (2) .... (never / try) it, but my brother (3) .... (do) it.
A Where (4) .... (he / do) it?
B He (5) .... (do) it on a beach in Cornwall last year.
A (6) .... (he / like) it?
B Yes, a lot. He was quite good at it.
A (7) .... (he / ever / try) paragliding?
B No, he (8) .... (have), he's scared of heights!

137

GRAMMAR REFERENCE UNIT 7

7.1 Present perfect with *just, already, yet*

We use the present perfect with *just* to talk about something that happened a short time ago:
Are you hungry?   No, I'm not. I've just eaten.
We use the present perfect with *already* to show that something happened before the expected time:
Shall I load the dishwasher?   It's OK, I've already done it.
We use the present perfect with *yet* in negative sentences to talk about something that hasn't happened at the time of speaking, but will happen in the future:
Is lunch ready?   No, I haven't made it yet.
We use the present perfect with *yet* in questions to ask about something we expected to happen:
Have you cleaned the car yet?   No, I'll do it now.   ▶ 7.1

7.2 Present perfect with *for, since*

We use the present perfect to talk about the duration of a situation that started in the past and continues into the present:
How long have you lived in Mexico?
I've lived here all my life.
We use the present perfect with *for* to talk about a period of time and with *since* to talk about a start point:
How long has she known David?
She's known him for six months.
She's known him since December last year.
In addition to years, months, etc., we can use *for* and *since* with other words and phrases:
I've known Carmen for a long time/ages.
She's lived there since she got married/her wedding.
We use the past simple to talk about the duration of completed situations in the past:
How long did you live in Madrid?
I lived in Madrid for ten years.
How long have you lived in Tokyo?
I've lived in Tokyo since 2020.   ▶ 7.2

7.3 Linkers

We use linkers to connect ideas. We can use them to join two sentences, or to show how one sentence relates to another:
My new phone wasn't expensive. It takes great pictures. The battery doesn't last long.
My new phone wasn't expensive and it takes great pictures. However, the battery doesn't last long.
We use the linkers *and, as well, also* and *too* to add information:
Everyone in our flat pays rent. We also share the bills.
The park is really nice. It's opposite the office, too.
We use the linkers *but, although* and *however* to contrast information:
Sharing a flat is great fun, but it's sometimes quite noisy.
Although my family live near me, I don't see them very often.
I love living in London. However, it's very expensive.   ▶ 7.3

7.1 a Put the words in the correct order to make sentences.

1 watered / I've / plants / already / the
....
2 you / yet / the / out / bins / taken / have ?
....
3 yet / hasn't / up / kitchen / she / the / tidied
....
4 his / gone / friend's / he's / just / to / house
....

b Complete the conversation with *just, already* or *yet*.

A Have you seen the new James Bond film (1) .... ?
B No, what about you?
A No, I haven't. Do you want to come?
B Sounds great. Shall we invite Jin and Hal?
A Jin's (2) .... seen it. I heard him talking about it last week.
B And Hal?
A I've (3) .... spoken to him. He hasn't finished his exams (4) ...., so he needs to study tonight.
B Oh, OK.

7.2 a Complete the sentences with *for* or *since*.

1 They've been married .... ages.
2 Peter has worked in Glasgow .... 2017.
3 He's been in a meeting .... 11.00 a.m.
4 Have you known her .... a long time?

b Complete the conversation with the present perfect or past simple forms of the verbs in brackets.

A How long (1) .... you (work) for this company?
B I (2) .... (be) here for almost a year now.
I (3) .... (start) in October last year.
A Where (4) .... you .... (work) before?
B I (5) .... (not work). I (6) .... (be) a student at Business School.
A How long (7) .... you .... (study) for?
B I (8) .... (be) there for three years.

7.3 Choose the correct linkers to complete the sentences.

1 *Although / However* I enjoy studying English, it's not my favourite subject.
2 Lena is her best friend *as well / and* she talks to her every day.
3 Glastonbury is a quiet town. *However / Also*, it's very crowded during the festival.
4 This laptop is really good. It's easy to carry, *although / as well*.

UNIT 8 GRAMMAR REFERENCE

8.1 -ing form and to + infinitive

When we use two verbs together, the second verb can be in the -ing form or to + infinitive:
I enjoy learning English.   I decided to learn English.
Many verbs that describe plans or intentions are followed by to + infinitive:

decide	I decided to write a blog.
agree	We agreed to help her.
hope	She's hoping to study Music next year.
learn	I'm learning to play the piano.
manage	I managed to find a place with a garden.
plan	They're planning to buy a new house.
prefer	Do you prefer to read the news online?
promise	They've promised to visit me.
want	He doesn't want to go to the festival.
would like	I'd like to meet new people.

Many verbs that express emotions are followed by the -ing form:

enjoy	She enjoys making her own clothes.
hate	I hate doing the ironing.
look forward to	He's looking forward to starting the job.
not mind	I don't mind waiting for the bus.
recommend	He recommended taking the train.
spend time	They spent a lot of time shopping.
can't stand	I can't stand doing the washing up.
suggest	He suggested changing courses.
finish	I've finished writing my essay.
miss	She really misses seeing her friends.

We can use some verbs in either form without any change in meaning:
It has started to rain. = It has started raining.
He continued to work. = He continued working.

▶ 8.1

8.2 Quantifiers

We use quantifiers to talk and ask about quantities of things:
How much food is there in the fridge?
There is some meat and a few eggs, but there isn't any milk.
We use different quantifiers with countable and uncountable nouns:

	Countable nouns	Uncountable nouns
Questions	How many …?	How much …?
Quantities	lots of/a lot of some a few not many very few not any	lots of/a lot of some a little not much very little not any

▶ 8.2

8.1 Choose the correct words to complete the sentences.

1 I'm really looking forward to *going / go* away this weekend.
2 I can't afford *going / to go* on holiday this year.
3 I love *doing / to do* exercise at the gym.
4 I've decided *looking / to look* for a new job.
5 I'd like *staying / to stay* at home this evening.
6 I miss *having / to have* more free time.
7 I promise *calling / to call* you every day.
8 I hope *finishing / to finish* the project next month.
9 I suggested *speaking / to speak* to the teacher about the problem.
10 I recommend *going / to go* to see that film.

8.2 a Complete the conversations with the words in the box.

| any (x2) | few | little | lots |
| many | much | some | |

1 A Have you had your lunch?
  B No, there wasn't ……… food in the fridge.
2 A Do you want sugar in your tea?
  B Yes, please, I'll have a ……… sugar and ……… milk.
3 A Did you take ……… holiday photos?
  B Yes, I took a ……… pictures of the mountains.
4 A Is there a good place to eat near here?
  B Not really. There aren't ……… restaurants in this town.
5 A How ……… time do we have before the exam?
  B We have ……… of time. It starts at 1.00.

b Look at the picture and choose the correct words to complete the sentences.

1 There are *lots of / much / a little* people on the beach.
2 There isn't *a little / much / many* space on the sand.
3 There aren't *much / many / a few* people in the water.
4 There are *a few / much / lots of* clouds in the sky.

GRAMMAR REFERENCE UNIT 9

9.1 too, too much/many, (not) enough

too, *too much* and *too many* have a negative meaning. We use them to say that there is more than we want or need. *Too* is used with adjectives, *too much* is used with uncountable nouns and *too many* is used with countable nouns:
This sandwich is too big, I can't eat it all.
There's too much salt in the soup, it's disgusting!
There are too many people here, I can't sit down.

We use *enough* to mean the right amount for what we want or need. *Enough* comes before nouns, but after adjectives:
We have enough money for the trip.
Do we have enough cups for everyone?
It's warm enough to sit outside.

We use *not enough* to say that the quality or amount is less than we want or need:
There aren't enough chairs at the table. We need more.
The music isn't loud enough. I can't hear it.

▶ 9.1

9.2 First conditional

We use the first conditional to talk about possible situations in the future. The first conditional has an *if*-clause and a main clause. The main clause shows the result of the action in the *if*-clause:

	If-clause (action)	Main clause (result)
+	If I pass my exams,	I'll go to university.
–	If he doesn't arrive soon,	we won't catch the train.

We use the present simple in the *if*-clause. We usually use *will* + infinitive in the main clause:
If you listen to me, you'll know what to do.
If she doesn't prepare for the interview, she won't get the job.

The *if*-clause can come first or second:
If I come first in the race, I'll win a prize.
I'll win a prize if I come first in the race.

▶ 9.2

9.3 Adverbs of manner

We use adverbs of manner to say how someone does something or how something happens:
She was talking loudly.
Her heart's beating slowly.

Most adverbs of manner are formed by adding *-ly* to an adjective:

Adjective
He's a quick learner.
Please be careful with the box.

Adverb
He learns very quickly.
Put the box down carefully.

If an adjective ends in *-le*, we remove the *e* and add *y*:
gentle → gently

If an adjective ends in *-y*, we remove the *y* and add *ily*:
easy → easily

Some adverbs of manner are irregular.
good → well, hard → hard, fast → fast

▶ 9.3

9.1 Look at the pictures. Complete the sentences with the words in the box and *too, too much/many* or *(not) enough*.

| big | money | people | sugar |

1 I .... have .... to buy lunch.
2 There are .... on the train.
3 There's .... in this coffee.
4 Those shoes are .... for you.

9.2 Complete the conversations with first conditionals and the verbs in brackets.

1 **A** How can I do better?
   B If you .... for half an hour every day, you .... very quickly. (play / improve)
2 **A** Have you seen Teo? I need to talk to him.
   B No, but I .... him you're looking for him if I .... him. (tell / see)
3 **A** Are you going on holiday this year?
   B I'm not sure, but if we .... it, we .... abroad. (can afford / go)

9.3 Complete the sentences with the correct verbs and adverbs in the boxes.

drive	eat	carefully	clearly
finish	speak	healthily	quickly
sleep	think	slowly	well

1 My head hurts and I'm tired. I can't ....
2 I don't understand – can you .... more .... , please?
3 She's gone back to bed. She didn't .... very .... last night.
4 We don't have much time so can you .... this .... ?
5 If you don't .... , you'll have an accident.
6 I've stopped buying meat – I want to .... more ....

140

UNIT 10 GRAMMAR REFERENCE

10.1 Second conditional

We use the second conditional to talk about imaginary situations in the future. We use the past simple in the *if*-clause. We use *would* + infinitive in the main clause:

	If-clause (imaginary situation)	Main clause (imagined result)
+	If I paid less rent,	I'd have more money.
−	If he didn't get a loan,	he wouldn't buy the car.

The *if*-clause can come first or second:
If I had a better job, I'd earn more money.
I'd earn more money if I had a better job.
We can use *were* instead of *was* in the *if*-clause with *I/he/she/it*:
If I was/were a politician, I'd try to help.
We often use *If I were you, I'd …* to give advice:
If I were you, I'd tell her the truth.

▶ 10.1

10.2 *so* and *such*

We use *so* and *such* to emphasize something that we are talking about: *I feel so stressed. It was such a hard exam.*
We use *so* before adjectives:
The weather was so warm yesterday.
We use *such a/an* before singular nouns. We often put an adjective before the noun:
The children make such a (big) mess.
Our trip was such an (amazing) adventure.
We use *such* before plural and uncountable nouns. We often put an adjective before the noun:
She gave me such (good) advice.
So and *such* are often followed by a clause with *that* which expresses a result:
He was so angry that he left the room.
It's such a good salary that I can afford to buy a car.

▶ 10.2

10.3 Indefinite pronouns

We use indefinite pronouns to talk about people, places and things without saying exactly who, what or where they are:
Everybody was late for class.   I have something to help you.
Do you know anyone from Peru?   There's nowhere like home.
We use *every-* to talk about all, *some-* and *any-* to talk about one, and *no-* to talk about none of the people/things/places:

	People	Things	Places
All	everyone/everybody	everything	everywhere
One	someone/somebody anyone/anybody	something anything	somewhere anywhere
None	no one/nobody	nothing	nowhere

We usually use indefinite pronouns with *any-* in questions and negative sentences:
Have you seen anyone with red hair?
I don't have anything for you.
We usually use indefinite pronouns with *some-* in positive sentences: *I need to go somewhere quiet.*
We use indefinite pronouns with *no-* in positive sentences:
There was nobody there. NOT *There wasn't nobody there.* ▶ 10.3

10.1 a Match the halves to make second conditional sentences.

1 I'd get a job in London if   ....
2 If I knew the answer, ...
3 If we didn't have all this furniture, ...
4 She'd come with us to the cinema if ....

a we'd rent a smaller flat.
b I'd tell you.
c she didn't have an exam.
d I wanted to speak more English.

b Complete the sentences with the correct form of the verbs in brackets to make second conditional sentences.

1 I .... more money if I .... every weekend. (save / not go out)
2 If I .... you, I .... a new computer. (be / not buy)
3 I .... happier if I .... for a different company. (be / work)
4 If I .... more on work, I .... less time. (concentrate / waste)

10.2 a Complete the sentences so that they mean the same. Use *so* or *such (a/an)*.

1 The journey took .... long.
   The journey took .... long time.
2 Did you know they had .... big flat?
   Did you know that their flat was .... big?
3 They serve .... delicious food.
   The food they serve is .... delicious.
4 Louisa's .... kind and generous person.
   Louisa's .... kind and generous.

b Complete the sentences with *so*, *such (a/an)* and the adjectives in the box.

| bad | close | good | sad |

1 I live .... to my office that it only takes me five minutes to walk there.
2 We had .... time on holiday that we didn't want to come home.
3 He had .... exam results that he had to repeat the year.
4 It's .... film that I cried when it finished.

10.3 Complete the sentences with the correct indefinite pronouns.

1 I heard a knock at the door, but there was .... there.
2 We need .... who speaks Portuguese very well.
3 There is a good Wi-Fi signal .... you go in this building.
4 The clothes shop didn't have .... in my size.

141

GRAMMAR REFERENCE UNIT 11

11.1 Passives
We use active sentences to focus on the subject of the sentence: *My brother designed this car.*
We use passive sentences to focus on the action or the object of the sentence: *This car was designed by my brother.*
We also use the passive when we don't know the subject or it isn't important: *This shirt was made in Italy.*
We use the prepostion *by* in passive sentences to refer to the subject: *This shirt was designed by Ralph Lauren.*
We form the passive with the verb *be* and past participle of the main verb:

	Present	Past
+	These oranges are grown in Spain.	The film was directed by Pedro Almodóvar.
-	My jacket isn't made of leather.	Fireworks weren't invented in Europe.
?	Are you paid in euros?	Was the project finished on time?
Y/N	Yes, I am./No, I'm not.	Yes, it was./No, it wasn't.

The past simple passive is often used in formal speech, in written reports and news articles:
The miners were rescued yesterday.
▶ 11.1

11.2 *used to*
We use *used to* + infinitive to talk about regular habits and situations in the past:

+	I	used to		swim every day.
-	She	didn't use to		eat meat.
?	Did	they	use to	live in France?
Y/N	Yes, they did.		No, they didn't.	

We don't use *used to* for actions that only happened once:
I went to the USA in 2019. NOT *I used to go to the USA in 2019.*
We only use *used to* for the past. We use the present simple (often with *usually*) to talk about habits in the present:
We usually play tennis twice a week. NOT *We use to play tennis twice a week.*
▶ 11.2

11.3 Past perfect
We use the past perfect to talk about something that happened before another action in the past:
I went to the swimming pool after I had finished work.
I didn't pass my exam because I hadn't studied enough.
Had you worked in Marketing before you started the job?
We form the past perfect with *had* and the past participle:

+	We	had	finished.
-	You	hadn't	finished.
?	Had	it	finished?
Y/N	Yes, it had.	No, it hadn't.	

▶ 11.3

11.1 a Complete the second sentences in the passive so they mean the same as the first ones.
1 Charles Dickens wrote *Great Expectations* in 1861.
  Great Expectations _____.
2 They make these shirts from organic cotton.
  These shirts _____.
3 Someone stole my wallet yesterday.
  My wallet _____.
4 People eat turkey for Thanksgiving in the USA.
  Turkey _____.

b Complete the text with the present or past passive forms of the verbs in brackets.

Häagen-Dazs makes ice cream, cakes and frozen yoghurt. The brand (1) _____ (create) by Reuben and Rose Mattus in 1961. Starting with only three flavours, its first store (2) _____ (open) in New York in 1976. Now, *Häagen-Dazs* has dozens of flavours and its products (3) _____ (sell) in more than 50 countries around the world.
The name *Häagen-Dazs* has no special meaning. They are just two words which (4) _____ (choose) because they sound Danish and because Denmark (5) _____ (know) for its dairy products. *Häagen-Dazs* ice cream (6) _____ (make) using quality ingredients to produce delicious ice cream.

11.2 Tick (✓) the correct sentences. Correct the sentences that are not correct.
1 I used to live in Hamburg, but now I live in Berlin. ☐
2 Did you used to watch cartoons as a child? ☐
3 Sheila didn't use to like olives, but she does now. ☐
4 Jim used to go to the supermarket yesterday. ☐

11.3 Complete the sentences with past simple or past perfect forms of the verbs in brackets.
1 The train _____ when I _____ at the station. (leave / arrive)
2 The kitchen _____ dirty and nobody _____ the dishwasher. (be / load)
3 We _____ a hotel, but we _____ a nice place to stay. (not book / find)
4 She _____ really hungry because she _____ anything for lunch. (feel / not have)

142

UNIT 12 GRAMMAR REFERENCE

12.1 Reported speech

When someone speaks, we call what they say 'direct speech'. When we talk afterwards about what they said, we call it 'reported speech':
'I don't like it.' → *She said that she didn't like it.*
We use the verbs *say* and *tell* to report speech. We use a noun or pronoun with *tell* to say who the person was speaking to. We can also use *that* in reported speech:
'I'm nervous.' → *He said/told me (that) he was nervous.*
The tenses of the verbs usually change when we report speech:

Direct speech		Reported speech
present simple 'I like you.'	→	**past simple** She said she liked me.
present continuous 'I'm buying dinner.'	→	**past continuous** He said he was buying dinner.
past simple 'I read all three books.'	→	**past perfect** She said she had read all three books.
present perfect 'I've made a cake.'	→	**past perfect** She said she had made a cake.
past perfect 'I hadn't seen it before.'	→	**past perfect** He said he hadn't seen it before.
am/is/are going to 'We're going to ask him.'	→	**was/were going to** They said they were going to ask him.
will/won't 'They won't come.'	→	**would/wouldn't** He said they wouldn't come.
can/can't 'I can help you.'	→	**could/couldn't** She said she could help me.

In reported speech, pronouns and possessive adjectives also change:
'My brother loves you!' → *He said that his brother loved me.*
Other common changes:
here → *there*
today → *that day*
tomorrow → *the next day*
yesterday → *the day before*

▶ 12.1

12.2 Uses of the *-ing* form and infinitive

We use the *-ing* and infinitive forms of verbs in different ways in English. The *-ing* form can be used after prepositions:
I'm interested in learning the flute.
She's afraid of flying.
The *-ing* form can also be used as the subject or object of a sentence:
Listening to music is the best way to relax.
I love playing the guitar.
The infinitive form can be used after most adjectives:
I'm happy to help you.
It's difficult to answer that question.
The infinitive form can be used to express purpose:
I'm ringing to ask if you'd like to come with us.
Will you use a credit card to pay for this?

▶ 12.2

12.1 a Read the sentences in reported speech and write the direct speech.

1 She said she wanted to meet more people.
'*I want to meet more people.*'
2 Luke and Nuria said they would be at the party on Saturday.
'_____'
3 Marie said that she was feeling good that day.
'_____'
4 Chris and Soo said they couldn't go to the cinema the next day.
'_____'

b Look at the picture and report the conversations.

1 *Paola told Jan that there was a party that night* .
2 Jan told Hugo that _____.
3 Hugo told Giulia that _____.
4 Giulia told Franz that _____.
5 Franz said that _____.

12.2 Complete the sentences with the *-ing* or infinitive forms of the verbs in the box.

| find out | get up | pay |
| play | take | work |

1 _____ video games is my favourite free-time activity.
2 I'm interested in _____ about the German lessons.
3 Ruth is saving money _____ for her holiday.
4 I think it's really difficult _____ as a waiter.
5 I don't like _____ early in the morning.
6 Simon is really worried about _____ his exams.

WRITING BANK — UNIT 1

A personal profile

1 In pairs, discuss the questions.
   1 Which social media sites do you use?
   2 What personal information can people see?
   3 Is there any information you don't want to share?

2 a Look at the social media profile. In pairs, guess the answers to the questions. Read Gloria's profile and check.
   1 Is it a professional or personal social media site?
   2 Where does Gloria live?
   3 What is her job?

   b What is your impression of Gloria?

3 Read the profile again. Match the paragraphs with the topics.
   1 Current job   ....
   2 Hobbies   ....
   3 Personal information and qualities   ....
   4 Hopes and dreams   ....

4 Choose the correct form of the verbs to complete the sentences. Check your answers in the text.
   1 I *currently work* / *'m currently working* at a school in the city centre.
   2 I *love* / *'m loving* reading – you *never see* / *'re never seeing* me without a book!
   3 I also enjoy dancing and I *go* / *'m going* to a dance class every Monday evening.
   4 I *grow* / *'m growing* some tomatoes and peppers on my balcony at the moment.

5 Read the Writing box. Write a personal profile for a social media site.

> ### a personal profile
>
> When you write a personal profile, think about who will read it and what information you want to share.
> - Use a different paragraph for each topic.
> - Use the present simple to talk about things in general and the present continuous for things that are happening now.
> - Your writing can be informal and you can use contractions.

HOME   ABOUT   CONTACT   NETWORK   JOBS   MESSAGES

GLORIA GONZÁLEZ

Update info

 Buenos Aires
 Teacher

A Hi, I'm 24, I'm Argentinian and I live in Buenos Aires. I'm a primary school teacher and, in the classroom, I'm cheerful and confident. I'm also very calm because I think that children learn best when they're relaxed.

B I'm currently working at a school in the city centre. It's a good job because the children are fun, and the other teachers are really friendly. I'm also learning a lot because most of the other teachers have a lot of experience.

C I'm happy in my job, but one day I'd like to be a head teacher because I'm very organized and I enjoy having responsibilities.

D In my spare time, I love reading – you never see me without a book! I also enjoy dancing and I go to a dance class every Monday evening. But my newest hobby is gardening. I'm growing some tomatoes and peppers on my balcony at the moment.

UNIT 2 WRITING BANK

An informal message

1 In pairs, discuss the questions.
1 How do you keep in touch with friends and family?
2 Which way of communicating do you like the most?
3 Which ways don't you like? Why not?

2 Look at the pictures and guess the answers to the questions. Read the messages and check.
1 What are Sandra and Luis doing?
2 Where are they?
3 What is the relationship between them?

3 Read the sentences from the messages. Are they used to start a message (S), end a message (E), ask for information (I), or attach a picture (P)?
1 I hope you're well.
2 Check out this picture of …
3 Well, that's all for now.
4 Here's a photo of …
5 It's great to hear from you!
6 Let me know …
7 How's everything going?
8 Speak soon.
9 Thanks for your message.
10 I just wanted to find out …
11 Take care.
12 Looking forward to hearing from you soon.

4 Which word do both Sandra and Luis use to start a new paragraph with a different topic?

5 a Read the Writing box. Then write an informal message to your partner telling him/her about your news and inviting him/her to meet up.

b Read your partner's message and reply.

✏️ an informal message

We write informal messages to friends to keep in touch and exchange news.
- Start and end the message in a friendly way.
- Mention earlier messages if you're replying.
- Use contractions and a spoken style: *Well, … Anyway, …*

Messages

Sandra
Hi Luis,
How's everything going? I hope you're well. Sorry for not getting in touch until now. I started a new job last month and I've been really busy. I'm working as a park ranger in Banff National Park in the Rocky Mountains. It's an amazing place. Here's a photo of me at work. 🙂
14.38

Sandra

Sandra
Anyway, I just wanted to find out what you're doing this summer. I'm renting an apartment in Calgary and I have lots of space for visitors, so it would be great to see you if you want to visit. Let me know if you're free and if you can come.
Well, that's all for now. Looking forward to hearing from you soon.
Take care.
14.42

Luis
Hello Sandra,
Thanks for your message. It's great to hear from you! I'm fine. I'm still working on my archaeology project at university. We went on a field trip to Guatemala a few months ago, which was fantastic. Check out this picture of me at work – always the hardworking student! 😉
15.01

Luis

Luis
Anyway, I'm really glad to hear that you have a new job. The national park looks beautiful and I'd love to come and visit you. I finish university on 28 June so I can come any time in July – just let me know which dates are best for you.
Speak soon.
15.03

WRITING BANK UNIT 3

A blog post

1 In pairs, discuss the questions.
   1 How much have you travelled in your country?
   2 What are the most iconic places to visit there?

2 Look at the pictures. In pairs, guess the answers to the questions. Read the blog and check.
   1 Which place did Jack visit?
   2 Is it an iconic place? Why?

3 Read the blog again and match the paragraphs with the sections.
   1 recommendations for readers ....
   2 journey to the destination ....
   3 reason for travelling ....
   4 what happened during the visit ....

4 a Complete the sentences with the linkers in the box. Check your answers in the text.

   | because   because of   so   that's why |

   1 I'm lucky to live in such a big and beautiful country. .... I get in the car and visit somewhere new.
   2 It's an iconic place for all Australians, ... I decided to visit.
   3 My friends told me to fly .... the distance, but I'm glad I drove.
   4 You aren't allowed to climb on the rock .... it's disrespectful to the Aboriginal people.

b Look at the sentences again and answer the questions.
   1 Which two linkers do we use to introduce a reason for something?
   2 Which of these do we use before a noun?
   3 Which two linkers do we use to introduce a result of something?
   4 Which of these starts a new sentence?

5 Read the Writing box. Then choose an interesting place you have visited and write a blog post about it.

✎ a blog post

When you write a blog, make it interesting and relevant.
- Start with a short introduction explaining why you are writing the post. Then write a paragraph for each idea.
- Use the linkers *because* (*of*), *so* and *that's why* to introduce reasons and results.
- Give your opinions and explain how you felt.

Hit the road, Jack

Hi, I'm Jack Kline and I'm from Sydney, Australia. I'm lucky to live in such a big and beautiful country. That's why I get in the car and visit somewhere new whenever I get the chance. I love visiting parts of my country that I've never seen before.

A ROCK THAT TAKES YOUR BREATH AWAY!

A This incredible rock is sometimes called Ayers Rock, but its Aboriginal name is Uluru. It's extremely important for the Aboriginal people who have lived there for thousands of years, but it's an iconic place for all Australians, so I decided to visit.

B We left Sydney on Tuesday and the journey took three days. My friends told me to fly because of the distance, but I'm glad I drove. Driving along miles of flat, empty roads made me realize that Uluru really is in the middle of nowhere!

C We arrived at lunchtime and we were all amazed at how big and beautiful it was. You aren't allowed to climb on the rock because it's disrespectful to the Aboriginal people, but that doesn't matter. In fact, I think it makes you appreciate its beauty even more. As the sun moved through the sky, Uluru changed colour, from yellow, to orange, to red! We couldn't stop taking photos! In the evening, we ate a picnic and looked up at thousands of stars. It was an amazing experience and now I really understand why this place is so special.

D If you get the chance, you should definitely visit Uluru. And don't just stay for one day. Spend one or two nights there so you can see the sunset and sunrise. You won't regret it! And if you can't go, you can now visit this iconic place on Google Street View!

Posted: 16 April

UNIT 4 WRITING BANK

A formal email

1 Look at the job search website. Which jobs are being advertised?

2 Read Stefan's email and answer the questions.
1 Which job is he applying for?
2 Do you think he will get the job? Why/Why not?
3 What is the style of the email?

3 Read the email again. Put the parts of the email in the correct order.
a ☐ why he is writing
b ☐ greeting
c ☐ when he can work
d ☐ ending
e ☐ his skills and experience

4 Choose the correct words to make formal phrases. Check your answers in the text.
1 Dear *Juliana,* / *Ms Wilson,*
2 I *am writing* / *'d like* to apply for …
3 … the *waiter job* / *position of waiter*
4 I *think* / *believe* that I am …
5 *In addition,* / *What's more* I like talking …
6 I *am able to* / *can* work from the beginning of July …
7 *Please find attached* / *Here is* my CV.
8 If you have any questions, *just ring* / *do not hesitate to contact* me.
9 *Looking* / *I look* forward to hearing from you.
10 *Yours sincerely,* / *All the best,*

5 Read the Writing box. Then write an email applying for one of the other jobs.

✏️ a formal email

We write formal emails to people we don't know. They are usually about important things.
- Use a formal greeting: *Dear Mr/Mrs Smith* or *Dear Sir/Madam*
- Explain why you are writing. Then use paragraphs to separate your ideas.
- Use formal words and phrases.
- Don't use contractions: *I have never worked …* NOT *I've never worked …*
- End the email formally: *Yours sincerely/faithfully.*

JobFinder — Sector > Tourism

Travel agent for independent travel company. Main responsibility: administration of transport and accommodation bookings.

The successful applicant will:
- be interested in travel
- have experience with computer programs
- speak more than one language

Contact: Kim.Smith@sun-travel.co.uk

We are looking for friendly, enthusiastic waiters to serve food and drinks at the Water Park Restaurant. No experience needed, but must be hard working and good with customers.
- Contract June–September
- Good rates of pay
- Flexible working hours

Please send CV to Juliana Wilson (HR Manager)

Friendly receptionist for city centre hotel. No experience necessary, but must be quick to learn and available to work evenings and weekends.
- Good salary
- 28 days holiday per year
- Career progression

Please apply to: staff@RH-Hotel.net

Dear Ms Wilson,

I am writing to apply for the position of waiter advertised on the JobFinder website. I am a university student, but I am looking for a temporary job this summer.

I have never worked in a water park, but I worked as a waiter in my uncle's restaurant for three months last year. I believe that I am a friendly, polite person and I enjoy working in a team. In addition, I like talking to customers and helping people.

I am able to work from the beginning of July, after my exams finish, until the end of August. Please find attached my CV. If you have any questions, do not hesitate to contact me.

I look forward to hearing from you.

Yours sincerely,

Stefan Krantz

WRITING BANK UNIT 5

An opinion essay

1 a Look at the pictures. In pairs, discuss the questions.
   1 What voluntary work are the people doing?
   2 Have you ever done a voluntary job?
   3 Is volunteering a good idea? Why/Why not?

   b Read the essay 'Is volunteering a good thing?' and compare your ideas with the writer's.

2 Put the parts of the essay in the correct order.
   a ☐ why volunteering helps society
   b ☐ conclusion
   c ☐ why volunteering helps volunteers
   d ☐ introduction

3 Look at the mind map. Which examples <u>didn't</u> the writer include in the essay?

4 Read the Writing box. Then choose a title and write an opinion essay.
   a Should we give money to homeless people?
   b Is having pets a good thing?
   c Will everyone speak English in the future?
   d Should we all become vegetarian?

✎ an opinion essay

In an opinion essay, we give arguments to support our point of view.

- Plan the essay by drawing a mind map with the main arguments and reasons to support them.
- Introduce the essay with your opinion and say what you will write about.
- Start a new paragraph for each argument and choose the best ideas from the plan to support them.
- Finish with a conclusion that summarizes the ideas.

Is volunteering a good thing?

I think that there are many advantages to volunteering. In this essay, I will look at some of the benefits to society and also to the volunteers.

Everyone needs help at some time in their life, but sometimes friends, family and the government can't help the people who need it. That's why volunteering is important. Volunteers can work for food banks – collecting food and giving it to people who can't afford to buy it. Some elderly people don't go out very often and can get lonely, but volunteers can visit and spend time with them or help them leave the house. And volunteers can also work together to clean public spaces so that people can enjoy them. All of these activities help to build a happier, stronger community.

Volunteering also helps the people who do voluntary work. Most volunteers say they feel happier and more confident when they help others and they also meet new people and make new friends. Volunteers often understand the world better because they see different parts of society and meet people from different backgrounds. And volunteers can even learn new skills, such as communication and management, which will help them in their careers.

In conclusion, I believe that volunteering is a very good thing. It helps society and makes the world a better place. In my opinion, everyone should try to volunteer because you'll enjoy it and learn from it.

UNIT 6 WRITING BANK

A web forum comment

1. Look at the title of the web forum post below. What do you think Eric's problem is? Read his post and check.

2. In pairs, answer the questions.
   1. Do you know anyone who moved cities for a job?
   2. What would you do in Eric's situation?
   3. What advice would you give Eric?

3. Read Emma's response. Was it similar to your advice? What do you think Eric will do?

4. Complete the sentences from Emma's reply with the sentence adverbs in the box. Check your answers in the text.

actually	clearly	hopefully
luckily	unfortunately	

   1. ……………, I was in the same situation last year.
   2. ……………, I was quite lonely for the first few months.
   3. ……………, I really enjoy my work and my new colleagues are great.
   4. ……………, if there aren't any design jobs in your area, you don't really have a choice.
   5. ……………, you'll find that life's just as good in the new city.

5. Read the Writing box. Then read Natalia's problem and write a response.

   ### ✎ a web forum comment

   People often discuss problems and give advice in web forums.
   - Be friendly and polite, but use an informal style.
   - Mention your own experience if it is relevant.
   - Give balanced advice to help the person make a decision.
   - Use sentence adverbs to get the reader's attention and emphasize your points.

   Natalia
   Posted 20 minutes ago

   Nightmare flatmate!
   I'm at university and sharing a flat with a friend of mine, but she isn't very clean and so I do all the housework. She cooks sometimes, but the kitchen is always a mess afterwards. When I complained once, she said she understood, but nothing has changed. What should I do?

WRITING BANK | UNIT 7

A promotional leaflet

1 Look at the pictures. In pairs, answer the questions.

1 What problems do they show?
2 Are any of these things a problem where you live?
3 What can local people do to solve problems like these?

2 Read the leaflet and answer the questions.

1 Who wrote it?
2 Why did they write it?
3 Who do they want to read it?

3 Match the three examples in the leaflet with the type of project. Can you think of other projects that would help your community?

1 Doing voluntary work   ....
2 Raising money   ....
3 Asking for help   ....

4 a Read the leaflet again. In pairs, find examples of:
1 addressing the reader as 'you'
2 rhetorical questions (questions that we don't expect an answer to)
3 imperatives (orders to do or not do things).

b Why does the writer do these things?

5 Read the Writing box. Then think of a project that would help your local community. Write a promotional leaflet encouraging local people to help.

✎ a promotional leaflet

In a promotional leaflet, you're trying to sell an idea.
- Use a title that catches people's attention.
- Address the reader as 'you' so it's more personal.
- Use rhetorical questions to make the readers think about the topic.
- Use imperatives to tell readers what to do.

YOUR NEIGHBOURHOOD NEEDS YOU! StreetWorks

Are you tired of seeing the same problems in your neighbourhood every day? Parking problems, potholes in the road, graffiti on the walls … Do you want your neighbourhood to be a better place to live? Don't wait for someone else to do something – the best person to make the change is YOU!

StreetWorks is a charity that helps you to help your neighbourhood. We give you support and advice at every step and we are completely free. Here are some examples of projects that StreetWorks has already helped with.

Street libraries – residents in Tamworth Street, Highbury started their own library! There are shelves of books in an old phone box and anyone can take one and leave another.

Slow zones – residents of south Grangetown were tired of cars driving too fast through their streets. So, they complained to the local government. Now there is a 20 mph limit in the whole neighbourhood!

Fun runs – many communities have organized running races, which raise money for the local area. The community chooses how to spend the money.

So, what are you waiting for? It's time to make a difference! Visit www.streetworks.co.uk today for more ideas and a starter pack.

UNIT 8 WRITING BANK

A for-and-against essay

1 Look at the picture. Which sentence do you think is true? Why?

The students are …
a using their phones to help them study.
b using their phones for entertainment.
c trying to study, but are distracted by their phones.

2 a In pairs, think of the advantages and disadvantages of students having phones in class.

Advantages	Disadvantages

b Read the essay. Which of your ideas did it include?

3 Put the topic sentences in the correct places in the essay. What is the writer's opinion? In which part of the essay is the opinion?

a Firstly, students can use their phones to learn things.
b In many countries, most people have a phone with internet access.
c In conclusion, I would say that phones can be a problem in class.
d On the other hand, phones can distract students from work.

4 Find phrases in the text with a similar meaning.

1 pros and cons of / arguments for and against / ....
2 to start with / in the first place / ....
3 in addition / another advantage is that / ....
4 however / whereas / ....
5 to sum up / taking everything into account / ....

5 Read the Writing box. Then write a for-and-against essay: 'Video games are a waste of time. Discuss.'

✎ a for-and-against essay

In a for-and-against essay you present both sides of an argument.
- Introduce the topic and explain there are different points of view.
- Explain the advantages and disadvantages in separate paragraphs, giving two or three reasons.
- Conclude the essay with your personal opinion.

Students should not be allowed to use their phones in class. Discuss.

❶ ....

People of all ages use them at home, in the office, on the bus and in the street. So why do many people believe students shouldn't use them in the classroom? There are advantages and disadvantages of using phones in the classroom.

❷ ....

We use the internet to check information all the time in the real world, and the way we learn should be the same. What's more, there are many good apps, dictionaries and websites for learners, so one small phone can replace lots of heavy books.

❸ ....

It's very difficult to listen to the teacher and other students if you receive messages and phone calls in class. Another disadvantage is that some students might use phones to cheat in a test, and so teachers won't know if students have learned what they need to.

❹ ....

Students need to listen and think on their own, and it isn't easy to ignore your phone. However, they are very useful for homework, so I think teachers should encourage students to use their phones for self-study.

WRITING BANK   UNIT 9

An invitation

1. Look at the pictures. Which event would you most like to go to? Why?

2. Read the emails. In pairs answer the questions.
   1. Which events does Cherie invite people to?
   2. Which events is Jamie coming to?
   3. Which events is Luna coming to?

3. Read the emails again. Are the sentences true (T) or false (F)? Underline the sentences in the emails that gave you the answers.
   1. Cherie has already bought the tickets for the group. ....
   2. She wants to have a picnic before the match. ....
   3. She only asks people to contact her if they want to come. ....
   4. Jamie can't come to the football match. ....
   5. Jamie knows what he is going to bring to the picnic. ....
   6. Luna wants to buy her own ticket for the match. ....

4. a Complete the sentences with the words in the box. Check your answers in the text.

bring	count	free
let	make	plans

   1. Are you .... on Saturday?
   2. Can you email me to .... me know if you are coming or not?
   3. The football sounds like fun, but I'm afraid I can't .... it.
   4. What should I ....?
   5. .... me in!
   6. I already have .... in the afternoon.

   b Which sentences are used in a) making b) accepting c) declining invitations?

5. a Read the Writing box. Then think of an event and write an invitation to your partner.

   b Swap invitations with your partner and write a reply.

✏️ an invitation

We often send informal invitations via text or email.
- When you write an invitation, include information about the event (date, time, location, etc.).
- Ask people to confirm if they will attend.
- When you reply, always thank the person for inviting you.
- When you accept, ask what to bring or wear.
- When you decline, it's polite to give a reason why.

To: Jamie, Luna, Petra, Sue +12 others
From: Cherie Golding

Hi guys,

Are you free on Saturday? A few of us are going to watch our local football team, the Lions, play Highbridge United. The match starts at 12.30 and there are still tickets available for £10 each. Afterwards, we're going to have a picnic in Victoria Park.

Can you email me to let me know if you are coming or not? Then I can buy all the tickets and you can pay me back.

I really hope you can all come. It should be fun!

Cherie

To: Cherie Golding
From: Jamie Harding

Hi Cherie,

Thanks for the invite. The football sounds like fun, but I'm afraid I can't make it. But I'd love to come to the picnic! What time will you be there, and what should I bring? I'm looking forward to seeing you.

Jamie

To: Cherie Golding
From: Luna Butron

Hi Cherie,

Great idea to support our local team – count me in! Is it OK if I pay you back on Saturday? I'd love to come to the picnic, but I already have plans in the afternoon.

Luna

152

UNIT 10 WRITING BANK

A complaint

1 In pairs, discuss the questions.
  1 What types of things do you order online?
  2 Have you ever had any of these problems?
   - the package arrived late
   - the package didn't arrive
   - the wrong product was sent
   - the product was damaged
   - the product was the wrong size/colour
   - the product wasn't good quality
   - a part was missing
   - the company charged you too much
  3 How do you complain when you have a problem?

2 Read Varinder's email and answer the questions.
  1 What did he buy?
  2 What three problems did he have?
  3 What does he want the company to do?

3 Put the sections of the complaint in the correct order. Check your answers in the text.
  a ☐ Describe the problem.
  b ☐ End your email in a formal way.
  c ☐ Start your email with a formal greeting.
  d ☐ Explain what you want to happen.
  e ☐ Give your reason for writing.

4 Complete the sentences with the words in the box. Check your answers in the text.

| complain | disappointed | expect |
| happy | please | unfortunately |

  1 I am writing to .... about …
  2 I am not .... with …
  3 I was .... to see that …
  4 ...., I also noticed that …
  5 .... could you send me …
  6 I also .... to receive a refund for …

5 Read the Writing box. Choose a product you have bought online and one or more of the problems from exercise 1 and write a complaint.

✎ a complaint

Written complaints should be formal so that you sound polite.
- Use a formal email style (see page 147).
- Include the order reference/date as subject.
- Say why you are writing, explain the problem(s) and say what you want the company to do.

To: info@highlands.clothing
From: varinder.harpal@x-mail.com
Subject: Problem with my order (H2886301)
Attachment 📎 jacket

Dear Sir/Madam,

I am writing to complain about a jacket that I ordered online from you last week. A friend told me that you sell high-quality jackets and have a good sales service, but I am not happy with the quality of the jacket or the service I received.

When I ordered the jacket, I paid £4.50 for next-day delivery, but I had to wait almost a week before it arrived. What's more, when it finally arrived, I was disappointed to see that the size was too big. I ordered a medium, but the jacket I received was a large. Unfortunately, I also noticed that there was a mark on the jacket. Please see the attached photo.

Please could you send me the correct jacket as soon as possible and tell me how to return the one I have. I also expect to receive a refund for the delivery cost.

I look forward to hearing from you soon.

Yours faithfully,

Varinder Harpal

WRITING BANK UNIT 11

A report

1 In pairs, discuss the questions.
1 Is it easy to find a job after you graduate?
2 What problems can graduates have looking for jobs?
3 What can graduates do to help them find a job?

2 Read the report and compare your answers.

3 Read the text again and put the headings in the box in the correct place.

> Investigation   Recommendations
> Results   Introduction

4 Choose the correct options to complete the sentences. Check your answers in the text.
1 The *aim / result* of this report is to show what problems graduates can have …
2 … a short *survey / question* was written …
3 Ten companies were *asked / interviewed* to understand the problems …
4 … the results were *analysed / shown*.
5 Our research showed that there is one *main / high* problem.
6 However, our research also discovered other *issues / interests*.
7 After looking at the *results / research* of the investigation, we can make three recommendations.
8 Students should get as much *job / work* experience as possible before they graduate.

5 Read the Writing box. Then write a report titled: 'Why people want to study English and how to improve courses.'

✏️ a report

A report is easy to read, shows the results of an investigation and often makes recommendations.
- Use headings to show what each section is about.
- We often use passives in a report: *A survey was written*. NOT ~~I wrote a survey~~.
- Use clear sentences and graphs to show results.

FROM UNIVERSITY TO WORK: A REPORT ON GRADUATE JOBS

By Sandra Smith and Maxi Pereira

These days, many graduates are still looking for work months, or even years, after graduating. The aim of this report is to show what problems graduates can have finding jobs and what students can do to improve their chances of getting a job.

To find out what the problems are, a short survey was written and was sent to twenty companies in the local area. There were sixteen responses. Ten companies were interviewed to understand the problems better and the results were analysed.

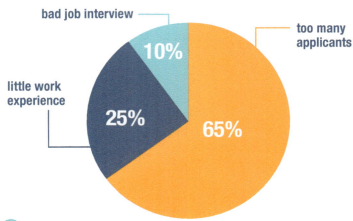

Our research showed that there is one main problem. Every company told us that there are too many applicants for jobs. However, our research also discovered other issues. Many graduates have little or no work experience and companies prefer to offer jobs to people who have worked before. Finally, some employers told us that graduates often did badly at job interviews.

After looking at the results of the investigation, we can make three recommendations:
- Graduates should not only look for work near their homes, but should apply for jobs in other areas of the country.
- Students should get as much work experience as possible before they graduate. This could be part-time work or volunteering at the same time as studying.
- Universities should help graduates by teaching them interview skills.

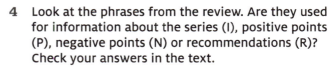

A review

1 Look at the picture. What kind of series is this? Read the review and check.

2 In pairs, discuss the questions.
 1 Have you seen the series?
 2 If so, did you like it?
 3 Which series do you enjoy watching?
 4 How do you decide which series to watch?

3 Read the review again and put the words in the box into the correct columns.

acting   music   scenery
special effects   suitability for children

Positive points	Negative points

4 Look at the phrases from the review. Are they used for information about the series (I), positive points (P), negative points (N) or recommendations (R)? Check your answers in the text.
 1 One of the best things about … is …   ....
 2 You won't be disappointed by …   ....
 3 I'm afraid to say that …   ....
 4 Overall, I highly recommend …   ....
 5 The story is based on …   ....
 6 If you like …, then you'll love …   ....
 7 It's about …   ....
 8 One criticism I'd make about the series is …   ....

5 Read the Writing box. Then write a review of a TV series, film or book that you have watched or read recently.

a review

In a review, we tell people about something and explain why we (don't) recommend it.
- Start with the general information.
- Mention the positive then the negative points.
- Express your personal opinion and give a recommendation at the end.

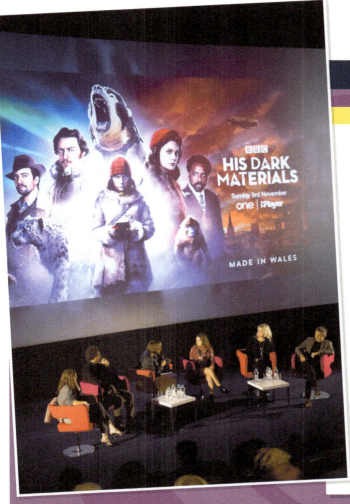

His Dark Materials is a fantasy series which lots of people are talking about at the moment. The story is based on Philip Pullman's famous novels. It's about two children, Lyra and Will, and their journey through different worlds to save their friends. Dafne Keen plays Lyra, the main character, and it also stars Scottish actor, James McAvoy. You can watch it on BBC or HBO.

The acting is fantastic, especially by the younger actors. However, one of the best things about this series is the amazing special effects. Every character has an animal which represents their personalities and you quickly forget that they're not real. You won't be disappointed by the scenery either. Although it's a fantasy series, it's set in a world very similar to our own, and it is filmed in the city of Oxford and other beautiful locations.

One criticism I'd make about the series is that although it looks like a children's series, some young children are frightened by it. I'm also afraid to say that the music isn't as good as other series on TV at the moment.

Overall, I highly recommend the series for teenagers and adults. If you like exciting fantasy worlds, then you'll love *His Dark Materials*.

EXAM PRACTICE UNIT 1

Writing an email

✓ exam information

In this part of the exam you write an email in response to another email.

1. Look at the exam task. In pairs, answer the questions.
   1. How do you know who to write to?
   2. What information must you include?

💡 tip

Notice if the email style is formal or informal.

Make sure you include an answer to each note in your email.

Don't add extra information that is not asked for.

Organize your email into paragraphs and link your ideas together logically.

2. Read the tip box and the exam task. In pairs, answer the questions.
   1. What is the relationship between you and Lee?
   2. What is the topic of the email?

3. Read the sample answers. In pairs, answer the questions.
   1. Which one replies to all four notes?
   2. Which one includes some unnecessary information?
   3. Which one is well organized and links ideas well?
   4. Which one is too formal?

4. Now plan your answer to the exam task. Make some notes before you write.

5. Write your email. Then, swap with a partner. Give each other advice about how to improve your emails.

A

Hi Lee

That's fantastic news about the job! I'm so happy about it!

July is good for me because university finishes at the end of June, and I'm not going on holiday until the end of September.

I'd love to work in the office. I had a job last summer working for a company that sells kitchens. I had to make phone calls and send emails so I'm quite good at all that now.

Personally, I'd prefer to work full time. That way we could earn more money. I know you're saving up for a car and I need money for my holiday.

Thanks and see you soon.

Luis

B

Dear Lee

I was very happy to get your email. I'd like a part-time job, please. I love running and other sports and I need time for that. I would like to apply for the job of theatre assistant. I am good at drama and I want to be an actor one day. I am in a drama club in my town. I played the lead role in the last play. Everyone said I was very good. If I can get enough money from this job, I'll pay for an acting course. An acting course will help in my career.

Thank you for your help.

Miguel

exam task

Read this email from your English-speaking friend Lee, and the notes you have made.
Write your email to Lee using all the notes. Write your answer in about **100 words**.

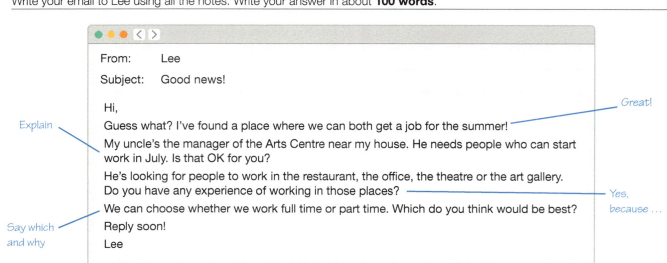

From: Lee
Subject: Good news!

Hi,

Guess what? I've found a place where we can both get a job for the summer! — *Great!*

My uncle's the manager of the Arts Centre near my house. He needs people who can start work in July. Is that OK for you? — *Explain*

He's looking for people to work in the restaurant, the office, the theatre or the art gallery. Do you have any experience of working in those places? — *Yes, because …*

We can choose whether we work full time or part time. Which do you think would be best? — *Say which and why*

Reply soon!

Lee

UNIT 2 EXAM PRACTICE

Completing a longer text

✔ exam information

In this part of the exam you read an article or a factual text. You choose the correct sentences to complete the text.

1 Look at the exam task. In pairs, answer the questions.
   1 How many gaps are there?
   2 How many sentences are there?

☀ tip

Read the text carefully then choose a sentence that fits.
Look for links between ideas in the text, for grammatical links and phrases that link ideas.
Check that none of the other options fit.
Read the complete text through to check it makes sense.

2 Read the tip box. Then complete question 1 of the exam task. In pairs, explain your answer.

3 Read three possible explanations for the correct answer for question 1. Which two explanations are correct?
   a 'However' in sentence G links to the text to contrast the 'incredible experience' with it being 'more challenging than … expected'.
   b The idea of the experience being challenging links to an example of why the experience was challenging (the difficult walk up the cliffs).
   c 'Also' in sentence G links to the text to give another example of why the experience was challenging.

4 Complete questions 2–5 of the exam task. In pairs, compare and explain your answers.

exam task

Five sentences have been removed from the text below.
For each question, choose the correct answer. There are three extra sentences which you do not need to use.

A week with the puffins of Shetland

Puffins are one of my favourite seabirds, but they are not doing well in the wild at the moment. So, when I was invited to spend a week on an island in north-east Scotland, helping scientists study them, I accepted immediately. I am glad I did, as it was an incredible experience. (1) .... Every day began with an hour-long walk up to the cliffs where the birds were nesting. We had to do this while carrying all the equipment and clothing we'd need for the day. (2) ....
The scientists' first step in helping the puffins is to discover what kind of fish they eat and where they go to find them. This meant we needed to catch the birds and attach tiny GPS transmitters to their backs. Catching them is obviously very difficult. We did it by putting up nets, which the puffins flew into as they returned to their nests.
(3) .... Although it was summer, the weather on our island never got very warm!
Of course, as well as helping the scientists, I was also there to produce art. I soon realized I would need a lot of patience, as the birds are naturally afraid of humans.
(4) .... In the end, I was able to make many drawings that I'm very proud of.
My week with the project was certainly hard work. We didn't finish until after midnight each day, and at that time of night it was freezing cold. (5) .... The scientists do this for a lot longer than a week, and they are simply amazing. Most of them are volunteers, giving up their time to help save the puffins. We should all be incredibly grateful to them.

A However, after a few days they began to come closer to me.
B In my case, that included my art things, which were quite heavy.
C Not all of them were as enthusiastic as this.
D I found myself actually looking forward to the long walk back to camp so I could get warm.
E No one understood why the number of puffins on the island was falling.
F They soon decided it wasn't going to be possible.
G However, it was also a lot more challenging than I expected.
H We spent many hours in the cold wind waiting for them to arrive.

EXAM PRACTICE UNIT 3

Understanding short texts

✓ exam information

In this part of the exam you read some short texts. For each one, answer a multiple choice question.

💡 tip

Read the text carefully and use any visual clues to help you.

Don't worry if you don't understand every word in the text.

Choose the option that matches the main idea most closely.

Check that the other two options are wrong.

1 Look at the exam task. In pairs, answer the questions.
  1 In which situation would you see each of the texts?
  2 How many options are there to choose from?

2 Read the tip box. In pairs, look at the text in question 1 of the exam task. Answer the questions.
  1 What is the relationship between Jed and Dan?
  2 Which sentence (A, B or C) matches the main idea of the message?
  3 Why are the other two options wrong?

3 Complete questions 2–4 of the exam task. In pairs, compare your answers.

exam task

For each question, choose the correct answer.

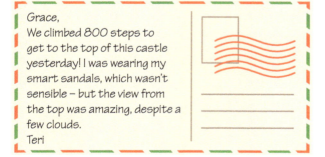

Dan: Jed, there are only a few places left on the university ski trip. I know it's expensive, but it's a lot of fun and we'll all miss you if you don't come! 18:31

1 What is Dan trying to do in this message?
  A warn Jed about the price of the ski trip
  B persuade Jed to go on the ski trip
  C offer to go on the ski trip with Jed

Notice to all kitchen staff

Please only put food that was supplied frozen into the freezer

2 This notice gives staff information about
  A what they are allowed to put in the freezer.
  B how much food they can put in the freezer.
  C which freezer they are allowed to use.

Grace,
We climbed 800 steps to get to the top of this castle yesterday! I was wearing my smart sandals, which wasn't sensible – but the view from the top was amazing, despite a few clouds.
Teri

3 What was Teri unhappy about yesterday?
  A the bad weather
  B her choice of shoes
  C the location of the castle

BITTACY FILM CLUB

Friday, May 24th

Eye in the Sky

Tickets £4 in advance, £5 on the door

Booking in advance guarantees you a seat, but remember that seats are not numbered.

4 A Extra tickets to see *Eye in the Sky* are now available.
  B Club members must pay extra if they wish to choose a seat number.
  C If you buy your ticket in advance, you will definitely be able to see the film.

UNIT 4 EXAM PRACTICE

Talking about yourself

✔ exam information

In this part of the exam you answer questions about you and your life.

💡 tip

Listen carefully so that you understand exactly what the examiner is asking you.

You don't have to give very long answers, but try to give reasons and examples.

1 4.8 Listen to part 1 of the speaking exam. Choose the topics the students are asked about.

free time   friends   hobbies   home
plans for the future   studying English   work

2 Match the questions and answers from the exam task. One of the questions has two answers.

1 Do you work or are you a student?
2 How long will you continue to study English?
3 What did you do last weekend?
4 What places would you like to visit in the future?

a I'm not sure, but I think maybe for another three or four years. I want to improve a lot before I stop.
b Oh, I was very busy.
c I'm a student.
d I like travelling a lot so I would like to see many parts of the world. I'd love to travel to Australia, for example, to see the Barrier Reef and all the sea life there.
e I have a job – I work in a bank in the centre of my city.

3 🔊 4.8 Read the tip box and listen again. In pairs, answer the questions.

1 Which answers in exercise 2 show a student giving reasons and examples?
2 Which answer doesn't exactly answer the question the examiner asked?
3 Which answers are very short?
4 What does the examiner do when the answer is very short?

4 a In groups of three, decide who is the examiner and who are Students A and B. Ask and answer the questions in the exam task.

b Swap roles and repeat the task.

exam task

Examiner: Ask both students the questions:

- What's your name?
- Do you work or are you a student?
- What do you do/study?

Examiner: Choose one or more questions from this list to ask each student:

- Why are you studying English?
- What are your plans for this evening?
- Tell me about a really good teacher you had.
- What do you like about the place where you work/study?
- Which season of the year do you like most?
- Where do you like to spend your holidays?
- How often do you do sports?
- What different things do you do during the day and in the evenings?

EXAM PRACTICE UNIT 5

Listening for specific information

✓ exam information

In this part of the exam you listen to some short dialogues and monologues. For each one, you answer a question by choosing the correct picture.

1 Look at the exam task. In pairs, answer the questions.
  1 What do you notice about the tenses used in the questions?
  2 Do the questions ask about specific details or the general idea?

2 Read the tip box. Then look at the three pictures for question 1 of the exam task. What can you see?

3 🔊 5.7 Listen once and complete question 1. Then listen again and check your answer.

💡 tip

Use the question and the pictures to get an idea about the topic.

You will hear each dialogue/monologue twice. Listen to the whole conversation once and choose an answer. The second time, check your answer.

Don't choose a picture just because the speakers mention it. Listen for the meaning.

4 In pairs, compare your answers. Explain how you chose your answer and why you think the other two are wrong.

5 🔊 5.8 Listen and complete questions 2–3 of the exam task. In pairs, compare your answers. Then listen again.

exam task

For each question, choose the correct answer.

1 What did the woman buy today?

A

B

C

2 What course does the man suggest?

A

B

C

3 What is wrong with the woman who is speaking?

A

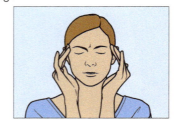
B

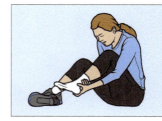
C

160

UNIT 6 EXAM PRACTICE

Describing a photo

✓ **exam information**

In this part of the exam you talk about a photo for about one minute.

1 In pairs, describe photo A using phrases 1–4 below.

A

1 The photo shows …
2 In the background/foreground, there is/are …
3 On the right/left of the picture, I can see …
4 He/She/They look(s) …

2 Read the tip box. Tick (✓) the things you and your partner talked about.

1 people's actions ☐   5 the objects ☐
2 people's feelings ☐   6 the place ☐
3 people's clothes ☐   7 the time of day ☐
4 the weather ☐   8 the background ☐

💡 **tip**

Imagine you are describing the photo to someone who cannot see it.

If you don't know the exact word for something in the photo, describe it using words you do know.

Use simple linkers to connect your sentences.

3 🔊 6.10 Listen to Roberto doing the same task. What things from exercise 2 does he mention?

4 🔊 6.10 Listen again. There is one thing Roberto does not know the name of. How does he describe it?

5 Complete the exam task with a partner. Describe one photo each. Take turns to be the examiner.

exam task

1

2

161

EXAM PRACTICE UNIT 7

Completing a factual text

✓ exam information

In this part of the exam you read a short text and choose the right word to complete each gap.

1 Look at the exam task. In pairs, answer the questions.
   1 What is the topic of the text?
   2 How many options are there for each question?

💡 tip

Read the text once to get an idea of the general meaning.
Choose the option that fits with the vocabulary, grammar and meaning around the gap.
Some options may be similar in meaning, but only one fits.
When you've finished, check the text makes sense.

2 Read the tip box. Then read the text once. In pairs, answer the questions.
   1 What is the main idea of each paragraph?
   2 What is the name of the bridge you can see in the picture?

3 Look at question 3 in the exam task. In pairs, answer the questions.
   1 What do the four options mean?
   2 Which options fit the meaning of the sentence around the gap? Which don't? Why?
   3 Which option also fits with the grammar and vocabulary around the gap?

4 Complete the exam task. Compare your answers with a partner and discuss why you chose each one.

exam task

For each question, choose the correct answer.

Fantastic footbridges

Over the past few years, many beautiful and unusual footbridges have been built all over the world. The **(1)** .... for this trend may be that pedestrian bridges are smaller and less expensive to build than road and rail bridges, and therefore architects are **(2)** .... to be braver and more creative with their designs.

Some of these incredible structures, such as Melbourne's Webb Bridge or London's Millennium Bridge, are there to **(3)** .... pedestrians to get from one part of a city to another. Others, such as China's famous glass bridges, are built as tourist **(4)** .... in areas of great natural beauty.

Cầu Vàng (or Golden Bridge) in Vietnam belongs in this group. This extraordinary bridge looks as if it is **(5)** .... up by a pair of enormous stone hands. It is located in the Bà Nà Hills, a popular tourist destination, and **(6)** .... visitors fantastic views of the surrounding mountains and the town below.

1	A suggestion	B thought	C reason	D opinion
2	A available	B able	C possible	D open
3	A agree	B let	C allow	D make
4	A sights	B scenes	C interests	D attractions
5	A held	B put	C taken	D given
6	A delivers	B passes	C offers	D sends

Writing a narrative

✓ exam information

In this part of the exam you write a story.

1 Look at the exam task. In pairs, answer the questions.
   1 How many words must you write?
   2 How do you know what to write about?

💡 tip

Read the sentence carefully. Check whether you need to write in the first person or use a name.

Make sure your story follows on from the sentence you are given, and that you don't change the topic.

Organize your story into paragraphs and link your ideas together logically.

Use past tenses to tell the events of your story, and include some direct speech: 'That's amazing,' he said.

2 a Read the tip box. Then read the sample exam question and order the paragraphs from 1–3 to make a story. There is one paragraph you do not need.

   b Which paragraph don't you need? Why doesn't it fit?

Your English teacher has asked you to write a story.

Your story must begin with this sentence:
Toby wasn't sure if the flying machine he had built would actually work.

Write your story in about **100 words**.

A ☐ The engine started, and the machine slowly lifted into the sky. Toby looked around him. He could see the roof of his house and his neighbours' gardens. He could see the roads too, and, as it was rush hour, all of them were full of traffic.

B ☐ After doing a lot of research, he began working on his machine. He spent every evening and weekend on it and finally, after six months, it was finished.

C ☐ 'One day, all those people down there will be able to fly to work instead of having to drive,' Toby said to himself. 'This invention of mine will change the world!'

D ☐ There was only one way to find out. He carried the machine into his garden, climbed inside, closed the door and put on his seat belt and helmet. Then he pressed the red start button. He felt very nervous, but also excited.

UNIT 8 EXAM PRACTICE

3 <u>Underline</u> the words and phrases that helped you put the paragraphs in order.

4 In pairs, look at the sample exam answer again and find examples of good vocabulary for the topic.

5 Now look at the exam task and plan your answer. Make some notes before you write. Think about these things:
   - What will happen in your story?
   - Is it possible to fit your ideas into 100 words?
   - What vocabulary do you want to include?

6 Write your story. When you have finished, swap with a partner. Give each other some advice about how to improve your stories.

exam task

Your English teacher has asked you to write a story.

Your story must begin with this sentence:

I felt excited as I collected my luggage at the airport.

Write your story in about **100 words**.

EXAM PRACTICE UNIT 9

Listening to a monologue

✓ exam information

In this part of the exam you listen to a longer monologue and complete the gaps in some notes.

1 Look at the exam task. What is the topic of the monologue?

2 Match the types of information with the gaps 1–6 in the notes.

   a the name of a sport
   b the name of a country
   c a telephone number
   d an age
   e a day or date
   f type of transport

3 🔊 9.10 Read the tip box and listen to the first part of the monologue. Look at question 1 in the exam task. In pairs, answer questions a–c.

   a Which three dates does the speaker mention?
   b Which one completes the gap correctly?
   c Why are the others wrong?

💡 tip

Read the notes and think about the context.

Look at the gaps and identify what type of information you need to listen for.

Listen carefully for this information and write the exact word or phrase you hear in the gap.

Sometimes you will hear more than one possible option, but only one is correct.

Any words spelled out for you must be written correctly.

4 🔊 9.11 Listen and complete questions 2–6 of the exam task. Then compare your answers with a partner.

---

exam task

For each question, write the correct answer in the gap. Write **one** or **two words**, or a **number**, **date** or **time**.

Summer Festival at Oaktree Park

Dates:
Three-day festival, beginning on
(1) ....

International food tent:
Try dishes from India, Indonesia,
(2) .... and Japan.

Live music:
Main Stage – established bands
Start-up Stage – new bands
To apply to appear on the Start-up Stage,
call (3) ....

Open-air theatre:
Name of show: *The Seagull*
Start time: 3 p.m.
Children who are aged
(4) ....
and over are welcome to attend.

Special event for Saturday:
Cars in the Park – an exhibition of old vehicles.
New this year: (5) ....

Sports Zone:
Football, cricket, tennis and a wheelchair sport
called (6) ....

UNIT 10 EXAM PRACTICE

Writing an article

✓ exam information

In this part of the exam you write an article of about 100 words.

1 Look at the exam task. In pairs, answer the questions.
1 What is the topic of the task?
2 How do you know what to write about?
3 How many questions must you answer?

☼ tip

Read the instructions and the notice carefully.

Try to interest and engage your reader by making your writing lively and fun.

Include examples and personal opinions, adjectives and superlatives.

Begin or end your article with a question addressed to the reader.

Organize your article into paragraphs and link your ideas together logically.

2 Read the tip box. Then complete the sample answer with the words and phrases a–h.

Markets in my country

People in the UK love markets, and we have (1) .... types. Some only sell one type of thing, whereas others are 'general' markets that sell (2) .... you can think of, at discount prices.

Farmer's markets sell (3) ...., such as cheese, meat and bread, directly (4) .... who produce it.

We (5) .... that sell vintage clothing, arts and crafts, and jewellery. Some of the (6) .... include Portobello Market and Camden Lock Market in London.

Markets are (7) .... where you can find the most unique and special things, and you don't have to spend your whole day indoors. I (8) .... to shopping centres, don't you?

a also have markets
b far prefer them
c just about anything
d most famous
e busy, exciting places
f from the people
g many different
h wonderful fresh food

3 Read the completed sample answer. In pairs, answer the questions.
1 Which parts of the text answer the three questions?
2 Does the text stay on topic?
3 How did the writer make the content interesting?
4 <u>Underline</u> where the writer has given examples and opinions.
5 How has the writer organized the information in the article?

4 Now plan your answer to the exam task. Make some notes before you write. Check it carefully when you finish.

5 Swap with a partner. Give each other some advice about how to improve your articles.

exam task

You see this notice on an English language website.

Write your article in about **100 words**.

ARTICLES WANTED!

MARKETS
● What kind of markets are there in your country?
● Do you prefer buying things in markets or in shopping centres? Why?

Write an article answering the questions and we will put it on our website!

EXAM PRACTICE UNIT 11

Listening to a radio interview

✓ exam information

In this part of the exam you listen to a radio interview and answer multiple choice questions.

1 Look at the exam task. In pairs, answer the questions.
   1 Who is being interviewed?
   2 What is the topic of the interview?

tip

Read the instructions and the questions carefully as this will tell you the content of the interview.

Some questions will be about details and some will be about opinions or attitudes.

2 Read the tip box and the exam task. Tick (✓) five things you think Tasha will talk about.
   1 her favourite fashion designers ☐
   2 her early thoughts about becoming a designer ☐
   3 how she got the training she needed ☐
   4 the job she is doing at the moment ☐
   5 her first job ☐
   6 her advice for young designers ☐
   7 things that were difficult for her ☐

3 🔊 11.7 Listen and complete the exam task. In pairs, compare your answers.

exam task

For each question, choose the correct answer.

You will hear an interview with a woman called Tasha Harper, a successful fashion designer.

1 When she was a child, how did Tasha feel about becoming a fashion designer?
   A She wasn't sure it would be enjoyable.
   B She didn't think it was a sensible ambition.
   C She had no idea how to make it happen.

2 What does Tasha say about her first job?
   A She hadn't realized how hard it would be.
   B It took her a while to get used to it.
   C She quickly realized it wasn't for her.

3 Tasha learned the skills she would need as a fashion designer
   A in her free time.
   B from the internet.
   C with her mother.

4 What does Tasha regret about training to become a fashion designer?
   A Being unable to see her friends.
   B Waiting so long before doing it.
   C Letting herself get so tired.

5 Tasha says she was not successful as a fashion designer until
   A she was brave enough to give up her receptionist job.
   B she found a good place to sell her clothes.
   C she changed the designs of some of her clothes.

6 What does Tasha say about her current job?
   A It's giving her the opportunity to learn something new.
   B She is happy to do it until a better offer comes along.
   C She has the right combination of skills and experience for it.

UNIT 12 EXAM PRACTICE

Understanding details in short texts

 exam information

In this part of the exam you read some short texts and some descriptions of people. You match the texts to the people.

 tip

Read the instructions and the descriptions of the people.

Underline the key information in the descriptions.

Read the texts carefully, and for each description, find the one that contains all the information you underlined.

Don't choose an answer unless it contains **all** the information in the description.

1 Look at the exam task. In pairs, answer the questions.
   1 What is the topic of the texts?
   2 Is the number of texts the same as the number of descriptions of people?

2 Read the tip box and the exam task. Underline the four key pieces of information in Tom's description.

3 Which texts contain some of the underlined information in the description of Tom?

4 Which text contains all of the information?

5 Complete questions 2–4 of the exam task. Compare your answers with a partner.

exam task

For each question, choose the correct answer.

The people below all want to listen to some live music.
Read the descriptions of six places to hear live music. Decide which place would be the most suitable for each person.

Places to hear live music this summer

A Tilbury House
The small summer concerts at Tilbury House aim to appeal to all generations. Famous performers from many different genres will perform against a backdrop of stunning trees and exotic flowers. Guests are welcome to bring their own food and drink, or can enjoy dishes from the many street food stalls.

B Lanterns Farm
These days lots of festivals are family-friendly, but only a few actually encourage you to bring your children. This one does, and has an equal number of activities for youngsters and adults. It's busy and popular, and the fields can get muddy in the rain, but there's lots of fun to be had by everyone.

C Music Central
This rock and indie music venue is over a century old, and is perfect for people on a budget – it's very popular with students. Bands play downstairs, and upstairs there's a reasonably priced restaurant. There's also a lounge room where you can relax if you get tired of dancing.

D Osprey Palace
This sixteenth-century palace is a fascinating museum, and worth a visit at any time of year. However, if you go during their summer music festival, you'll be able to check out the building and its gorgeous gardens before enjoying the latest hits from well-known popstars in its lovely concert hall.

E Northside Park
Northside Park is known for its excellent modern open-air theatre and cinema, but it's also possible to listen to live music here. There are free concerts by the lake throughout the summer. Come early, especially if you plan to eat at the nearby café first, because it's popular and you may not get a place to sit. Expect jazz, classical, blues and more.

F Henley Castle
900-year-old Henley Castle holds an outdoor festival every year. This summer it has music and much more – a circus, film screenings, a health and wellness tent, readings by famous authors and cookery demonstrations. There will also be several bands playing, although be warned that you aren't likely to see any big names from the rock or pop world at this venue.

1 ☐ **Tom** is interested in history and would love to have the opportunity to combine some sightseeing with a concert. He prefers pop or rock music to classical or jazz and would like to see some famous performers.

2 ☐ **Oliver** would like to go to an event that offers live music, but that also has a range of other activities he can take part in. He's particularly interested in films, plays, books and food.

3 ☐ **Suzy** doesn't have much money, but would love to see some live music performed outdoors. She'd like to be able to have a meal just before the concert.

4 ☐ **Maria** wants to take her two children to an outdoor concert in a beautiful garden setting. She dislikes crowds and would like to be able to have a picnic while listening to the music.

IRREGULAR VERBS

Infinitive	Past simple	Past participle
be	was, were	been
become	became	become
begin	began	begun
break	broke	broken
bring	brought	brought
build	built	built
buy	bought	bought
choose	chose	chosen
come	came	come
cost	cost	cost
do	did	done
drink	drank	drunk
eat	ate	eaten
fall	fell	fallen
feel	felt	felt
find	found	found
fly	flew	flown
forget	forgot	forgotten
get	got	got
give	gave	given
go	went	gone, been
have	had	had
hear	heard	heard
hold	held	held
keep	kept	kept
know	knew	known
learn	learned	learned
leave	left	left
lose	lost	lost

Infinitive	Past simple	Past participle
make	made	made
meet	met	met
pay	paid	paid
put	put	put
read /riːd/	read /red/	read /red/
ride	rode	ridden
ring	rang	rung
run	ran	run
say	said	said
see	saw	seen
sell	sold	sold
send	sent	sent
show	showed	shown
sing	sang	sung
sit	sat	sat
sleep	slept	slept
speak	spoke	spoken
spend	spent	spent
stand	stood	stood
swim	swam	swum
take	took	taken
teach	taught	taught
tell	told	told
think	thought	thought
throw	threw	thrown
wake	woke	woken
wear	wore	worn
win	won	won
write	wrote	written